Field Guide to

SEAFOOD

How to Identify, Select, and Prepare Virtually Every Fish and Shellfish at the Market

By Aliza Green

QUIRK BOOKS

PHILADELPHIA

Copyright © 2007 by Quirk Productions, Inc.
All rights reserved. No part of this book may be reproduced in any form without written permission from the publisher.

Library of Congress Cataloging in Publication Number: 2006933771

ISBN: 978-1-59474-135-7

Printed in Singapore

Typeset in Adobe Garamond, Franklin Gothic, and Impact

Designed by Karen Onorato
Photographs by Steve Legato
Iconography by Karen Onorato
Edited by Erin Slonaker
Production management by Stephanie O'Neill McKenna

All photographs copyright © 2007 by Quirk Productions, Inc.

Ditributed in North America by Chronicle Books
85 Second Street
San Francisco, CA 94105

10 9 8 7 6 5 4 3 2 1

Quirk Books
215 Church Street
Philadelphia, PA 19106
www.quirkbooks.com

Contents

285 **PRESERVED FISH AND SEAFOOD**

Introduction

From Antarctica to the Arctic Circle and everywhere in between, all kinds of creatures of the sea are caught by people for eating. I have put together a small book packed with the essentials of identifying, choosing, storing, preparing, and cooking fish and seafood. Because the same species may be known by many different names, I include scientific names to avoid confusion. The scientific family name, in bold at the end of the Other Names, is also included. The yields listed indicate the approximate percentage of usable meat for each species.

There are many diverse harvesting methods, each having different effects on the fish or seafood itself and on the environment.

Aquaculture and shellfish culture: Finfish and shellfish are raised to market size in a controlled environment, then processed and shipped within hours of harvesting. They can be grown in ocean pens, in freshwater ponds or tanks, in earthen saltwater ponds, or suspended off the ocean floor.

Dredge: A dredge is a heavy metal rake that is dragged across the ocean floor. Dredging is used mainly for shellfish. The negative effect of dredges on ocean floor habitats is of concern, though some dragging methods work more like a lawnmower and are more environmentally responsible.

Diving and gathering: Individual divers gather shellfish such as scallops and clams by hand. This method is considered very environmentally conscious, and the product yields a high price.

Drift net: A drift net is a huge net suspended with floats that is allowed to drift freely in the ocean. The United Nations has banned drift nets in international waters because they capture indiscriminately.

Gill net: A gill net allows only the heads of fish to pass through the mesh, catching them by their gills. Many U.S. states have banned gill nets because they are nonselective. Gillnetting is efficient, but because it kills on capture, quality can be compromised.

Harpoon: Harpooning targets individual larger fish using a handheld or gun-fired harpoon. It is a traditional method that is rare today.

Hook and line: Recreational fishers use a rod and fishing line with one or more hooks, attracting a large variety of fish with lures or bait. This is considered an environmentally responsible fishing method because unwanted catch can be quickly released.

Longline: A main line (a longline) up to 40 miles long carries up to several thousand short lines, each baited with a hook; it is pulled across the water. The fish, usually still alive, are brought on board one at a time and processed quickly, so quality is high.

Pole: Large numbers of surface-swimmers are attracted to bait thrown into the water and are caught on hooks attached to a pole.

Purse seine: One or two boats circle a school of fish with a large net, then the bottom of the net (the seine) is pulled closed like a purse to catch pelagic (open-sea) fish such as mackerel, herring, and sardines. Quality is related to volume: the more fish, the lower the quality.

Traps and pots: Traps are designed to catch a particular species, such as bottom-dwelling fish. Pots, used to catch lobsters, shrimp, and crabs, are cages or baskets with one or more openings that are laid on the ocean floor and connected by ropes to buoys on the surface.

Trawl: A trawl is a net with a wide mouth tapering to a pointed end that is towed behind a boat. It is used to harvest large numbers of ground fish such as cod and flounder. The product may be damaged and there may be a great deal of bycatch.

Trolling: Several unconnected lines, each hooked and baited, are slowly dragged behind a vessel. Troll-caught fish is of high quality (and usually high price) because one fish is hooked at a time, then cleaned, bled, and stored on ice or frozen onboard.

Knowing how fish and seafood are harvested is only the start. The next task is to choose the best fish and seafood market. The product should be neatly, even artfully, displayed and surrounded by crushed ice. The counter and surrounding areas should be sparkling clean with a fresh, briny smell. Your order should be handled with care. A fish and seafood specialty store will have high product turnover and experienced staff, making it a better choice than most supermarkets.

When handling fish and seafood, avoid cross-contamination by keeping raw juices away from other foods. If your immune system is compromised, avoid eating raw fish or seafood. Cook seafood to an internal temperature of 145°F. Be sensitive to seafood allergies, and avoid eating any seafood that causes you to have an allergic reaction.

To make it easier to make environmentally conscious choices, Oceans Alive provides a Pocket Seafood Selector. Download it from www.environmentaldefense.org/documents/1980_pocket_seafood_selector.pdf. The Monterey Bay Aquarium provides downloadable pocket seafood guides according to region. Go to www.mbayaq.org/cr/seafoodwatch.asp.

For comments and questions, please write to me at www.alizagreen.com.

Aliza Green

Fish

As our oceans become depleted of once abundant fish, choosing a fish is an important decision. For farmed fish, closed production systems are considered best. Individually line-caught (by trolling) fish will generally be of higher quality than net-caught. All fresh fish should be iced properly and kept cold all the way to market. Some recommended nonendangered fish are American farmed catfish, Arctic char, flounder, halibut, mackerel, mahimahi, Alaska pollock, black cod, wild salmon, sardines, Pacific sole, hybrid and wild striped bass, farmed sturgeon, and tuna.

Much of the fish that we eat has actually been frozen, which is usually a good thing. Most fish used for sushi, in a market that demands the highest quality, has been frozen. The best frozen fish is called clipper grade, which is frozen on board as soon as it is caught. Lower-quality frozen fish is frozen at fluctuating temperatures or not fast enough to prevent ice crystals from forming in the flesh and damaging its cell structure.

Most fish is quite lean, so it can easily get overcooked and dried out. The fish is ready when it's barely done in the middle, so it's still juicy. When sautéing, get the pan very hot, so the fish browns well and cooks quickly. In many restaurants, tuna is only seared on the outside, and salmon is served medium-rare like a steak. At home, you might want to cook the fish fully. A rule of thumb is to cook fish ten minutes for every inch of thickness.

Many fish have a set of small pin bones crosswise to the backbone starting from the head end and running about one-third of the way along the length of the fish. There is one pin bone per muscle layer. Those at the head end of the fish will be larger and tougher to pull out. Ask the fishmonger to remove them or use needlenose pliers, a pair of tweezers, or special stainless steel fish pliers to pull them out.

Whole round fish have been gutted and scaled, and perhaps the fins trimmed, but otherwise left alone. For most fish, allow one full pound per serving. Dressed fish have been gutted and scaled with the head, tail, and fins removed. Allow $1/2$ to $3/4$ pound per serving. Fish steaks are pan-ready crosswise slices cut from larger fish, such as salmon, halibut, or cod. Allow $1/3$ to $1/2$ pound per serving. Fish fillets are pan-ready portions of fish cut lengthwise from the fish with the backbone removed. Fish with the skin on will cook up juicier; that without the skin will shrink and dry out more quickly. Fish with soft flesh, such as bluefish, are not skinned, because they would fall apart. Fish with inedible skin, such as catfish, is sold skinned. Deep-skinned fish have had the fatty, strong-tasting layer that lies just below the skin removed.

Whole fillets, less common in the United States, include the entire side of a fish with only the backbone removed, including the belly and the nape (the lower side of the fillet below the center line at the head end of the fish). For V-cut fillets, the backbone and small pin bones are removed along with a thin central section from the head end that contains darker meat. In J-cut fillets, the backbone and small pin bones are removed along with the nape, yielding a J shape. The thin belly meat just behind the nape may also be removed. Tail meat is thin and stringy and curls up in cooking, so it is less visually appealing. It can easily be overcooked. The tail may be completely removed or "cropped," trimmed to make a squared-off end. Allow 6 ounces to $1/2$ pound of fillets per serving.

Choosing fresh whole fish: Look for shiny skin; any coating should be transparent. Limp fish should be avoided. The flesh should be firm and taut: When pressed, the flesh should spring back. The fish should smell briny and oceanlike or, for freshwater fish, like a clean pond. The scales should adhere tightly. Lift up the gill cover and examine the gills: They should be cherry-red, not at all brown. With exceptions for a few deep-water fish, the eyes should be clear and protruding. The tail should be moist and flat, not dry or curled up. Red bruises on the flesh indicate that the fish was injured during capture.

Choosing fresh fish fillets: Look for moist-looking fillets. Any red to pink color should have no brown tint. The freshest fillets are the most translucent. The grain should be dense without gaps. If the fish is in a plastic-wrapped container, make sure no liquid has leaked from the fish.

Choosing and defrosting frozen fish: Check that the fish is somewhat shiny and has no white freezer-burn spots. It should be rock-hard with no evidence of previous defrosting. Buy frozen fish where the turnover is high. The freezer itself should be cold, clean, and with minimal frost. The package should be well sealed, and it should be a maximum of three months old. Thaw frozen fish in the refrigerator overnight. Once mostly thawed, cook as quickly as possible, because frozen fish will tend to give off its juices. Fully thawed fish may be dry and mushy when cooked.

To clean, trim, and scale a roundfish:

1. **Starting near the tail end of the fish and using heavy kitchen shears, cut along the belly all the way to the base of the head.**

2. **Reach inside the body cavity and pull out and discard all the innards.**

3. **Snip off the fins with heavy kitchen shears, rinse the fish thoroughly under cold running water, and pat dry.**

4. **To scale, grab the fish by its tail, using a kitchen towel or work glove to get a better grip. Using the edge of a chef's knife or a special fish scaler, scrape away from your body at a slight angle to the fish to remove the scales while leaving the skin intact. Rinse under cold water again, and pat dry.**

To fillet a roundfish:

1. **With the fish belly facing you and the head at your left (if you're left handed, start with the head at your right) and using a sharp, flexible,**

thin knife, make a diagonal cut from the base of the head at the belly end, up through the thick flesh on top, cutting down to the bones.

2. Insert the knife at the top edge of the cut and slice along the length of the back, just above and paralleling the backbone, cutting about ¹/₂ inch into the flesh. Continue cutting until the entire fillet has been detached.

3. Turn the fish over and around so that it faces in the opposite direction. Make another diagonal cut at the base of the head down to the bones.

4. Starting at the tail end this time, slice along the length of the back, just above and paralleling the backbone, about ¹/₂ inch into the flesh. Repeat until the second fillet is released. Trim off and discard the bony part of the fillets at the head end. Pull out the pin bones if present. Trim off the last inch or so of stringy flesh at the tail end and discard.

To fillet a flatfish:

1. Place the cleaned, scaled fish with the head away from you and the dark (upper) side up. Use kitchen shears to remove the fins, including the long thin ones running along the top and bottom edge of the fish.

2. With the fish head facing you and using a sharp, flexible, thin knife, make a diagonal cut at the base of the head down to the bones.

3. Open up the cut at the base of the head and find the backbone. Insert the knife just on top of the backbone and cut over the backbone from the head to the tail end, always keeping the knife just over the backbone.

4. Slice toward the thicker portion of the fillet at the top end of the fish, cutting all the way through the small side bones, then cut toward the

thinner end of the fillet at the belly end of the fish and cut all the way through the side bones.

5. Turn the fish over and repeat on the other side.

6. Using a knife or kitchen shears, trim off the outer edges, including the fin bones of each fillet.

To skin a fish fillet:

1. Place the fillet skin-side down and make a small cut across the fish through the flesh only near the end of the tail. Grasp the tail end with your left hand (or right hand, if you're left handed) and, with the knife at a slight angle to the flesh, start cutting the flesh away from the skin, cutting down toward the skin. As you're cutting, pull the tail end.

2. Cut and pull until the fillet is cut completely away from the skin. If there are any skin patches left, cut them away, always pressing your knife toward the skin rather than into the flesh.

To make fish stock:

1. Rinse the fish frame (everything that's left after filleting) thoroughly, pulling out and discarding any bloody portions or internal organs.

2. Use kitchen gloves or pliers to pull out the gills. The gills carry a great deal of blood and are the first part to deteriorate. For truly fresh fish you caught yourself, it is not necessary to remove the gills.

3. Rinse thoroughly under cold water, then place in a pot. Cover with cold water and white wine and/or lemon juice or several wedges of lemon. Bring to a boil; skim off any white foam.

4. Add finely cut aromatics such as light green celery and fennel trimmings, white onion or trimmings, carrot slices, and white mushroom stems. Add whole peppercorns, sprigs of thyme, 1 to 2 bay leaves, sprigs of dill or tarragon, and coriander or fennel seeds.

5. Bring to a boil again, skimming as necessary, then reduce the heat to very low and simmer 30 minutes, or until the fish bones break up into smaller pieces and any flesh is easily pulled off the bones. Strain through a sieve or a conical strainer, discarding the solids. Cool and then chill, or freeze up to three months.

1. **ANCHOVY**

Other Names:	**Mediterranean anchovy:** *Acciuge* (Italian); *aladroc* (Catalan); *anchoa* (Spanish); *anchoïo* (Provençal); *anchois* (French); *anshouwa* (Tunisia); *ansjos* (Danish); *biqueirão, enchova* (Portuguese); *gávros* (Greek); *hamsi* (Turkish); *katakuchiiwashi* (Japanese); *khamsa* (Russian); *sardelle* (German). **Engraulidae.**

General
Description:

The small, narrow, silvery-skinned European or "true anchovy" (Engrulis encrasicolus) has richly flavored, soft, dark flesh. The majority of the European anchovy catch is preserved (p. 285). Anchovies swim in huge schools and are caught by deepwater trawlers. The gutsy flavor of anchovies is indispensable in cuisines from the Mediterranean to Southeast Asia.

The Pacific anchovy (*E. mordax*) has a long snout overhanging a large, sharklike mouth. Commercial fishers take large quantities of these anchovies for processing into fish meal and oil, though they are also good for eating, albeit a bit stronger and more oily than "true" anchovies.

Locale and
Season:

The European anchovy is found in the Black Sea, the Mediterranean, and the warmer waters of the eastern Atlantic. The Pacific anchovy ranges from British Columbia to Baja California. Fresh anchovies are in season in April, May, and June.

Characteristics:

Anchovies are commonly 3 to 4 inches long with finely grained off-white or grayish flesh; soft, smooth texture; and rich, distinctive, lightly oily flavor.

How to Choose:	Look for whole fresh anchovies in French, Spanish, and Portuguese markets. A fresh anchovy should be silvery—not blue or dark. Look for unbruised whole fish, which can be hard to find because they are quite fragile. Sardines and anchovies are often confused: For sardines, the lower jaw protrudes, whereas the opposite is true for anchovies. Yield is 45 percent.
Storage:	Fresh anchovies are highly perishable and should be cooked within 1 day. Once filleted and lightly salted, they may be kept 1 more day, always refrigerated.
Preparation: 1.	**Slit the anchovies open along the belly, then remove and discard the innards. Rinse under tepid water and pat dry.**
2.	**To fillet, use your fingers to gently pull off the fillets on either side of the backbone. Discard the backbone along with the head.**
3.	**Bake, broil, pan-fry, grill, or hot-smoke. Anchovies are not appropriate for most soups or stews because their flesh is too soft and oily.**
Suggested Recipe:	**Fried Anchovies** (serves 4): Use 1 pound cleaned and boned anchovies with their tails intact. Sprinkle with salt and pepper inside and out. Roll in cornmeal and fry in hot olive oil until browned, about 6 minutes. Serve 6 to 8 anchovies per person as an appetizer with lemon wedges, holding by the tail to eat while hot.
Flavor Affinities:	Capers, dill, fennel, garlic, lemon, olive oil, olives, orange, parsley, tomato, white wine.

2. **ARCTIC CHAR**

Other Names:
Alpine char; alpine trout; Arctic charr; blueback trout; charr (Canada); *eqaluc* (Greenlandic); *fjaeldørred* (Danish); *golec* (Russian); Hudson Bay salmon; *omble chevalier* (French); Quebec red trout; *röding* (Swedish); *røye* (Norwegian); *saibling* (German); *salmerino alpino* (Italian); *salvelino* (Spanish); sea trout. **Salmonidae**.

General Description:
Arctic char (Salvelinus alpinus) *resemble small salmon and are the most commonly sold northerly freshwater fish.* Wild Arctic char live only 500 miles south of the North Pole. This species is a close relation to the brook trout (p. 174). The Inuit of Canada have long enjoyed char, which they freeze, and the fish are a favorite at Canadian government dinners. The land-based, closed-cycle systems used to farm Arctic char are considered environmentally responsible.

Locale and Season:

Wild-harvested char come from remote, icy waters of Europe (especially alpine lakes), Asia, and North America. They appear as far south as Newfoundland, Iceland, and Norway. Most of the char on the market today are frozen. Farmed char are available year-round. Wild char are available in limited quantities in the fall. Landlocked freshwater char are highly prized and are found in England, France, and Switzerland.

Characteristics:
Char's mild but rich flavor is more pronounced than that of trout and less than that of salmon. These fish have moderately firm flesh with a finer flake than

either trout or salmon. With their high fat content, Arctic char stay moist in cooking and can be successfully broiled or grilled. The flesh ranges in color from pale pink to deep red, depending on the fish's diet. Wild Arctic char can grow to 25 pounds, but market weight for farm-raised fish averages 4 pounds.

How to Choose: Char from the late summer or fall will be fattier and more flavorful. Two-thirds of the world's supply of char is farm-raised. Farm-raised char has reddish skin with cream-colored spots; wild char has silvery skin.

Storage: Refrigerate Arctic char in a perforated pan over another pan to catch the drips. Top with crushed ice for up to 2 days after purchase. Like other anadromous fish, char can contain parasites, which are killed by freezing for at least 2 days or by cooking.

Preparation: • **The skin becomes leathery when cooked. It can be removed either before or after cooking.**

• **When broiling or grilling, leave the skin on. Using a sharp knife, cut the skin in a crisscross pattern, making ¹/₂-inch-deep cuts into the flesh.**

• **Cold- or hot-smoke, pan-fry, poach whole, grill, broil, or bake.**

Suggested Recipe: **Salt-Baked Char** (serves 4): Place 2 teaspoons each chopped chives, parsley, and rosemary; 1 sliced lemon; and the zest of 1 lemon inside a trimmed whole 3-pound Arctic char. Whip 3 egg whites to soft

peaks and mix with 3 pounds kosher salt to the texture of damp sand. Spread a 1/2-inch layer of the salt
mixture on a large baking pan. Place the fish on top
of the salt and cover with the remaining salt to
enclose completely in a 1/2-inch thick layer. Bake at
400°F for 25 minutes or to an internal temperature
of 140°F. Remove from the oven and let the fish rest
for 5 minutes. Crack the crust with a rolling pin,
remove the salt chunks and the skin, and serve.

Flavor
Affinities:

Basil, butter, chervil, chives, cream, curry, curry leaf,
ginger, lemon, mushroom, parsley, rosemary, sesame,
shallot, tarragon, white wine, wild lime.

BARRACUDA

Other Names:

Amerikanischer pfeilhecht (German); *barrcouda,
brochet de mer* (French); Commerson's sea pike;
espeton, picuda, picua, picúa corsaria (Spanish);
gaviana (Portuguese); *kadd* (Arabic); *kaku, kupala*
(Hawaiian); *kucul, tenak* (Malay); *luccio marina*
(Italian); *ono* (Tahitian); *snoek* (Dutch); *zub-saalim*
(Somali). **Sphyraenidae.**

General
Description:

The barracuda is a large, fearsome-looking game fish.
With long slender bodies, forked tails, and vicious
sharp teeth, barracudas live in the western Atlantic,
the Caribbean, and the Pacific. Firm-fleshed barracuda
fillets and steaks hold together well during grilling
and broiling, the preferred cooking methods for this

fish. It holds up well to marinades and flavorful sauces. Pacific barracuda (*Sphyraena argentea*) are one of about 20 species of fish in this family. They are found from Baja California to Alaska. Atlantic barracuda (*S. barracuda*) are rarely eaten because of their tendency to carry ciguatera toxins, although natives of the Bahamas and the Caribbean claim that fish weighing less than 5 pounds are safe.

Locale and Season:

Barracuda are in season from April through September on both coasts of Canada and the United States and the western coast of Mexico.

Characteristics:

The flesh of a barracuda is creamy tan when raw and off-white when cooked. The meat is firm, with a large flake, moderate fat content, and full, meaty flavor. Yield is 35 percent.

How to Choose:

The Atlantic barracuda has dark bars and scattered black splotches on greenish skin. Atlantic barracuda are often found in markets in the Caribbean. The Pacific barracuda is the only one marketed in the United States. Average market weight is 3 to 6 pounds, but the fish can reach 100 pounds.

Storage:

☐ x 2

Barracuda spoils easily, so keep it well chilled in the refrigerator, and cook it within 2 days of purchase.

Preparation: •

Grill, broil, or sauté; use for fish tacos.

Suggested Recipe:

Barracuda Tacos (serves 4): Marinate 2 pounds barracuda sections with 1 tablespoon each kosher salt, chili powder, and the juice of 1 lime for 2 hours. Grill or broil for 15 minutes or until the fish flakes. Break into bite-sized pieces and spoon into warm flour tortillas. Top with finely shredded red cabbage, sour cream, and fresh salsa.

Flavor
Affinities:

Bell pepper, black pepper, celery, chiles, chili powder, chipotle, cilantro, fennel, garlic, lemon, lime, onion, orange, oregano, scallion, thyme, tomato.

3.

BARRAMUNDI

Other Names:

Akame (Japanese); barra; cock-up; giant perch; *lates* (Polish, Russian); Nile perch; Palmer perch; *perca gigante* (Spanish). **Centropomidae.**

General
Description:

Barramundi (Lates calcarifer), with moist flesh and delicate flavor, are native to Australia's northern tropical wilderness and are now being raised by aquaculture. Barramundi have gained a reputation as one of Australia's finest eating fish. One company, Australis, is now raising barramundi for the American market in a Massachusetts fish farm. Australian-born fingerlings are flown in live and then grown to portion-sized fish, which are harvested to order. Whole fresh barramundi are farmed in an environmentally responsible way.

Locale and
Season:

Farm-raised barramundi are available year-round. Wild fish are found year-round in Northern Australia.

Characteristics:	An average barramundi weighs 12 pounds, but they can weigh up to 130 pounds. Prized for its sweet, buttery taste and succulent, delicate texture, barramundi is comparable to wild sea bass but moister and more delicate. The white flesh has a fairly high oil content, cooking up white with good-sized flake. Eat with the skin on or off; the skin crisps up beautifully. Fish that have spent time in turbid, muddy water can have muddy-tasting flesh.
How to Choose:	Farm-raised barramundi are sold in three sizes: small, 1 to 1¼ pounds; medium, 1¼ to 1½ pounds; and large, 1½ to 2¼ pounds.
Storage:	Store whole barramundi up to 2 days refrigerated.
Preparation:	• **Cut 3 slashes at the thicker head end in each side of whole barramundi before grilling or baking whole.**
	• **Grill, bake, roast, or steam whole; grill, sauté, pan-fry, or broil fillets.**
Suggested Recipe:	**Barramundi in Banana Leaf** (serves 4): Chop 1 red chile, 2 shallots, and the cleaned roots of 1 bunch cilantro. Combine with 2 tablespoons Asian fish sauce, 2 tablespoons brown sugar, the juice of 2 limes, and a large pinch of Australian lemon myrtle (or substitute grated lemon zest), mixing until sugar dissolves. Arrange 2 whole scored barramundi on banana leaves, cover with some of the sauce, wrap, and skewer shut. Grill packets 10 minutes on each side. Serve with remaining sauce.

| Flavor Affinities: | Arugula, Asian fish sauce, bok choy, brown sugar, cilantro, garlic, green chiles, lemon myrtle, lemon verbena, lime, mizuna, scallion, shallot, soy sauce, tatsoi. |

BELTFISH

| Other Names: | *Bottersnoek* (Afrikaans); *çatalkuyruk bal* (Turkish); *coutelas*, *sabre argenté* (French); cutlassfish; *degenfish* (Norwegian); *espada branca* (Portuguese); *espadiella*, *pez cintro*, *sable* (Spanish); frostfish; hairtail; *lepidop* (Russian); *para* (Maori, New Zealand); *pesce sciabola* (Italian); ribbonfish, scabbardfish (Great Britain); southern frostfish (Australia); *spadopsaro* (Greek); *strumpfbanfisch* (German). **Trichiuridae**. |

| General Description: | *The long, narrow beltfish* (Lepidopus caudatus) *does indeed resemble a belt.* This rather scary-looking fish has a serpentine shape and sharp teeth. Most beltfish are about 3 feet long—only the front half is fleshy enough to be worth filleting. The flesh is excellent and commands a high price, especially in Asian markets and in New Zealand. They may be pan-fried without the skin, cooked in sections, or grilled with the skin on. Beltfish are now endangered. |

| Locale and Season: | These important commercial fish are caught in the eastern North Atlantic, mainly off Portugal and Morocco, and are also caught by trawls off Namibia and New Zealand. |

Characteristics:	Beltfish may be up to 6 feet long and weigh up to 18 pounds. The flesh is rather oily.
How to Choose:	Fresh beltfish may be found at Asian markets. Choose bright, silvery fish. Beltfish are often found frozen.
Storage: ☐ x 2	Store beltfish up to 2 days refrigerated. Defrost frozen beltfish overnight in the refrigerator.
Preparation: •	**Steam, braise, grill, pan-fry in sections, or use for stews.**

Suggested
Recipe:

Beltfish with Rice and Ginkgo Nuts (serves 4):
Rinse 1 1/2 cups Japanese short-grain rice with cold water until the water runs clear. Cover rice with cold water again and soak for 20 minutes. Drain and reserve. Meanwhile, bring a small pot of water to a boil over high heat. Add 1/4 cup ginkgo nuts and cook for 5 minutes. Drain, skin, and reserve. Fillet and bone 1 1/2 pounds beltfish, then cut each fillet in half crosswise. Cut the backbone into thirds. Set fillets and bones aside. Put rice into a large rice cooker or a large pot. Lay bones and fillets on rice. Add 1 1/2 cups dashi, 1/4 cup sake, 2 tablespoons soy sauce, and 2 teaspoons grated ginger. Bring to a boil and cook, uncovered, until liquid barely covers rice, about 5 minutes. Cover and cook at medium-low for 15 minutes, or until the rice is tender. Remove the pot from the heat. Add shelled ginkgo nuts, cover, and set aside for 10 minutes. Carefully remove and discard the bones. Gently stir the rice to distribute the fish, rice, and nuts, and serve.

| Flavor Affinities: | Dashi, garlic, ginger, ginkgo nut, kombu (seaweed), pine nut, sake, scallion, sesame, soy sauce. |

5.   **BLACK SEA BASS**

| Other Names: | Blackfish; *fantre noir d'Amérique* (French); *perchia striata* (Italian); *schwarzer sägebarsch* (German); *serrano estriado* (Portuguese, Spanish). **Serranidae**. |

| General Description: | *Black sea bass* (Centropristis striata) *are small, bottom-feeding fish that live in the western Atlantic between Florida and Cape Cod.* Unlike their cousins the striped bass and white bass (p. 161), black sea bass are purely oceanic. These stout-bodied fish are a deep, smoky gray-black with a lighter belly. The fish are often small enough to cook whole, and their firm, white, lean meat makes them a kitchen favorite. Take care not to overcook, because the lean fish can easily dry out. When fried whole in Chinese restaurants, it is called Hunan fish. Sea bass have been declining in size and numbers but are still relatively inexpensive. |

| Locale and Season: | Black sea bass are most abundant between New Jersey and North Carolina, from September to March. |

| Characteristics: | Black sea bass may weigh up to 5 pounds, but market average is 1 to 2 pounds. Its lean flesh is moderately firm with small, tight white flakes. Its flavor is delicate, with undertones of crustacean. Yield is 40 percent. |

How to Choose:	Look for whole black sea bass in Asian markets. They are sometimes sold from live tanks. The fish should have deep color, bright eyes, and rosy-pink (not brown) gills.
Storage:	Refrigerate fillets in a plastic ziplock bag topped with crushed ice for up to 2 days.

Preparation: **1.** **For whole black sea bass, use scissors to snip off all fins. Scrape backward on the flesh of the fish to remove any remaining scales. Rinse and pat dry.**

 2. **For fillets, use fish pliers or needlenose pliers to remove the pin bones.**

3. **Steam or deep-fry whole fish or fillets (boneless, skin-on, or skinless). Bake fillets in parchment paper or foil packets. Pan-fry fillets or whole small fish. Braise whole fish or fillets.**

Suggested Recipe: **Black Sea Bass in Parchment** (serves 4): Arrange 4 (6- to 8-ounce) skin-on sea bass fillets on individual squares of parchment paper or aluminum foil. Top each with 1/4 cup tomato sauce, 3 to 4 thin slices of lemon, and 1 tablespoon each halved oil-cured black olives, capers, and chopped parsley. Wrap up and bake for 15 to 20 minutes at 425°F or until bubbling.

Flavor Affinities: Asian black bean sauce, bay leaf, capers, chiles, ginger, lemon, marjoram, olive oil, oregano, rice wine, scallion, sesame, soy sauce, thyme, tomato, white wine.

BLOWFISH

Other Names:

Blowfish: Blowie; *egelvis* (Dutch); fugu; globe fish, puffer (Great Britain); *ryba shar* (Russian); *shosaifugu, fugu* (Japanese). **Sea squab:** Blowfish; pufferfish; swellfish. **Tetraodontidae.**

General Description:
☠

Blowfish (Takifugu vermicularis *and others), which contain the deadly poison tetrodoxin, are a genus of fish popularly known by their Japanese name,* fugu. The fish defend themselves by puffing up and poisoning their predators. There are 25 species worldwide, mostly in saltwater, but also in fresh or brackish water. Blowfish have long been eaten in Japan and are featured prominently in Japanese art and culture. The poisonous parts of blowfish differ according to species, and the poison is not affected by cooking. The consumption of the liver and ovaries is prohibited in Japan, but since miniscule amounts of the poison in these parts impart a numbing sensation on the tongue, they are desired by thrill-seeking gourmets. Some people feel that eating blowfish testes in a glass of hot sake is the best aphrodisiac. It is said that the most poisonous type of blowfish, *tora-fugu,* is also the most delicious. The most common species, *Fugu rubripes,* contains poison that is 1,250 times more deadly than cyanide, and the toxin found in one average blowfish can kill up to 30 adults. Death comes within 4 to 24 hours for most victims, who remain fully conscious but are paralyzed and subsequently asphyxiate. If the victim survives the first 24 hours, he or she usually recovers completely. There is no known antidote.

Japanese chefs must undergo a rigorous apprenticeship before they can prepare blowfish. Despite these precautions, some deaths still occur, both from preparing blowfish and from eating it. The most popular dish is *fugu sashimi*, also called *fugu sashi* or *tessa*, sliced so thin that the pattern of the plates can be seen through the meat. Most Japanese cities have *fugu* restaurants, and it is considered safer to eat it there. There are only seventeen restaurants in the United States, mostly in New York City, licensed to sell blowfish. Scientists in Japan have managed to raise non-poisonous blowfish by changing their diet.

The related sea squab (*Spheroides maculatus*), fished off the Atlantic coast, is not nearly so dangerous to eat, especially if purchased at a reputable fishmonger where all possible poisonous parts have been removed. Sea squab "fillets" resemble tiny chicken drumsticks, with a single bone running between two morsels of flesh. They are eaten as finger food.

Locale and Season:

Blowfish prices rise in the fall and peak in winter, when the fish are at their fattest and best. Most blowfish are harvested in the spring during spawning season and then farmed in floating cages in the Pacific Ocean. The high demand has led to overfishing, and strict regulations are now in place. Sea squab are found in the warmer waters of the western Atlantic and are most common in New Jersey in summer.

Characteristics:

Blowfish is lean and white like chicken breast: It is meaty rather than flaky. The fish are so small that they must be cooked very quickly over high heat.

Sea squab have fine, firm, succulent flesh. Yield is 60 percent.

How to Choose:	Only highly trained chefs can clean blowfish. Cleaned blowfish may be found in fish markets in Japan. Sea squab is available on the U.S. East Coast.
Storage:	Cook the day the fish is purchased.

Preparation: **1. To clean sea squab, wear gloves for protection against any poisons.**

2. Cut a slit through the flesh just behind the head. Grasp the backbone and pull it out through the slit while turning the skin inside out, pulling out the innards at the same time. The fillets on either side of the backbone are the edible portion.

NOTE: **Do not prepare blowfish at home. Eat blowfish only at the most reputable establishments that specialize in this fish, and be aware that it is a risky undertaking.**

Serving Suggestions: For *fugu-chiri*, vegetables and *fugu* are simmered in kombu dashi soup and served with ponzu sauce. For *fugu kara-age*, the fish is floured and deep fried. For *fugu hire-zake*, the fins are grilled, then served in hot sake. Sea squab works well in recipes for frog legs, scallops, or shrimp.

Flavor Affinities: Dashi, Japanese vegetables, kombu, ponzu, sake, sesame, soy sauce, yuzu.

6. **BLUEFISH**

Other Names: *Amikiri, okisuzuki* (Japanese); *anchoa de bando,
                 anjova, chova* (Spain); *anchova, tasergal* (Portuguese);
                 blaabars (Danish); *blaufish, tassergal* (German); *blauw-
                 baars, zeepiranha* (Dutch); *coupe fil, tassergal* (French);
                 gofári (Greek); *karradh* (Tunisia); *lüfar* (Turkish); *pesce
                 serra* (Italian); tailor. **Pomatomidae.**

General   *Bluefish* (Pomatomus saltator) *are great sport fish known
Description: for their voracious appetite and tremendous fight.* Young
                 bluefish eat crustaceans, so they are milder and sweeter,
                 while mature bluefish eat menhaden fish, giving them
                 their pronounced flavor. Around the Mediterranean,
                 especially in Turkey and Tunisia, bluefish are a
                 favorite at waterside restaurants. Brining or rubbing
                 with lemon before cooking firms up the sometimes
                 soft flesh and cuts its oiliness.

Locale and   Because bluefish deteriorate so rapidly, they are sel-
Season: dom found far from where they are landed. World-
                 wide, they are found in the western Atlantic and
                 throughout the Mediterranean. In the United States,
                 bluefish travel the East Coast from Florida to Maine,
                 progressing northward, from spring to summer to fall.
                 The main American catch is in the fall in the mid-
                 Atlantic, with a winter catch off North Carolina. Peak
                 season for bluefish is late summer, though they are
                 available year-round.

Characteristics: Bluefish are most common at 5 pounds, though they
                 may reach more than 30 pounds. Raw bluefish flesh

ranges from light putty to bluish-gray, becoming lighter when cooked. Large bluefish have full-bodied flavor that is too strong for many people. Their coarse-textured, moist meat is rich in beneficial omega-3 fatty acids, and they have edible skin. Yield is 45 percent.

How to Choose:

Look for small, brightly colored, firm bluefish for mild flavor and fine grain. Snapper blues are the smallest, harbor blues are medium size, and horse blues are the largest. The fish will be much milder if gutted and bled as soon as they are landed. If handled poorly, bluefish are subject to scombroid poisoning. Large blues may contain high levels of PCBs (poly-chlorinated biphenyls) and should be avoided, especially by those with weakened immune systems.

Storage:

Bluefish deteriorate quickly, so keep the fish refrigerated, preferably covered by a bag of crushed ice. Cook this inexpensive fish the day you buy it, or marinate and then cook the next day.

Preparation: 1.

Cut away the strong-tasting strip of dark meat under the skin for a milder flavor and more appealing look.

2.

Using fish pliers, pull out the pin bones.

3.

Bake, broil, grill, pan-sear, sauté, or hot smoke.

Suggested Recipe:

Turkish Baked Bluefish (serves 4): Rub 4 (6- to 8-ounce) bluefish fillets with the juice of 1 lemon; set aside. Sauté 2 cups red onion strips and 2 teaspoons chopped garlic in olive oil. Add 1 pound diced tomatoes, 3 bay leaves, and 2 teaspoons paprika. Cook 5 minutes and stir in 1/4 cup chopped Italian parsley. Spread half the mixture in a shallow baking dish, top with fish fillets, and cover with remaining mixture. Pour 2 tablespoons olive oil and juice of 1 lemon over the fish and sauce, cover, and bake at 400°F for 20 minutes, or until the fish flakes.

Flavor Affinities:
Bay leaf, cayenne, cumin, garlic, lemon, lime, marjoram, mustard, orange, oregano, paprika, red onion, red wine, red wine vinegar, rosemary, thyme, tomato.

7. **BLUENOSE BASS**

Other Names:
Antarctic butterfish; blue-eye trevalla; big-eye trevalla; blue-eye cod; blue-nose warehou; bonita; bream trevalla; deep-sea trevalla; Griffin's silverfish; sea trevally; stoney-eye; trevalla. **Centrolophidae.**

General Description:
Bluenose bass (Hyperoglyphe antarctica) *are stout-bodied fish, with blunt noses and small scales, that make for excellent eating.* They are versatile enough to steam, fry, broil, or bake. Bluenoses were first taken off Tasmania in the early 1950s. They are exported to Japan for sashimi because of their firm flesh. In New Zealand, the fish are controlled by a quota management system to maintain their viability. High-quality bluenoses are caught by longline and immediately gilled and gutted, then packed on ice into small tubs and rushed to market. Bluenose is now becoming

popular on American restaurant menus, though it is not yet commonly available at retail.

Locale and Season: ❄	Bluenoses are found in rocky beds on the continental shelf in temperate waters, primarily off the coasts of southern Australia, New Zealand, and Tasmania as well as South Africa and Argentina. They are found year-round, depending on weather conditions, but are most common in winter (summer in the Southern Hemisphere).
Characteristics:	The meat is firm textured and light colored. It has a mild, pleasing taste and large flakes when cooked.
How to Choose:	Bluenoses weigh up to 10 pounds and are sold fresh or frozen whole, headed and gutted, and as skinless fillets in the United States, Australia, and New Zealand. Choose firm fish with translucent-looking flesh and a briny, sweet smell.
Storage: ▯ x 2	Store whole fish up to 2 days refrigerated. Store fillets up to 1 day refrigerated.
Preparation: • Suggested Recipe:	**Sauté, pan-fry, steam, poach, bake, or use for fish soup.**

Panko-Crusted Bluenose Bass topped with Crab Salad (serves 4): Dust 1¹/₂ pounds (4 fillets) bluenose bass with flour, then dip in a mixture of 2 lightly beaten eggs with 2 tablespoons milk, then coat with panko crumbs. Refrigerate 30 minutes to set. Heat 2 tablespoons each butter and olive oil in a large skillet. Brown the fillets on both sides until firm, 2 to |

3 minutes per side. Serve topped with Crab Salad:
Combine 12 ounces fresh crabmeat with 1/4 cup
mayonnaise, the juice of 2 limes, the zest of 1 lime,
2 tablespoons chopped shallots, 1/4 cup each finely
chopped fennel and celery, and season to taste with
salt, pepper, and cayenne.

Flavor
Affinities:

Basil, bay leaf, butter, capers, cilantro, cucumber,
cumin, Dijon mustard, garlic, grapefruit, lemon, lime,
olive oil, orange, rice wine vinegar, shallot, shrimp,
tangerine, tarragon, thyme, tomato, white wine.

BONITO

Other Names:

Bonet à dos rayé (French); *bonit atlántico, sarda*
(Spanish); *boniter* (Dutch); *bonito* (Portuguese);
egalushe (Basque); *hagatsuo, kitsungegatsuo* (Japanese);
lakerda (Bulgarian); *obynknovennaya bonita* (Russian);
palamída (Greek); *palamita* (Italian); *palamut, torik*
(Turkish); *pelamide* (German); *rygstribet pelamide*
(Danish); *sarrajão* (Portuguese). **Scombridae.**

General
Description:

*Bonito belong to the mackerel family and resemble small
tuna (p. 176), with which they are often confused.* Bonito
are extremely fast swimmers and aggressive feeders,
swimming in shoals often 15 to 20 miles from shore
and frequently leaping out of the water while feeding.
Atlantic bonito (*Sarda sarda*) have silvery bellies and
sides and a steel to purplish-blue back with dark blue
slanting stripes. Pacific bonito (*S. chiliensis*) are silvery

brown and about the same size as their Atlantic cousins. The slightly larger striped bonito (*S. orientalis*) is found along the Pacific coast of North and South America. Fresh bonito are quite popular in Turkey, and they are highly prized in the north of Spain. In Basque country, this fish is served in *marmite kua* or *marmitako*, a fisherman's stew ideally prepared and eaten at sea. Bonito is well-suited to escabeche. In Spain, the word *bonito*, especially *bonito del norte*, refers to the closely related albacore (p. 176); the term *oceanic bonito* is also used for skipjack tuna (p. 176). Bonito's tasty meat is used fresh, dried, salted, smoked, and canned and may be cooked like mackerel (p. 93) and bluefish (p. 22).

Locale and Season:
Atlantic bonito are found as far north as Cape Cod in the western Atlantic and the southern coast of Great Britain in the eastern Atlantic. They are in season in New England in late July. Pacific bonito are found off the western coasts of North and South America from Chile to the Gulf of Alaska. The largest southern catches of Pacific bonito are in late summer and early fall; to the north, commercial fishing is mostly in the summer and fall.

Characteristics:
Market average weight is 5 pounds. Bonito meat is firm, compact, and light in color with moderate fat content. The skin is not eaten.

How to Choose:
This underrated fish may be had inexpensively on the U.S. East Coast in the summer. Bonito are often confused with skipjack tuna, but bonito have stripes on

their backs, while skipjack have them on their under-side. The flesh of the bonito is pale pink, while that of the skipjack is dark red.

Storage:

□ x 1

Store bonito up to 1 day refrigerated.

Preparation: •

Bake, broil, grill, hot smoke, or stew. Remove the skin after cooking and before serving.

Suggested
Recipe:

Grilled Bonito (serves 6): Sprinkle a 5- to 6-pound bonito with salt, oregano, black pepper, and olive oil. Cut slits into the meat and insert sliced garlic. Score the sides of the fish, brush with oil and lemon juice, sprinkle with more oregano, and grill using indirect heat with the lid on until the flesh is opaque, about 30 minutes. Remove the skin before eating.

Flavor
Affinities:

Bay leaf, bell pepper, capers, cayenne, garlic, lemon, lime, olives, olive oil, oregano, paprika, parsley, potato, red wine vinegar, roasted red pepper, thyme.

CARP

Other Names:

Common carp: *Carpa* (Italian, Portuguese, Spanish); *karpfen* (German); *kyprinos* (Greek). **Big-head carp:** *Belli-gende* (India); *cá mè hoa* (Vietnam); *carpa cabezona* (Mexico); *carpe chinoise* (France); *carpa dalla testa grande* (Italy); *dai tau* (Hong Kong); *gefleckter silberkarpfen* (Germany); *kapoor-e-sargondeh* (Iran); *kokuren* (Japanese); *marmarokyprinos* (Greece);

pestryi tolstolob (Russian); *tolpyga pstra* (Polish).
Cyprinidae.

General
Description:

The common carp (Cyprinus carpio) *is a bottom-feeding river and lake fish with a plump body.* These fish are beloved by Jewish grandmothers for making gefilte fish (ground fish balls). They are also found in fancy colors as highly prized koi in Japanese ponds, not meant for eating, of course. Carp are native to the Danube and other rivers flowing into the Black Sea and the Aegean, but they have been widely introduced elsewhere because they grow quickly and are well suited to aquaculture. Carp were mentioned by Aristotle about 350 BCE. In classical times, carp were widely cultivated and highly regarded. When imported into American waters in 1831, they became a textbook case of the dangers of introducing invasive foreign species when they decimated local wildlife populations. Carp are excellent when smoked, and the roe is edible. Big-head carp (*Aristichthys nobilis*) are native to Asia and are the world's most widely distributed freshwater fish. They are extensively aquafarmed in Southeast Asia.

Locale and
Season:

Carp live in temperate freshwaters throughout the world. Because most carp are farm-raised, they may be found year-round.

Characteristics:

Carp have small eyes, thick lips, two barbels at each corner of the mouth, large scales, and serrated spines. They are olive-green to silver-gray on top, fading to silvery yellow on the belly. Big-head carp are darker and have larger heads. Carp are quite bony. The flesh is grayish and richly flavored but tends to be coarse in larger fish. Carp from stagnant ponds may acquire a muddy taste. Yield is 25 percent.

How to Choose: Carp are usually purchased live, because they spoil quickly. Look for small carp for their finer, lighter flesh, and choose one with bright eyes. Average size is 3 pounds, though they can be much larger.

Storage: Keep a live carp in a water-filled bathtub for up to 1 day before cooking. Otherwise, have the fish market clean and fillet the fish. Use within 1 day of purchase.

x 1

Preparation: 1.   **It's important to remove the skin and dark flesh, which are both unappetizing and tough. To skin, see directions on page 5.**

2.   **Bake whole fish, steaks, or fillets; hot-smoke, or grind for fish balls.**

Suggested Recipe: **Carp Baked in Sour Cream** (serves 4): Butter a baking dish. Season a 3-pound cleaned whole carp with salt and pepper. Brush with butter, top with 3 bay leaves, and cover with 1 cup sour cream and the juice of 1 lemon. Bake at 350°F for 40 minutes or until the fish flakes.

Flavor Affinities: Bay leaf, butter, caraway, dill, garlic, ginger, lemon, lemongrass, onion, paprika, red chiles, shallot, sour cream, tarragon, turmeric, white wine.

8.   **CATFISH**

Other Names: **Channel catfish:** *Katfisch, wels* (German); *lobo*
(Spanish); *namazu* (Japanese); *pesce gatto* (Italian);
poisson chat (French). **Vietnamese catfish:** Basa;
bocourti; giant Mekong catfish; Pacific dory. **Sutchi
catfish:** China sole; river cobbler; swai; tra. **Ictaluridae.**

General
Description: *Catfish is the name given to fish from both freshwater
and saltwater that have cat-whisker-like barbels, no
scales, and a somewhat flattened head.* The most important catfish, from an American cook's point of view,
are blue or Mississippi catfish (*Icatalurus furcatus*) and
channel catfish (*I. punctatus*), which are farm-raised
by a highly successful industry that began in Arkansas
in the 1960s. Channel catfish are one of the fastest-
growing catfish in the world. In the American South,
catfish are commonly dusted with cornmeal and fried
and served with hush puppies (spiced fried cornmeal
dumplings) and coleslaw. Unlike many other fish,
farmed catfish are preferred to wild, which may have
a muddy flavor.

The world's largest catfish are found in the Amazon
basin and in the European rivers east of the Rhine,
where European catfish (*Siluris glanus*) weighing more
than 400 pounds have been caught. Mekong giant
catfish (*Pangasianodon gigas*) may weigh more than
700 pounds. The reddish eggs, referred to as Laotian
caviar, are eaten on rice cakes. Giant catfish have
been listed as critically endangered, so they are to be
avoided. Vietnamese and Cambodian farmers have
long raised basa or Vietnamese catfish (*Pangasius*

bocourti) in cages along the Mekong River, but the coarser and grainier swai (*Pangasius hypothalamus*), or tra, has become the preferred species because it grows faster.

Locale and
Season:

Most American catfish farms are located in the Mississippi Delta, Alabama, and Arkansas. Catfish are available year-round as fillets. Marinated or seasoned fillets are quite common in retail markets. Look for basa and swai at Asian markets.

Characteristics:

Market-size channel catfish weigh 1 to 1 1/2 pounds. Fresh catfish meat will be white to off-white with a pinkish tint, noticeable translucence, and iridescence. A grain diet gives the fish an aroma like raw chicken. Cooked catfish will be opaque and bright white. Basa is a flavorful fish with delicate texture and white flesh. Tra are coarser and grainier than basa and are tan to beige in color. All catfish have tough skin, which is not eaten. Yield is 40 percent.

How to Choose:

The quality of catfish can fluctuate with water conditions and feed. Watch out for "specials" that may feature less-desirable wild river catfish. Do not confuse ocean catfish (p. 190) with farmed channel catfish. Avoid catfish fillets that are reddish or yellowish. Standards for basa and tra vary greatly, so buy carefully.

Storage:
x 2

Store seasoned catfish up to 2 days refrigerated. Store boneless, skinless fillets up to 1 day refrigerated.

Preparation: • **Barbecue, bake, broil, sauté, or bread and fry.**

Suggested Recipe:

Mustard-Pecan Crusted Catfish (serves 4): Mix 1/2 cup mayonnaise with 1/4 cup Dijon mustard and the juice of 1 lemon. Season 4 catfish fillets with salt and pepper and arrange on a buttered baking dish. Spread the mayonnaise mixture over the fish and sprinkle with 1/4 cup finely chopped pecans. Bake at 425°F for 12 minutes or until the fish flakes.

Flavor Affinities:

Cajun seasoning, celery, cornmeal, garlic, green chiles, lemon, olive oil, onion, paprika, pecan, red pepper, scallion, seasame, soy sauce, thyme, tomato, vinegar.

9a–b. 📷

CHILEAN SEA BASS

Other Names:

Antarctic cod; *austromerluza negra* (Spain); *austromerluzzo nero* (Italian); *bacalao de profundidad, mero* (Latin America); *colin antarctique, légine antarctique* or *australe* (French); icefish; *marlonga negra* (Portugal); *ookuchi* (Japanese); Patagonian toothfish; *patagonische ijsvis* (Dutch); *schwartzer seehecht* (German); *sort patagonisk isfisk* (Danish). **Nototheniidae.**

General Description:

Chilean sea bass (Dissostichus eleginoides) *is a South American fish originally known as Patagonian toothfish, renamed to increase its market appeal.* This large, slow-growing species is a member of an unusual family of fish found only in the Southern Hemisphere. Far less plentiful now because of overfishing, this slow-growing fish has also been decreasing in size. Many are caught by illegal pirate fishermen, who take fish that are less than eight years old, before they begin to reproduce. The high oil content makes this firm, bright white fish grill beautifully. Handle carefully so the fillets, sold skinless, do not fall apart. The fish is richly flavored, so avoid heavy sauces.

Locale and
Season:

The fish are caught off the coasts of southern Chile and South Africa. Those from Chile tend to be larger. March to July is the slow season.

Characteristics:

Chilean sea bass have large pectoral fins and the glassy sunken eyes of a deep-water dweller. Most are gutted and headed before they are shipped to the United States and are usually frozen. Average market weight is about 20 pounds. Both raw and cooked meat are bright white with rich, melt-in-the-mouth flavor. It is usually sold as skinless steaks or fillets, which need minimal trimming, if any.

How to Choose:

Defrosted fillets should be shiny and resilient. Frozen fillets should not have any freezer burn or discoloration. Many restaurants and home cooks are choosing to pass on this fish to conserve depleted stocks.

Storage:
x 2

Store up to 2 days refrigerated.

Preparation: •

Broil, bake, braise, or sauté. The fish is too oily for deep-frying.

Suggested
Recipe:

Lemongrass-Crusted Chilean Sea Bass (serves 4):
Process together 1/2 cup sliced shallots, 1/4 cup sliced
lemongrass, and 2 tablespoons sliced ginger to a
chunky paste, then add 1/4 cup cilantro and process
again. Stir in 1/4 cup canola oil, 1/2 cup sesame
seeds, and 1 cup panko. Pat 4 fish fillets with the
mixture. Bake at 425°F for 15 to 20 minutes or
until the fish flakes.

Flavor
Affinities:
Basil, chives, cilantro, garlic, ginger, lemon, lemongrass, lime, mango, miso, olive oil, orange, sesame,
shallot, soy sauce, tarragon, tomato, white wine.

10. **COBIA**

Other Names:
Black kingfish; black salmon; *cá bop* (Vietnamese);
cabio; crabeater; *dalag-dagat* (Filipino); *esmedregal*
(Mexico); *fogueteiro galego* (Portuguese); *foringjakfiskur*
(Icelandic); *kobia* (Russian); lemonfish; ling; *mafou*
(French); *offizierfisch* (German); *pla chawn thaleh*
(Thai); runner; sergeant fish; *sichil* (United Arab
Emirates); *sugi* (Japanese). **Rachycentridae**.

General
Description:
Cobias (Rachycentron canadum), *which resemble
mackerel, are known as fast and voracious game fish
and are the only member of their family.* This large fish
has a long, slim body; a broad, sunken head; and a
protruding lower jaw. They may be substituted for
Spanish mackerel (p. 93) in recipes. Cobias command
a high price for their firm texture. The fish's solitary

nature means there is no exclusive fishery for it. In Mexico, cobia is the fish of choice for weddings and celebrations. Aquafarming is done successfully in Asia, especially in Taiwan.

Locale and
Season:

Cobias are found around the world and are pelagic fish, living in the open seas. They inhabit warm tropical waters in winter and move to more temperate waters in the spring, summer, and fall.

Characteristics:

Cobias can weigh up to about 135 pounds, but 20 to 40 pounds is average. Their flesh is white, firm, and well-flavored. Yield is 50 percent or more.

How to Choose:

Cobias are usually sold fresh. Because they are subject to visible parasites, they should be inspected carefully before purchase.

Storage:

Store cobia for up to 2 days refrigerated.

Preparation: 1.

Cut away the blood line (dark flesh near the backbone) and the tough skin.

2.

Grill, broil, sauté, or poach fillets, or cube for kebobs.

Suggested
Recipe:

Marinated Grilled Cobia (serves 4): Cut 3 pounds of cobia fillets into 4 servings. Mix together 1/4 cup each olive oil and lemon juice. Add 1 1/2 teaspoons each dry mustard and minced garlic, and salt and pepper to taste. Use to marinate at room temperature 15 minutes. Drain, reserving marinade, and grill, basting often with marinade. Discard remaining marinade.

| Flavor Affinities: | Almond, banana, Cajun seasoning, cayenne, cilantro, coconut, garlic, kiwi, lemon, lime, mango, mustard, olive oil, onion, orange, star fruit, thyme. |

11.

COD

| Other Names: | *Bacalao* (Spanish); *bakaliáros gádos* (Greek); *cabillaud, morue commune* (French); *dorsch, kabeljau* (German); *kabeljautorsk* (Danish); *madara, taiseiyo tara* (Japanese); *merluzzo bianco* (Italian); *morina* (Turkish); *torsk* (Norwegian). **Gadidae**. |

| General Description: | *Three hundred years ago, Atlantic cod* (Gadus morhua) *was a hugely important, indeed essential, source of food.* Historians theorize that the enormous stocks of cod in the western North Atlantic spurred European colonization of America. Fresh cod became the fish of choice in New England, while salted cod (p. 290) was exported across the ocean. Today, Atlantic cod stocks are much depleted.

Pacific cod (*G. macrocephalus*) are similar to Atlantic cod. While the two species are often sold interchangeably, Pacific cod are moister and not as firm. Cod have a mild flavor, so they take well to rich sauces and strong flavors and tastes. The cod family also includes cusk (p. 44), grenadier (p. 60), haddock (p. 67), hake and whiting (p. 69), pollock (p. 121), and scrod (p. 67). Much cod is processed and made into frozen foods such as fish sticks. |

Locale and Season:	Atlantic cod are fished from North Carolina to Greenland and are available year-round. Wild Atlantic cod are caught in late fall and early winter, transferred to net pens or sea cages, fed on a natural diet of fish, and kept for 3 to 4 months until they reach market size. Pacific cod are found from California to Alaska and from northern Japan to Russia; they are in season from January 1 until quotas are reached.
Characteristics:	Cod are brown or green-gray with dark brown mottling. Market average for Atlantic cod is 4 to 6 pounds; for Pacific cod it's 5 to 15 pounds. Cod are mild in flavor, somewhat gelatinous, and lean. When cooked, their texture is moderately firm with large, moist flakes and delicate, sweet flavor. Cod cheeks have firm, dense, yet succulent meat, and the tongues are a delicacy. Yield is 30 to 40 percent.
How to Choose:	Fresh whole cod can be recognized by the single barbel (whisker) jutting out of the chin and the clear white lateral line that curves up toward the head. They may be purchased whole with head on or off, as skinless or skin-on fillets, as center-bone steaks, or they may be salted. Lesser-quality cod from New England is often treated with sodium tripolyphosphate to help it retain moisture. The quality of cod varies greatly depending on how well it has been handled. Excellent quality cod comes from longliners that process and freeze the fish immediately upon harvest. Pacific cod may have been twice frozen, once when headed and gutted and a second time when filleted. Because Alaskan trawlers do not bleed their fish on

board, their fish is usually not as white. Remove the skin before cooking to avoid parasites.

Preparation:

• **Bake, broil, fry, microwave, or add to soups, chowder, and sauces.**

Suggested Recipe:

Braised Cod Cheeks (serves 4): Trim 8 cod cheeks, pat dry, and season with salt and pepper. Mix 2 eggs with 1 cup heavy cream, 1 tablespoon Dijon mustard, and 2 tablespoons each chopped dill and basil in a bowl and coat cheeks in the mix. Fry the cheeks in butter until brown, about 5 minutes per side. Remove from the pan and keep warm. Return the pan to the heat, pour in 1 cup fish stock and 1/4 cup Madeira, and boil until syrupy. Add 1/4 cup chopped leeks and the cheeks to the pan and simmer 5 minutes longer. Serve with boiled potatoes.

Flavor Affinities:

Arugula, bacon, bay leaf, butter, capers, celery, celery root, cranberry beans, cream, dill, lemon, mustard, potato, salt pork, shallot, thyme, tomato, white wine.

12a–c. 📷 **CROAKERS AND DRUMS**

Other Names:

Atlantic croaker: *Atlantischer umberfisch* (German); *corvinón brasileño* (Spanish); grumbler; hardhead; *iskine* (Turkish); *ombrina* (Italian); golden croaker; *guchi* (Japanese); *rabeta brasileira* (Portuguese); *tambour* (French). **Spot:** Goody; Lafayette or Norfolk spot; *punkttrommefisk*

(Denmark); *roncadeira-pinta* (Portuguese); spot croaker (Great Britain); *tambour croca* (French); *verrugato croca* (Spain); *zebra-umberfisch* (German). **Yellow croaker:** *Guchi* (Japanese); Japanese sea bass; yellow flower fish; yellowfish. **Meagre:** *Bocca d'oro* (Italian); *corvina* (Spanish); *maigre* (French); *mayáticos aetós* (Greek); *sariagiz* (Turkish). **Corb:** *Corbeau, poisson juif* (French); *corvo* (Italian); *corvallo* (Spanish); *eskina* (Turkish); *skiós* (Greek). **Red drum:** Channel bass; redfish. **Southern grunt:** Croaker (Great Britain); *corvina* (Latin America). **Drum:** *Adlerfisch* (German); oyster cracker; *tambour* (French). **Corvina:** *Cagna chilienne* (French); croaker (Great Britain); *ronco chileno* (Spanish); *scienide* (Italian). **Freshwater drum:** Bubbler; croaker; grinder; grunt; lake drum; sheepshead; thunder pumper. **Suzuki mulloway:** Butterfish; jewfish; mulloway; suzuki sea bass. **California white sea bass:** *Corbina blanca* (Mexico); king croaker; sea trout. **Sciaenidae.**

General Description:

There are 270 species of the drum and croaker family living in temperate and tropical seas worldwide, noted for having large otoliths (wavy flat "stones" in the ears) and air bladders that males can resonate, producing a sound. Those called croakers make a croaking sound, and those called drums make a drumming sound when they pop their heads above water. Drum and croaker otoliths resemble ivory and have been worn as protective amulets, made into jewelry, and traded.

Atlantic croaker (*Micropongonius undulatus*) is the smallest member of the drum family and almost always sold whole; they are best pan-fried or broiled whole. These golden-silver fish, popular from New York to Florida, are inexpensive and tasty, with moderately firm, lean flesh, but are famously bony. Spot (*Leiostomus xanthurus*) is the smallest member of the croaker family found at the market and has a spot right behind the gill opening. They are best pan-fried whole. Yellow croaker (*Pseudosciaena crocea*) is sought after in Asia, especially China, and is dried in Korea as gulbi (p. 289).

Meagre (*Argyrosomus regius*)—a large, dark Mediterranean drum with a golden throat and white, bone-free flesh—may be cooked as for sea bass (p. 17) and tastes good both hot and cold. Corb (*Sciaena umbra*), a small Mediterranean drum with a plump body, is good fried in slices. The red drum (*Sciaenops ocellata*) got its fame from chef Paul Prudhomme, who used it for his Cajun blackened redfish. That one dish became so popular that a moratorium was placed on the fish. Today, large black drum (*Pogonias cromis*) is usually substituted. Corvina (*Cilus montti*) is popular in Peru for ceviche and is found off the Pacific coast of South America.

The only freshwater drum, *Aplodinotus grunniens*, is a bottom-dwelling species found in lakes and rivers. It is an important commercial crop on the Mississippi River. The suzuki mulloway (*Argyrosomus hololepidotus*) is a farm-raised sashimi fish sought after in Japan. The fish are stunned and bled immediately for low-stress harvest and best quality. The prized California white sea bass (*Atractoscion nobilis*) is the largest member of the drum family found on the American Pacific coast. Most are sold to high-end restaurants. Regionally it is known as corbina and king croaker; the FDA-approved name is sea trout.

Locale and
Season:

Atlantic croaker is found along the coast from Cape Cod to Mexico, although in recent years it has not been as plentiful or widely distributed as the smaller spot. It is in season from March through October. Red drum is now imported from Mexico, Argentina, Ecuador, and Central America and fetches high prices. Farmed red drum from Texas, Taiwan, and Ecuador is also available. Black drum is more plentiful and lower-priced and is found from Virginia to the northern Gulf of Mexico, though restrictions have tightened supplies. Black drum is most abundant in cooler months. Suzuki mulloway is found in Japan and South Australia, where it is farmed in the cold, clear waters of the Southern Ocean. California white sea bass range from Alaska to southern Baja and are in season from June through September.

Characteristics:

Atlantic croakers average 1 pound; the raw meat is bright white and may have a reddish tint. The cooked meat is lean, white, and full-flavored and similar to the black drum; the skin is edible. Red and black drums have mild, sweet flavor and firm, moist flesh similar to red snapper. Market average for red drum is 1 to 2 pounds. The flesh of small, very fresh red drum fish has an almost emerald-green tint, while the meat of larger red drums is white with a red tint.

Black drum is the largest in its family and may weigh up to 30 pounds. The raw flesh of black drum is whiter in color than red drum, but both cook up snow white. Freshwater drums generally weigh 5 to 15 pounds, although they may become quite large in rivers. Spots weigh only about 1/4 pound. Suzuki mulloway has rich, white, full-flavored flesh with medium-firm and tight-grained texture. It weighs 1 to 10 pounds. California sea bass market weight is about 15 pounds; the meat is moderately fatty, white, and flaky with fine texture. Yields average 40 percent.

How to Choose: Small puppy drums are considered sweeter and flakier than larger bull drums. While black and red drum can be used interchangeably, black drum is firmer and meatier. Red drums are smaller, with distinctive black spots. Red drums have barbels on their chins; black drums do not. Choose small red drums with coppery sheen and pronounced scales.

Storage: Store whole drums and croakers in the refrigerator up to 2 days on ice and surrounded by ice. Store fillets 1 day in the refrigerator.

Preparation: • **Pan-fry, deep-fry, pan-sear, "blacken," smoke, bake, broil, grill, sauté, or steam.**

NOTE: **Do not overcook. The low oil content means that fillets dry out much more quickly than other, oilier fish.**

Suggested Recipe: **Panamanian Ceviche de Corvina** (serves 4): Cut 1 pound well-trimmed California sea bass fillets into very small cubes and place in a glass bowl. Mix with 1 cup lime juice, 1 tablespoon red wine vinegar, 1/2 cup finely diced sweet onion, 1/4 cup finely diced celery,

2 teaspoons minced fresh green chile, and salt and
pepper to taste. Leave in the refrigerator for at least
1 hour and up to 12, depending on how cured you
like the ceviche. Serve with saltines.

Flavor
Affinities:

Bacon, celery, cilantro, cornmeal, ginger, lemon, lime,
mustard, onion, paprika, rice wine, scallion, sesame,
soy sauce, tarragon, tomato, white wine.

CUSK

Other Names:

Atsukawadara, torusuku (Japanese); *brosme* (French);
brosmio (Italian, Spanish); *brósmios* (Greek); *keila*
(Icelandic); *lumb* (German, Swedish); *menyok*
(Russian); moonfish, torsk (Great Britain); ocean
whitefish; oyster fish; tusk; usk. **Lotidae.**

General
Description:

*The large cusk (Brosme brosme) are bottom-dwellers
related to cod (p. 37) that are slow-growing solitary
swimmers living in northern coastal waters.* Often
regarded as a lesser substitute for cod, cusk's firm,
slightly chewy flesh has its own good, sweet, mild
flavor. Whole cusk are long and slimy with large,
whiskered mouths and a strong smell. Their firm flesh
holds together well, so it makes a superb fish chowder
and takes well to frying. The dense flesh takes longer
to cook through than cod or haddock (p. 67).

Locale and
Season:

Cusk are found along the western Atlantic, from
Newfoundland to Cape Cod (especially the Gulf of

Maine). In the eastern Atlantic, major fishing grounds lie off the northern coast of the British Isles, Denmark, and the Murmansk coast, with the largest catches in Norway and Iceland. Because they do not swim in schools, these fish are often landed as a bycatch of haddock and cod fishing. They are found year-round, especially in northern Europe.

Characteristics: Cusk may be recognized by the single long dorsal fin that runs the length of their back, giving them an eel-like appearance. Their color may be red-brown, green-brown, or yellow-gray, shading to cream below. Market weight ranges from 1 1/2 to 5 pounds. They have firm, lean flesh that is moderately oily and juicy with good flavor and large flakes when cooked.

How to Choose: Small 2- to 3-pound fish, known as squirrels, are caught by longliners, and 15-pound fish are caught by draggers. They are sold fresh whole or filleted, but also dried, salted, and brined.

Storage: Store up to 2 days refrigerated.

Preparation: • **Bake, broil, pan-fry, deep-fry, poach, stew, sauté, or cube for kebobs.**

Suggested Recipe: **Baked Cusk** (serves 4): Cut small incisions into the flesh of a whole (2- to 3-pound) cusk and insert strips of rinsed salt pork inside. Stuff the belly cavity with a mixture of 2 cups bread crumbs, 2 beaten eggs, 1 cup chopped parsley, and 4 tablespoons chopped fresh herbs such as thyme, rosemary, and marjoram, and

then close with skewers or toothpicks and lay on a
bed of salt pork strips. Bake at 375°F for about 30
minutes or until fish flakes.

Flavor
Affinities:

Bay leaf, butter, celery, chervil, chives, cream, marjoram,
onion, potato, salt pork, tarragon, thyme.

DENTEX

Other Names:

Dentex: *Capatão legitímo, dentão* (Portuguese); *dendiq*
(Tunisia); *denté commun* (French); *dentice* (Italian);
dentón commún, sama dorada (Spanish); dog's tooth
bream (Great Britain); *sinarit* (Turkish); *synagrída*
(Greek); *zahnbrassen* (German). **Pink dentex:** *Dentice
corassiere* (Italian); *denté couronné, gros denté rose*
(French); *koronáti tsaoússis* (Greek). **Sparidae.**

General
Description:

Dentex (Dentex dentex) *are one of the more delicate
fish in the sea bream family (p. 147).* A small, short,
plump fish, their color varies according to age. Young
adults have steel-blue backs and silver sides with red-
tinted pectoral fins; very large fish may be wine colored. Crimson dentex (*D. maroccanus*) are found in
the western Mediterranean. Pink dentex (*D. gibbosus*)
are common in the waters near Gibraltar and prized
by anglers. They are rosy in color.

Locale and
Season:

These fish are found in the warmer waters of the
Mediterranean, especially to the west.

Characteristics:	Dentex have fine, delicate flesh with edible skin and succulent, tasty meat.
How to Choose:	Young dentex are gray, changing to reddish pink then steel blue with a few spots as they mature. They are best when they weigh about 1 1/2 pounds. Dentex are usually sold whole.
Storage:	Store whole dentex up to 1 day refrigerated.
Preparation:	• **Grill whole, stuff, or bake. Large fish should be cut into steaks before grilling or pan-frying.**
Suggested Recipe:	**Italian Dentex with Orange** (serves 2): Combine the grated zest of 2 oranges, 1/2 cup breadcrumbs, and 2 tablespoons each chopped parsley, chopped cured black olives, capers, and olive oil. Add the juice of 1 orange. Stuff the cavities of 2 (1-pound) cleaned whole dentex. Cut three slices into the flesh on the side of each fish and insert a half-moon slice of orange. Wrap the fish in foil and bake at 350°F for 20 minutes or until bubbling.
Flavor Affinities:	Anchovy, bay leaves, butter, capers, dill, fennel, garlic, lemon, olive oil, olives, orange, tomato, zucchini.

13. **DOVER SOLE**

Other Names:	*Dil* (Turkish); European sole; *glóssa* (Greek); *lenguado* (Spanish); *linguado legitimo* (Portuguese); *morskoy*

yazyk (Russian); *seezunge* (German); *shitabirame* (Japanese); *sogliola* (Italian); *sole commune* (French); *tong* (Dutch); *tunge* (Danish, Norwegian). **Pleuronectidae**.

General Description:

Dover sole (Solea solea) *is truly deserving of its culinary fame.* A cousin of the flounder, it is extremely well-flavored. A true Dover sole can be skinned by peeling the skin off, something that can't be done with any other member of their family. In spite of confusing names like lemon and gray sole, there are no true soles in American waters. These world-famous fish get their common name from the town of Dover on the English Channel, which historically supplied the greatest numbers of these fish to the main London fish market at Billingsgate. In Italy, the more delicate sole from the shallower and less salty Adriatic is preferred. Dover sole are landed by trawlers. They have long been a mainstay of high-end French and Continental restaurants because they yield thin, firm fillets that don't fall apart whether rolled and stuffed, sautéed meunière style, or broiled. They are best cooked on the bone and are often filleted at the table in fine restaurants.

Locale and Season:

The best fishing grounds are in the North Sea and the Bay of Biscay, but Dover sole are also harvested in west Africa, France, Italy, Belgium, the Netherlands, and Great Britain. Sole are available fresh and frozen year-round, but late in the year, supplies can be tight.

Characteristics:	Dover sole are long and elliptical with tough, dark top skin that is usually peeled off before cooking; the lighter bottom skin may be left on. Average weight is 1 pound. The raw meat is glistening white, firm, and dense, cooking up white with pleasing, mild, sweet flavor that is well adapted to rich sauces. Yield is 40 percent.
How to Choose:	The smaller the sole, the more delicate the flavor. Choose fish of less than 1 pound that are firm and have a sweet, briny smell. Dover sole are normally sold whole and frozen in America and are all imported.
Storage: ☐ x 2	Store whole Dover sole up to 2 days refrigerated; store fillets up to 1 day refrigerated.
Preparation:	• **Peel the skin off by cutting a slit at the tail end, then lifting up the edge and pulling it off the fish.**
	• **When sautéing whole, place a slice of raw potato under the thin tail end so that it cooks more evenly.**
	• **Poach, steam, grill, broil, bread and pan-fry, sauté, bake, or use for sushi.**
Suggested Recipe:	**Sole Meunière** (serves 4): Season 4 sole fillets (6 to 8 ounces each) with salt and pepper. Dust with flour and brown in butter, 1 to 2 minutes per side. Remove from the pan and keep warm. Pour off any fat, add 2 tablespoons fresh butter to the pan, heat until bubbling, then add 2 tablespoons chopped parsley and a squeeze of lemon juice. Swirl to combine, then pour over the fish.

<table>
<tr><td style="text-align:right">Flavor
Affinities:</td><td>Almond, butter, capers, chervil, crabmeat, crayfish, cream, dill, lemon, lobster, mushroom, pine nut, shallot, shrimp, spinach, tarragon, truffle, white wine.</td></tr>
</table>

14.   **EEL**

<table>
<tr><td style="text-align:right">Other Names:</td><td>**American eel:** *Amerikanischer aal* (German); *anguilla americana* (Italian); *anguille d'Amérique* (French).
European eel: *Aal, flussaal* (German); *anguila* (Spanish); *anguilla, ragano* (Italian); *anguille* (French); *enguia* (Portuguese); *ferskvandsaal* (Danish); *héli* (Greek); *unagi* (Japanese); *yilan bilagi* (Turkish).
Young eel: *Angula* (Spanish); *civelle, piballe* (French); *cieche* (Italian); elver; glass eel; *txitxardin* (Basque).
Conger eel: *Congre* (French); *congrio* (Spanish); *grongo* (Italian). **Anguilidae** (freshwater eel).
Congridae (conger eel). **Muraenidae** (moray eel).</td></tr>
</table>

<table>
<tr><td style="text-align:right">General
Description:</td><td>*There are more than 20 members of the freshwater eel family, all long, slim, snakelike fish with smooth, slippery skin, microscopic scales, and spineless fins.* The American eel (*Anguilla rostrata*) and its close cousin the European eel (*A. anguilla*) live part of their life in freshwater and part in saltwater; most are caught at their freshwater stage. In America, adult eels are known as yellows, silvers, or bronzes depending on the stage of maturity. Eels date from early prehistoric times; it is said that the Gulf Stream they follow on their migrations once circled Atlantis.

    In Spain, some eels are taken to freshwater nurs-</td></tr>
</table>

eries (*viveros*), where their spines darken, producing the choice *angulas de lomo negro* (black-backed eels). Baby eels, first popularized in Spain by the Basques, are a great delicacy there and in Italy. Elvers are cooked whole. Spanish restaurants provide special wooden forks to avoid any metallic taste and to get a better grip on the smooth-skinned eels. Mature eel is good simmered in stew and goes well with acidic flavors to cut its richness. It is not served raw.

The conger eel (*Conger conger*) is a large sea eel popular in Europe. This scary-looking creature with a pointed head and sharp teeth is found in temperate and tropical areas. It can grow to almost 10 feet long, though 2 to 5 feet is average. In Europe, conger goes into soups and stews, especially bouillabaisse. Although edible, moray eels (*Muraena helena*) have bony and rather coarse flesh.

Locale and Season:

Wild eels are caught off eastern Canada, the American eastern seaboard, and Greenland. Farm-raised eels come from China, Japan, and Taiwan. The American eel fishery supplies Asian and European aquafarms with baby eels to raise to adulthood; there is a separate fishery for adult eels. In Europe, live baby eels are caught in the spring and served in restaurants from late October through February. Adult eels are found from September to November. Conger is in season from early spring to autumn.

Characteristics:

Eel meat is quite firm with a high fat content and full-bodied, distinctive flavor. The raw flesh is gray but turns lighter when cooked, and it has a small, fine flake.

The skin is not eaten. The flavor of elvers is so subtle that it can easily be lost; they must be cooked briefly. Yield is 60 percent skinless fillets from whole eel.

How to Choose:

There may be more than 1,000 elvers in 1 pound. Adult eels are at their plumpest and best in autumn, when they have turned silver with almost black backs. Females weigh three times as much as males. Eels harvested from stagnant water or held too long in tanks can have a muddy flavor. Look for live eel tanks in Asian markets. Eel is best bought while still alive, or the flesh can be soft and mushy. Conger is usually sold cut into chunks or steaks. Ask for a middle cut; the tail end is quite bony.

Storage:

Eels can survive several days out of water if kept in a damp environment.

Preparation: •

Ask the fishmonger to skin and cut eels into shorter lengths.

  •

Roast, poach, braise, or hot-smoke.

Suggested
Recipe:

Angulas à la Bilbaina (serves 4): Heat 1 cup olive oil with 6 cloves sliced garlic and a piece of dried red chile pepper in a *cazuela* (shallow earthenware casserole) until the garlic turns golden. Plunge 1 pound washed and well-drained baby eels directly into the oil, stirring with a wooden spoon. Season with salt and pepper, remove the dish from the heat, cover with a plate, and bring sizzling to the table.

| Flavor Affinities: | Cilantro, garlic, chiles, lemon, lime, olive oil, parsley, pepper, sage, salt, sesame, shallot, soy sauce, truffle, white wine. |

 ESCOLAR

| Other Names: | *Barakuta* (Japanese); butterfish; *escolar negro, sierra* (Spanish); *escolar-schlanenmakrele, snoek* (German); *escolier* (French); *foguete, senuca* (Portuguese); snoek (Great Britain); *snoekmakreel* (Dutch); *tirsite* (Italian); *walu* (Hawaiian); white tuna. **Gempylidae.** |

| General Description: | *Escolar is a lusciously rich Pacific fish popular in Hawaii, where it is known as* walu. Two different fish are sold as escolar: *Lepidocybium flavobrunneum*, considered to be the true escolar, and *Ruvettus pretiosus*, the so-called oilfish or castor oil fish, known for its purgative qualities. Though both are purgative, the association of true escolar with the oilfish has given the former a bad reputation. Escolar are excellent for grilling, and their distinctive taste holds up well to strong flavors. |

| Locale and Season: | Found in tropical and temperate waters worldwide, escolar is nearly always a bycatch of tuna longline fisheries. Escolar is fished in Australia, Ecuador, and Indonesia. In the United States, it comes primarily from the Gulf of Mexico or is imported from Ecuador and Fiji. Escolar is mostly available from late winter through spring. |

Characteristics:	Escolar are similar to Chilean sea bass and black cod with their oil-rich, slightly gelatinous, intensely flavored flesh. Raw escolar is bright white to light cream and cooks up juicy and snow white.
How to Choose:	Avoid buying oilfish, which may be sold as escolar. This fish will be much lower in price but is so high in oil that it makes people sick. Escolar fillets will be dark, similar to bluefish in color; oilfish fillets will be reddish in color. True escolar flesh will be bright white. The flesh of escolar should spring back when pressed—if it doesn't, the fish is old.
Storage:	Store escolar fillets up to 2 days refrigerated.
Preparation:	• **Broil, steam, pan-sear, grill, hot-smoke, or bake. The skin is not eaten.**
Suggested Recipe:	**Grilled Escolar** (serves 4): Combine 3 tablespoons honey, 2 tablespoons red wine, 1 tablespoon Worcestershire sauce, 1 tablespoon ground coriander, 1 teaspoon ground cumin, 1/2 teaspoon ground black pepper, and salt to taste. Marinate 4 (6- to 8-ounce) escolar fillets in the mixture 2 to 4 hours, then grill in indirect heat (with the lid closed) about 20 minutes, or until opaque.
Flavor Affinities:	Apple, Cajun seasoning, cilantro, coriander, cumin, curry, ginger, honey, lemon, mint, mushroom, olive oil, orange, red wine, rice vinegar, saffron.

16. 📷 EUROPEAN SEA BASS

Other Names:
Bar, loup de mer (French); *branzino, spigola* (Italian); *hata, suzuki-no-rui* (Japanese); *havabbor* (Norwegian); *lavráki* (Greek); *levrek baligi* (Turkish); *lubina, robaliza, róbalo* (Spanish); *qarous* (Tunisian); *robalo* (Portuguese); *seebarsch, wolfsbarsch* (German). **Moronidae.**

General Description:
The famed European sea bass (Dicentrarchus labrax) *are as sought after today as they were in Roman times.* They are found in the sea, saltwater lakes, and the lower reaches of rivers in Europe. In Roman times, those from the rivers were preferred; today those from the sea are considered best, but fish from aquafarms in Norway and Greece are becoming common. They are one of the most prized of all Mediterranean fish and have always been expensive. This handsome and voracious fish is indeed very good eating.

Locale and Season:
European sea bass are found throughout the Mediterranean and north to Great Britain, Iceland, and Norway. They are available year-round from aquafarms and are best in spring and early summer, before they spawn.

Characteristics:
European sea bass typically weigh $1^1/2$ to 3 pounds and have a silvery skin much like striped bass without the stripes. They have firm, white, mild-flavored flesh without small bones and hold their shape well.

How to Choose:
Line-caught wild sea bass have the best flavor and texture but are rare. The fish are mostly aquafarmed.

Choose fish with bright, silvery, shiny skin and clear, bright eyes.

Storage:

Store whole sea bass up to 2 days refrigerated; store fillets up to 1 day refrigerated.

Preparation: •

Grill, bake, stuff and bake, braise, poach, pan-fry, sauté, steam, or poach whole.

Suggested Recipe:

Baked Sea Bass with Potatoes (serves 4): Arrange an overlapping layer of 1 1/2 pounds thinly sliced Yukon gold potatoes in a baking dish coated with olive oil. Sprinkle with a mixture of finely chopped thyme, garlic, salt, pepper, and extra-virgin olive oil. Repeat to make a second layer. Cover and bake 20 minutes at 400°F. Season a whole (2-pound) sea bass with salt and pepper and rub with olive oil. Lay the fish over the potatoes and sprinkle 2 cups diced fresh tomatoes and 1/4 cup chopped cured black olives around the fish. Bake for 30 minutes or until the fish flakes and the potatoes are soft.

Flavor Affinities:

Butter, capers, cured black olives, fennel, ginger, lemon, mayonnaise, olive oil, orange, Pernod, potato, scallion, sesame, shallot, tarragon, thyme, tomato.

17a–c.

FLOUNDER AND DAB

Other Names:

Dab: American or Canadian plaice; *ising*, *slette* (Danish); *kliesche* (German); *limande* (French); *sandflyndre*

(Norwegian); *sandkoli* (Icelandic); *schar* (Dutch).
Summer flounder: *Carta de verão* (Portuguese);
chomatída tou kalokairioú (Greek); *cardine du Canada*
or *d'été* (French), *falso halibut del Canadá* (Spanish);
fluke; *hirame* (Japanese); *letnyaya kambala* (Russian);
rombo dentato (Italian); *sommerflunder* (German).
Yellowtail flounder: *Gelbschwanzflunder* (German);
karei (Japanese); *limanda* (Italian); rustytail; yellowtail dab. **Winter flounder:** *Akagarei* (Japanese);
Amerikanische winterflunder (German); *chomatída*
(Greek); lemon sole; *limanda americana* (Italian);
platija americana, solla roja (Spanish); *plie rouge*
(French); *schollen* (German); *zimnyaya kambala*
(Russian). **Pleuronectidae.**

General Description:

Flounder are the most important flatfish family and are found mostly in northern waters. Their Latin name, *Pleuronectidae*, means "sideswimmer" because they start out as round fish, but as they mature and become bottom-dwellers, one eye migrates to the same side of the head as the other eye and the fish actually swim on their sides. There are right-eyed and left-eyed flounders, though all commercially impor-tant species in North America (except fluke) are right-eyed. Flounder use color adaptation to match the bay or ocean floor and may partially bury themselves for camouflage. On the American Atlantic coast, yellow-tail is the most important flounder; on the Pacific coast it is petrale sole.

Winter flounder (*Pseuopleuronectes americanus*) are the most common shallow-water flatfish in North America. They are brown-skinned, right-eyed flounder.

On some fish, the tail area on the underside is yellow, so they are often called lemon sole. They may weigh up to 8 pounds. Winter flounder produce both a white and a gray fillet, but both turn pure white when cooked. Summer flounder (*Paralichthys dentatus*) have brownish skin with conspicuous black spots on the top side; the bottom side is almost white. They are usually sold under the name *fluke* and are left-eyed. They are one of the larger flounders, weighing up to 26 pounds. The meat is delicately flavored, bright white, and firm. They are also used for sushi.

Sand dab (*Limanda limanda*) grow up to 5 pounds and may be sold as flounder or, if filleted, as sole. In the Jutland area of Denmark, sand dab is salted and dried and also smoked. Gray sole (*Glyptocephalus cynoglossus*), or witch flounder, is an American East Coast favorite. Their skin is pale gray. Gray sole can weigh up to 5 pounds and are elongated rather than rounded, with perfectly white fillets. Because of the small yield, only 28 percent, this is an expensive fish. It is best eaten whole with skin on. Yellowtail flounder (*L. ferruginea*) weigh only 1 to 2 pounds but are one of the most important species in the Atlantic. Numbers have been diminishing in recent years. Petrale sole (*Eopsetta jordani*) is one of the best-tasting flounders on the American Pacific coast. They can grow as large as 5 pounds but are most common at 1 pound. The rex sole (*G. zachirus*) is a delicious small flounder once common in Pacific waters but increasingly hard to find. They can weigh up to 1 pound but are most common at $1/2$ pound, so they are sold whole. California halibut (*Paralichthys californicus*), or fluke-halibut, is actually a large and tasty flounder sought after for sport and the table. Overfishing has diminished stocks of this flatfish, which makes for excellent eating unless caught near Los Angeles, where fish may be contaminated by pollutants.

Locale and Season:

Flounder are caught in Canada, Iceland, the Netherlands, Portugal, Russia, Spain, the United Kingdom, and the United States. Peak season is May to October for Pacific sand dab, November to April for gray sole, November to May for lemon sole, and May to June and October to November for yellowtail. California halibut range from British Columbia to Baja California.

Characteristics:

Gray and rex sole have long, slender fillets. Yellowtail flounder, lemon sole, fluke, and sand dab have broader, thicker fillets. Market size is from 1 to 5 pounds, according to species. Flounder are renowned for their fine, tender, yet firm texture and have delicate, sweet flavor. Yield is 30 percent.

How to Choose:

Note that some processors used tripolyphosphates to increase moisture levels and extend the shelf life of frozen, defrosted flounder fillets. This also adds water weight to the fish. If the fillets are abnormally wet (or overly inexpensive) they may have been treated. Inexpensive yellowtail fillets may be frozen in blocks.

Storage:
x 2

Store whole flounder up to 2 days refrigerated; store fillets up to 1 day refrigerated.

Preparation: •   **Fillets from large fish may be stuffed, rolled and baked, baked, or coated and pan-fried. Smaller whole fish may be grilled, broiled, or baked.**

NOTE: **Flounder is quite lean, so do not overcook it. As soon as the flesh is opaque, it is done. Because it flakes easily, fillets are not suitable for stir-frying or grilling.**

Suggested Recipe: **Broiled Crumbed Flounder** (serves 4): Sauté 1/4 cup finely chopped onion with 1/4 cup chopped green and red pepper in 1 tablespoon butter. Remove from heat and combine with 1/4 cup sliced scallions, 1 teaspoon chopped garlic, and 1/2 cup fine dry bread crumbs. Season 4 (6- to 8-ounce) flounder fillets with salt and pepper, spread with a thin layer of mayonnaise, and top with the crumb mixture. Broil about 6 minutes, or until the fish flakes.

Flavor Affinities: Bell pepper, butter, chervil, chives, cream, dill, fennel, gruyère cheese, lemon, mint, mushroom, parmesan cheese, parsley, shallot, spinach, tarragon, tomato, white vermouth, white wine, zucchini.

GRENADIER

Other Names: *Granadero* (Spanish); *granatiere* (Italian); *grenadier de roche* (French); *grenadierfisch* (German); *isgalt* (Norwegian); *lagartixa da rocha* (Portuguese); *langhale* (Danish); *langstart* (Swedish); onion-eye, roughhead grenadier, smooth-spined rat-tail (Canada); *shiira* (Japanese); *siewiernyj* (Russian); *snarphali* (Icelandic). **Macrouridae.**

General Description:
Grenadier (Macrourus berlax, Coryphaenoides rupestris, and others) is a deep, cold-water relative of cod. Ash gray in color, these long, thin fish are taken by bottom- and midwater trawlers in Canada, where there is a significant fishery. Processing has been a problem in the past because the scales have ruined knives—today, the fish are filleted by mechanical means. Other species live in the cold waters of the Southern Hemisphere. Grenadiers feed mostly on shrimp, small fish, and squid, so they have richly flavored meat.

Locale and Season:
Grenadiers are found off Labrador, the Georges Bank, and the Grand Banks, frequently as bycatch of Greenland turbot. Their main season is May to December, but frozen fillets are available year-round.

Characteristics:
Grenadiers have large heads, tapering bodies, whiplike tails, and sharp scales and are commonly over 2 feet long. Their tough, inedible skin protects snow-white, firm, and flavorful meat that is sweet and succulent. The flesh can be as much as 1 inch thick at the head and paper thin at the tail. Yield is 20 percent.

How to Choose:
Choose firm, white fillets with a clean, briny smell; choose frozen fillets with no signs of freezer burn.

Storage:
x 1
Store grenadier fillets 1 day refrigerated; defrost frozen fillets overnight in the refrigerator.

Preparation: •   **Grenadier stands up well to sauces. Bake, sauté, fry,
or use in chowder.**

Suggested
Recipe:

Creamy Grenadier Chowder (serves 6): In a large
soup pot, slowly cook 1/4 pound diced salt pork until
crisp. Remove the meat, reserving the fat in the pot.
Add 2 tablespoons butter, 1 1/2 cups diced onions,
1/2 cup diced celery, and 1 tablespoon chopped thyme
and/or marjoram and cook until the onions are soft.
Add 2 pounds diced peeled potatoes and 1 1/2 quarts
fish stock or clam broth and bring to a boil. Season
with salt and pepper and simmer until the potatoes
are almost cooked through. Add 3 pounds cut up
grenadier fillets and simmer until the fish flakes,
about 8 minutes. Stir in 2 cups light or heavy cream
and 2 tablespoons chopped parsley, and serve.

Flavor
Affinities:

Bacon, bay leaf, butter, celery, chives, cream, lemon,
marjoram, onion, parsley, potato, salt pork, savory,
shallot, thyme, white wine.

18a–b.

GROUPER

Other Names: *Cernia* (Italian); *garoupa, mero* (Spanish); *hata, mero*
(Japanese); *mennani* (Tunisia); *mérou, serran* (French);
rophós (Greek); *serrano* (Portuguese); *zackenbarsch*
(German). **Serranidae.**

General
Description:

Grouper are part of the large sea bass family. They are
large, solitary, predatory fish that inhabit rocky, shallow

tropical waters. These excellent, meaty fish have few bones and are sought by sport fishermen. In the American South, grouper fillets are often blackened: coated with Cajun seasoning then pan-seared at high heat so that it is crusty on the outside and moist on the inside. These wild fish maintain their moisture even if overcooked, making them a favorite for restaurants, especially in Florida and the American South.

The red grouper (*Epinephelus morio*), most common in the American marketplace, is valued for its availability, flavor, and size and is recognizable by its mottled brown-red color. Red grouper can weigh up to 50 pounds, but average is 5 to 10 pounds. Black grouper (*Mycteroperca bonaci*) are caught mostly off the coast of Florida and in the Caribbean and can weigh as much as 100 pounds, but 10 to 15 pounds is average. They have dark brown or gray blotchy skin with black spots and squiggly, pale lines. Because of limited supplies of true black grouper, they have been replaced in markets by gag (*M. microlepis*), which are similar in flavor and consistency.

Jewfish (*E. itajara*), once very popular in Chinese restaurants and markets, are the largest of all groupers, weighing about 200 pounds. Because of overfishing, there is currently a moratorium on this species. Nassau grouper (*E. striatus*) are large and abundant with very tasty meat. They are found off the coast of Florida and in the Bahamas. They grow to more than 50 pounds, but 5 to 10 is average. The strikingly beautiful giant hawkfish (*Cirrhitus rivulatus*) from the Pacific coast is known in Spanish as *chino mero*, or "Chinese grouper," because its markings are thought to resemble Chinese characters. The excellent table fish may weigh up to 9 pounds.

Locale and
Season:

Grouper are found in temperate waters from the mid-Atlantic states and Florida to the Gulf of Mexico, Central America, and South America and in the Mediterranean. They are usually caught by hook and line and are most abundant in late summer and fall.

Characteristics:

Red grouper are sweeter and milder than black grouper. The meat of both red and black grouper is white and lean with few bones. Cooked, the meat is firm with white, moist, heavy flake.

How to Choose:

Because of its large size and thick skin, grouper is usually sold filleted and skinned. Grouper, especially large red grouper, are prone to parasites in the summer, but once cooked, there is no health risk. Because they are a reef fish, they can also cause ciguatera poisoning, though this is rare.

Storage:

Store grouper fillets up to 2 days refrigerated.

x 2

Preparation:

• **This versatile fish can be fried, grilled, skewered for kebobs, pan-fried, breaded and fried, sautéed, or used to make chowders and fish stews.**

• **Larger whole groupers are suitable for roasting. Fillets from large groupers should be butterflied to reduce the thickness of the dense flesh.**

Suggested Recipe:

Cornmeal-Fried Grouper with Papaya Salsa
(serves 4): Combine 1 papaya cut into small cubes with 1 tablespoon honey, the juice of 1 lime, 1/2 cup diced red onion, 1/2 cup diced red bell pepper, and 1 finely minced Scotch bonnet or other chile pepper, and reserve. Sprinkle 4 boneless, skinless grouper fillets with salt and pepper. Dip first in flour, then in beaten eggs, and finally in cornmeal. Fry in a heavy skillet in 1/2 cup hot canola oil until browned on both sides and the fish flakes. Drain well and serve topped with the papaya salsa.

Flavor Affinities:

Capers, chiles, cilantro, coconut, lime, mango, olives, papaya, passion fruit, pineapple, red onion, star fruit, sweet onion, tartar sauce, tomato.

GURNARD AND SEA ROBIN

Other Names:

Grey gurnard: *Benekli kirlangic* (Turkish); *borracho, cuco, perlón* (Spanish); *cabra morena, ruivo* (Portuguese); *carpone gorno, gallinella* (Italian); *crooner* (Scotland); croonack, gowdie (Great Britain); *crúdán* (Irish); *grauer-knurrhahn* (German); *grauwe poon* (Dutch); *grondin gris, trigle gris* (French); *hono-no-rui* (Japanese); *kaponi* (Greek); *knurr* (Norwegian). **American gurnard:** *Grondin carolin* (French); *rubio carolino* (Spanish); sea robin. **Red gurnard:** *Blauflossen-knur-rhahn* (German); *carbra kumu* (Portuguese); *capone* (Italian); *grondin, perlon* (French); *minamihôbô* (Japanese). **Piper:** *Capone lira* (Italian); *garneo*

(Spanish); *grondin lyre* (French); *öksüz* (Turkish). **Tab gurnard:** *Bacamarte, cabra-cabaco* (Portuguese); *bejel, perlón* (Spanish); *capone, gallinella* (Italian); *grondin galinette, perlon* (French); *rød knurhane* (Danish); *rode poon* (Dutch); *seeschwalbe* (German); *selachi* (Greek). **Triglidae.**

General
Description:

Gurnard are small fish commonly known as sea robins in the United States because of their large, winglike pectoral fins. These odd-looking fish, with scaly, huge heads, creep along the sea bottom. Gurnard produce audible grunts like snoring to keep in touch with each other, a skill noted in classic Greek times by Aristotle.

The piper (*Trigla lyra*) is a large member of this family, with a red back, rosy-pink sides, and a silvery belly. They have firm white flesh that is free of small bones, though the flesh tends to dry out when cooked. Grey gurnard (*Eutriglia gurnardus*) are popular filleted and fried in Holland. Large tub gurnard (*T. lucerna*), or tub-fish, are the largest and one of the best tasting of these fish. They are popular in the Black Sea. Red gurnard (*Aspitrigla cuclus*) are common in the waters of Great Britain and make for good eating. The American gurnard (*Prinotus carolinus*), or sea robin, has delicately flavored, quite firm flesh.

Locale and
Season:

Gurnard are found in the Mediterranean, the Black Sea, the southern Atlantic, and the Gulf of Mexico and off the coasts of Africa, Great Britain, and Japan.

Characteristics:

Gurnard flesh is white, firm, and lean; the skin is edible. Their roe is also eaten. Yield is 35 percent.

How to Choose:	Gurnard are bony with innocuous flavor and tend to be inexpensive. They are usually sold whole. Ask the fishmonger to remove the spiny fins and the skin. In France, gurnard may be substituted for the superior red mullet (p. 129). Allow 1 pound per person.
Storage:	Store gurnard fillets up to 1 day refrigerated.

Preparation:

• **For small fish, cut off the head, clean the tail section, and skin like monkfish (p. 103). Cook the tail whole.**

• **Bake, fry, poach, or use for fish stew.**

Suggested Recipe:

Gurnard with Turkish Almond Sauce (serves 4): Poach a whole (2-pound) gurnard in court bouillon (white wine, lemon, thyme, bay leaf, coriander seed, shallots simmered with enough water to cover the fish). Cool and serve with Turkish Almond Sauce: Blend 1 cup blanched almonds with 1 slice crustless white bread, 3/4 cup extra-virgin olive oil, and the juice of 1 lemon until thick and smooth. Season with salt and pepper.

Flavor Affinities:

Almond, cilantro, chiles, garlic, lemon, mayonnaise, olive oil, onion, paprika, parsley, pine nut, potato, saffron, tomato, vinegar, white wine.

19. **HADDOCK**

Other Names: *Aiglefin, ânon, églefin* (French); *anon, eglefino, liba* (Spanish); *arinca* (Portuguese); *bakaliáros* (Greek);

eglefino (Italian); *hyse, kolje* (Norwegian); *kuller* (Danish); *montsukidara* (Japanese); *piksha* (Russian); *schellfisch* (German); *schelvis* (Dutch); *ysa* (Icelandic). **Gadidae**.

General
Description:

Haddock (Melanogrammus aeglefinus) *are perhaps the most prized member of the cod family because of their delicate flavor and melt-in-the-mouth texture.* They are similar in appearance to the much larger Atlantic cod, though with less mottled skin, and can be identified by the black mark on the head area just above the pectoral fin. Scrods are small, head-on, gutted haddock between 1 1/2 to 2 pounds. Smaller haddock are called snapper haddock; those over 2 1/2 pound are large haddock. Haddock is cold-smoked as Scotland's famous finnan haddie (p. 288). Haddock are caught by longlines and trawl nets. This tender, mild fish is quite versatile in the kitchen.

Locale and
Season:

Haddock are wild-caught fish found on both sides of the North Atlantic. They are fished in Canada, Iceland, Norway, Russia, the United Kingdom, and the United States. Fresh haddock fillets are most abundant in June, though they are imported from Iceland year-round. Peak season in the United States and Canada is June through October.

Characteristics:

Market weight is 2 to 5 pounds. Overfishing makes haddock relatively scarce and also expensive. Haddock meat has a delicate, fine flake and slightly sweet flavor; once cooked, the firm yet tender meat holds together. The meat is lean. The raw meat is white, and when cooked, it is even whiter.

How to Choose: Haddock fillets are smaller and have a finer flake than cod. When sold filleted as scrod, they usually have their skin. Choose haddock with firm, resilient flesh.

Storage: Store whole haddock up to 2 days refrigerated; store
☐ × 2   fillets 1 day.

Preparation: • **Small fillets can be sautéed or breaded and pan-fried; large fish are suitable for soups, stews, and chowders and can also be poached or pan-fried.**

Suggested   **Broiled Haddock with Egg Sauce** (serves 4):
Recipe: Sprinkle 2 pounds haddock fillet with salt and pepper and dot with butter. Arrange in an oiled baking pan and broil 5 to 10 minutes, or until the fish flakes. Remove the fish from the oven and pour off any cooking juices into a small pot, keeping the fish warm separately. Boil the juices until syrupy. Whisk in 3 tablespoons butter, 2 tablespoons each chopped marjoram, thyme, and parsley, and 3 chopped hard-cooked eggs. Serve over the fish.

Flavor   Bacon, butter, chervil, chives, cream, egg, onion, parsley,
Affinities: potato, scallion, shallot, thyme, white wine.

20a–b.   **HAKE AND WHITING**

Other Names: **Hake:** *Heiku* (Japanese); *merlu* (French); *merluza* (Spanish); *nasello* (Italian); *seehecht* (German). **Chilean hake:** Argentine whiting; capensis. **Pacific whiting:**

Merlu du Pacifique (French); *nordpazifischer seehecht*
(German); Pacific hake; South African whiting.
Atlantic whiting: Atlantic hake; *bakaliáros tou
Atlantikoú* (Greek); *merlu argenté* (French); *merluza
norteamericana* (Spanish); *nasello atlantico* (Italian);
noordwestatlantische heek (Dutch); *pescada prateada*
(Portuguese); silver hake (Great Britain). **Merlucciidae**.

General
Description:
*Hake (Merluccius merluccius) is a deepwater member
of the cod family.* The fish have mild-tasting and
sweet meat, with creamy flesh and a rather coarse,
watery texture. Capensis, from South Africa, is the
firmest type of hake, followed by Atlantic and
Argentine hake. Atlantic whiting (*M. bilinearis*)
are sold inexpensively in U.S. fish markets simply
as whiting, often whole with their heads. In New
England, they are salted like cod. Though there are
subtle differences between hake and whiting, they
are sold interchangeably and make a good, less
expensive substitute for pollock (p. 121) or cod
(p. 37).

While both hake and whiting have a reputation
for mushy texture, fresh and well-handled fish does
not suffer from this. They are fairly bland fish that
take well to all sorts of seasonings. They are often
used for commercial fish sticks. White hake (*Urophycis
tennuis*), also known as Boston ling or steakfish, is
large hake that can weigh up to 30 pounds, though
market weight is 1 to 2 pounds. Antarctic queen (*M.
australis*), or New Zealand hake, has firmer flesh than
other hake and mild flavor.

Locale and Season:	Atlantic whiting from the northwest Atlantic are the most common species in the United States and are in season from October to December. Pacific whiting are found from the Bering Sea to Baja California. The United States also imports large quantities of Argentine whiting (*M. hubbsi*) and Chilean hake (*M. gayi*). Argentine hake is in season from November through February. Pacific whiting is in season in May and June. Cape capensis is in season year-round.
Characteristics:	These fish range in size from small (1- to 2-pound) Pacific whiting to large (6-pound) capensis. Hakes and whiting have fragile white meat with small flake that is highly perishable, so much of the Pacific catch is immediately frozen.
How to Choose:	Whiting are best in February and March, just before they spawn. There is a wide range of hake species, and because these fish are quite soft and fragile, there is a great deal of variation in quality from excellent to poor. Large whiting may be sold filleted.
Storage:	Store hake and whiting up to 1 day refrigerated.
x 1	
Preparation:	• **For fillets, pull out the pin bones and remove the skin, if desired. Or cut into steaks.**
	• **Bake, broil, deep-fry coated in bread crumbs or batter, sauté, or pan-fry.**
Suggested Recipe:	**Spanish Hake with Spinach** (serves 4): Wilt 1 1/2 pounds fresh spinach briefly, then squeeze out water

and chop. Season 1¹/₂ pounds whiting fillet with salt and pepper and then dust with flour. Fry in 2 tablespoons hot olive oil until brown on both sides. Remove fish to a plate. In the same pan, heat 2 tablespoons more olive oil, add 1 cup finely chopped onion, and cook over low heat 10 minutes, or until softened. Stir in 2 teaspoons chopped garlic, cook 1 minute, then add the spinach and salt and pepper, and toss together. Spoon the spinach mixture into a shallow baking dish and top with the fish. Sprinkle with 2 tablespoons pine nuts, ¹/₂ cup dry sherry, and 1 tablespoon olive oil. Bake at 375°F for 15 minutes, or until the fish flakes.

Flavor
Affinities: Anchovy, balsamic vinegar, bay leaf, capers, cilantro, coriander, cumin, cured black olives, garlic, lemon, marjoram, mayonnaise, olive oil, orange, preserved lemon, thyme, tomato, white wine.

21a–b.   **HALIBUT**

Other Names: **Atlantic halibut:** *Flétan* (French); *heilbot* (Dutch); *helleflynder* (Danish); *hipogloso negro* (Spanish); *ippóglossa* (Greek); *ippoglosso Atlantico* (Italian); *karasu-garei* (Japanese); *kveite* (Norwegian); *pi-mu-yu* (Taiwan); *schwartzer heilbutt* (German). **Pacific halibut:** *Belokory paltus* (Russian); *ohyô* (Japanese). **Greenland turbot:** *Alabote-de-gronelandia* (Portuguese); *flétan noir* (French). **Pleuronectidae.**

General Description:	*Halibut are the largest of all flatfish, up to 9 feet long.* Halibut have a large mouth, a forked tail, and are dark green-brown on their upper side and gray-white below. They are bottom-dwelling strong swimmers and may be caught by longline. Small fish are called chicken halibut, while large adults are whales. Halibut command a high price for their firm, white meat.
	Pacific halibut (*Hippoglossus stenolepsis*) are closely related to Atlantic halibut; some scientists consider them to be the same species. Northwest Indians carved special fish hooks for halibut with designs to bring good luck and large fish. Atlantic halibut (*H. hippoglossus*) are caught close to shore and are now being farmed.
	Greenland turbot (*Reinhardtius hippoglossoides*) are closely related to the halibut. They are economical, versatile fish loaded with omega-3 fatty acids.
Locale and Season:	Alaska produces 80 percent of Pacific halibut. They are in peak season April through October. Russian and Japanese halibut may be had from March 15 through November 15. Atlantic halibut are caught from Labrador to Maine. Supplies of halibut dwindle in early winter. Greenland turbot are harvested from deep waters near Newfoundland and Labrador and are in season from May to October.
Characteristics:	Halibut may weigh more than 600 pounds, although 5 to 10 pounds is average. The lean, snow-white meat is finely textured, dense, and has few bones; it retains its moisture well when frozen. When cooked it is tender and flaky, though still firm, but it is important

not to overcook this lean fish. Its dark skin is edible though often removed. Pacific halibut is larger and softer in texture than Atlantic halibut. Halibut can harbor undetectable microorganisms that can make it mushy when cooked. This is uncommon, and the microorganisms are killed by cooking to 140°F.

How to Choose: Halibut are sold whole, as steaks and fillets. Meat from large halibut is a bit coarse. Choose halibut with white, glossy, almost translucent flesh, avoiding any that is dull, yellowish, or dried out. Greenland turbot is sold whole, as fresh or frozen fillets, and as steaks.

Storage: Store large sections of halibut up to 3 days refrigerated;
⊟ x 3   store fillets up to 2 days refrigerated.

Preparation: •   **Poach, bake, broil, sauté, steam, grill, pan-roast, sear, or cube and skewer.**

Suggested   **Baked Halibut with Tarragon** (serves 4): Arrange 4
Recipe: halibut fillets in a shallow baking dish. Sprinkle with salt, pepper, 2 tablespoons chopped tarragon, and 1/4 cup chopped shallots. Dot with 2 tablespoons butter, spread with 2 tablespoons sour cream, and bake at 375°F until the fish flakes, about 20 minutes.

Flavor   Almond, asparagus, butter, capers, chervil, chives, dill,
Affinities: fennel, ginger, lemon, orange, ponzu, potato, shallot, tarragon, white wine, wine vinegar.

22a–b. **HAMACHI**

Other Names:
Buri, mojyako, tsubasu yazu (Japanese); *charuteiro do Japão* (Portuguese); *gelbschwanz, Japanische seriola* (German); Japanese amberjack; *Japansk ravfisk* (Danish); king amberjack; racing tuna; *ricciola giapponese* (Italian); *seriola coreana, serviola* (Spanish); *sériole du Japon* (French); yellowtail; *zheltokhvostaya lakerda* (Russian). **Japanese kingfish:** Gold striped amberjack; *hiramasa* (Japanese); yellowtail kingfish. **Carangidae.**

General Description:
Hamachi (Seriola quinqueradiata), commonly known as yellowtail, is a prized, expensive, rich, flavorful fish in the jack and pompano family. Some fish are caught wild, but a substantial amount is farmed for use in sushi. In May, Japanese farmers scoop up the small wild fry (called *mojako*) from under floating seaweed and grow them in cages in the sea. The closely related Japanese kingfish (*S. lalandi*), commonly known by its Japanese name, *hiramasa*, is found in the cool, temperate waters of the Pacific and Indian Oceans and is now farmed in Japan and Australia. Firm with full-bodied flavor, the fish is highly esteemed for sashimi.

Locale and Season:

Wild hamachi are found in Hawaii; they are farmed off central Japan. Another species, *S. lanlandei*, are harvested off Baja California and may be sold as farmed hamachi, though they are not suited to sushi.

Characteristics:
Hamachi have both dark and light meat, though wild fish vary in color depending on fat content. Lighter

fish are higher in fat. Raw, they have subtle flavor and yielding texture. Cooked, the flesh is white and firm with mild, sweet, buttery flavor. Wild hamachi, not farmed, may contain parasites.

How to Choose:

Whole hamachi average 12 pounds; single sides are shipped from Hawaii in well-sealed packages. Line-caught whole hamachi from California are also available. In Japan, fish of 3 kilos (6.6 pounds) are called hamachi, at 5 kilos (11 pounds) they are called buri.

Storage:

Refrigerate hamachi in its package under crushed ice. Do not use cubed ice, which could bruise it.

Preparation: 1.

Cut away any dark meat along the edge. Trim very well and use every bit, especially the delicious firm meat near the head.

2.

To slice for sushi, wrap hamachi fillets in plastic and freeze 30 minutes, or until firm and somewhat stiff.

3.

Using a very sharp knife with a long, thin blade, and starting at the head end, cut straight across into very thin slices to about three-quarters of the way down the fillet. The tail end is too stringy to use.

4.

Broil, grill, sauté, or use for sushi or sashimi.

Suggested
Recipe:

Hamachi with Red Grapefruit and Mint (serves 4):
Combine 6 ounces of very thinly sliced fresh hamachi with 4 thin slices red onion and 2 tablespoons small diced red grapefruit. Combine 2 teaspoons lime juice,

1 teaspoon canola oil, 1 teaspoon ponzu sauce, and salt and pepper to taste. Toss the fish with most of the marinade, leave for 5 to 10 minutes to cure, then drain. Combine with remaining marinade, thinly sliced mint and scallions, and serve very cold.

Flavor
Affinities:

Avocado, bell pepper, cucumber, ginger, lemon, lime, mint, orange, ponzu, red grapefruit, red onion, rice vinegar, scallion, sesame, soy sauce, yuzu.

HERRING AND SPRAT

Other Names:

Herring: *Ammassassuaq* (Greenlandic); *arenque* (Portuguese, Spanish); *aringa* (Italian); *Atlanticheskaya seld* (Russian); *hareng* (French); *haring* (Dutch); *hering* (German); *nishin* (Japanese); *régha* (Greece); *ringa* (Turkish); *sild* (Danish, Norwegian); *sledz* (Polish). **Sprat:** *Breitling* (German); *espadín* (Spanish); *esprot* (French); *nishi-no-rui* (Japanese); *papalina* (Italian). **Clupeidae.**

General
Description:

Herring (Clupea harengus) are one of the world's most important fish, especially in northern Europe. The small, iridescent herring are enjoyed worldwide fresh, cured, pickled, smoked, or for their roe (p. 289). The humble herring was once important enough to determine the fate of empires: The powerful German and Scandivanian Hanseatic League collapsed in the fifteenth century when the lucrative fish stopped spawning in the Baltic Sea. Treaties worth millions of dollars were negotiated

for herring rights in the New World. There are two
types of commercially significant herring: The Atlantic
herring (*C. harengus*) and Pacific herring (*C. harengus
pallasi*). Sprat (*Sprattus sprattus*) are smaller, closely
related fish.

Locale and
Season:

The best fresh herring are available in spring and
summer, just before spawning. Herring are found in
colder waters of the western and eastern Atlantic.

Characteristics:

Fresh herring have deep green coloring along their
backs and bright silvery scales that slide off easily.
They are bony with off-white, soft, rich meat; they
average less than 2 pounds. Small herring are rich and
delicate in flavor; large herring are coarse and oilier.
They are sold whole. Yield is 45 percent.

How to Choose:

Choose bright herring with firm bellies. The higher
the fat content, the more flavor.

Storage:
x 2

Herring are highly perishable. Store on ice, refrigerated,
up to 2 days.

Preparation: •

**Slit open along the belly from the head nearly to the
tail, pulling out the head, guts, and backbone, but
leaving the tail in place to hold the fish together.**

 •

Grill, pan-fry, bake, hot-smoke, or broil.

Suggested
Recipe:

Baked Herring with Mustard (serves 4): Combine 3
tablespoons oil with 1½ tablespoons soy sauce, 3
tablespoons Dijon mustard, 1 finely chopped onion,

and salt and pepper to taste. Pour over 2 pounds herring fillets and marinate 1 hour refrigerated. Place herring in an oiled baking dish and broil 20 minutes or until the fish flakes, turning it halfway through.

Flavor
Affinities:

Allspice, bacon, bay leaf, butter, coriander seed, cream, dill, garlic, mustard, onion, parsley, potato, soy sauce, sugar, tarragon, vinegar, white wine.

HOKI

Other Names:

Blue grenadier; blue hake; *langschwanz-seehecht* (German); *merlu à longue queue* (French); *merluza azul* (Spanish); *nasello azurro* (Italian); New Zealand whip-tail; New Zealand whiting. **Merlucciidae**.

General
Description:

Hoki (Macruronus novazelandiae) *are a commercially important species from Australia and New Zealand.* These elongated fish taper to a point and have joined fins, a large mouth, and tiny scales. Hoki are best fried or baked because they are quite lean. They are used for fish sticks at McDonald's restaurants in Australia and New Zealand. They make a good alternative to cod and haddock. Most hoki are consumed where caught, but some are exported.

Locale and
Season:

Hoki are caught off the coasts of Australia and New Zealand. Peak season is June through September.

Characteristics:	The versatile hoki have white, flaky, and lean but succulent flesh with few bones and mild flavor. Outside of Australia and New Zealand, hoki are usually found as frozen, skinless fillets. The flesh remains white when cooked. Hoki are well suited for commercial processing and are commonly formed into a block for further processing, as for breaded fish sticks.
How to Choose:	Hoki fillets are long and thin. Stocks have greatly declined because of large-scale deepwater trawling, so many conscientious consumers avoid this fish.
Storage:	Defrost hoki fillets overnight in the refrigerator and cook within 1 day.
Preparation:	**1.** **Remove the fat line that runs down the center of the fillet to improve shelf life and flavor. Once the fat is removed, the fish will be fragile, so handle with care.**
	2. **Cook fillets directly from the freezer except when breading or stuffing.**
	3. **Fry, bake, poach, sauté, broil, or microwave.**
Suggested Recipe:	**Oven-Fried Hoki** (serves 4): Sprinkle 1 1/2 pounds skinless hoki fillets with salt, pepper, and lemon juice, adding cayenne, oregano, dill, or hot pepper sauce if desired. Dip in evaporated milk, then roll in cornflake or panko crumbs and drizzle with oil. Bake at 450°F for 8 to 10 minutes, or until it flakes.

Flavor Affinities:	Almond, celery, chiles, coconut, dill, leek, lime, olive oil, orange, oregano, pine nut, rice wine, scallion, sesame, snow pea, soy, tarragon, thyme, tomato.

23.

JOHN DORY AND OREO DORY

Other Names:	**John Dory:** *Christópsaro* (Greek); *dülger baligi* (Turkish); *gallo*, *pez de San Pedro* (Spanish); *galo negro*, *peixe galo* (Portuguese); *kuznets* (Russian); *matôdai* (Japanese); *poule-de-mer*, *Saint Pierre* (French); Saint Peter's fish; *Sanktpetersfisk* (Danish). **Oreo dory:** *Ôme-matodai-zoku* (Japanese); *samonete* (Spanish); *tiefsee Petersfisch* (German). **Zeidae**.

General Description:	*John Dories* (Zeus faber) *are famed in many places as Saint Peter's fish because of the prominent gold-ringed black spot that is the supposed mark of Saint Peter.* They are the most prized and expensive member of their family and have rich-textured, firm, well-flavored flesh. They are an odd-looking, primitive, spiny-finned flatfish (not related to flounder) with a very small proportion of meat. One French name, *poule de mer*, means "chicken of the sea" (not the tuna).

American dories (*Zenopsis ocellata*) swim in the western Atlantic and are just as delicious as their European counterpart, but because they are not fished commercially, they are only occasionally found for sale. The similar, though unrelated, black oreo dory (*Allocyttus niger*) and the smooth oreo dory (*Pseudocyttus maculatus*) from New Zealand are occasionally found for sale in the United States. They are trawl-caught, both as targeted fish and as bycatch of the orange roughy fishery in New Zealand. The firm meat of oreo dory holds together in cooking, so it is a good choice for soups, chowders, and stews.

Locale and
Season:

John Dories are found in the Mediterranean and off the coast of Great Britain and the western coast of Africa. Oreo dories are found off the coasts of Australia, New Zealand, and South Africa. Although they are found year-round, supply is low in the summer.

Characteristics:

John Dories weigh up to 15 pounds, but average size is much less. Market size for oreo dories is 1 to 2 pounds. The skin is not eaten. Yield for John Dory is 25 percent. The lean flesh of oreo dory easily dries out.

How to Choose:

John Dory has smooth, silvery skin with a dark spot behind the pectoral fin. Black oreo dory has rough black skin; smooth oreo dory has brown skin and is more highly regarded. Because the fish are harvested far offshore, they are generally sold as skin-off frozen fillets, making it hard to tell the species apart.

Storage:

Cook John Dory the same day it is purchased. Defrost oreo dory fillets overnight in the refrigerator and cook within 1 day.

Preparation: •

Roast or bake a whole cleaned John Dory.

• **Pan-fry, steam, or sauté John Dory or oreo dory fillets or use in soups and stews.**

Suggested
Recipe:

Pan-Fried John Dory (serves 4): Lightly beat 2 eggs and season with salt, pepper, and cayenne. Make fresh bread crumbs from crustless Italian bread and mix with finely chopped oregano. Dust 4 skinless fillets with flour, then dip in the egg, and then in the crumbs. Pan-fry in olive oil until crisp and brown on both sides. Drain and serve with lemon wedges.

Flavor
Affinities:

Avocado, basil, butter, cilantro, fennel, lemon, lobster, marjoram, olive oil, orange, oregano, Pernod, red onion, tarragon, thyme, tomato, white wine.

KINGKLIP

Other Names:

Kingklip: *Abadèche* (French); *abadeco* (Italian); *abadejo* (Spanish); Chilean ling; *congrio* (Latin America); cusk-eel; *kingu* (Japanese); *schlangenfisch* (German). **Ophidiidae. Ling:** *Barruenda, maruca* (Spanish); *julienne, lingue* (French); *korojimanagadara* (Japanese); *lange* (Norwegian); *leng* (German); *molva* (Italian); *valkoturkska* (Finnish). **Lotidae.**

General
Description:

The long, slender kingklip is a member of the cusk eel family with four species: red (Genypterus chilensis), *golden* (G. blacodes), *South African* (G. capensis), *and black* (G. maculatus). This eel-like fish can be up to 6 feet long. They are popular for a Chilean-style bouillabaisse called *caldillo congrio*; these fish work well in soups and stews because the dense meat holds its shape. However, the meat's density means that it takes a while to cook. They are caught by trawlers, often as a bycatch. In Europe, kingklip is sold as cusk eel.

Ling (*Molva molva*), resembling the kingklip, have good flavor, comparable to that of monkfish. The salted roe is a delicacy in Spain; in Scandinavia, ling is salted and dried. A smaller Mediterranean ling (*M. dypterygia*) is known as blue ling.

Locale and Season: Kingklip are found in the Southern Hemisphere off Argentina, Chile, Australia, New Zealand, and South Africa. The supply is lightest between November and February. Ling are in season September to July.

Characteristics: Kingklip can weigh up to 50 pounds, but 10 pounds is average, with fillets ranging from 1 to 4 pounds. Kingklip are rather slimy on the outside. The raw meat of red and golden kingklip is pink to creamy white and cooks up white. Their long fillets are mild and slightly sweet with a dense though tender texture, large flake, and few bones. Yield is 40 percent.

How to Choose: Red and golden kingklip are considered best for flavor and texture. Black kingklip has narrower fillets; they will cook up darker and won't be as tender. They can be identified by their yellow spots and dark flesh.

Storage: Store kingklip up to 2 days refrigerated.

x 2

Preparation: • **Bake, broil, grill, steam, fry, poach, or sauté.**

Suggested Recipe:

Baked Kingklip in Foil (serves 4): Combine the juice of 4 lemons and 2 oranges with 2 tablespoons soy sauce, 1/2 cup olive oil, 1 diced red onion, and a handful of chopped cilantro. Marinate 4 kingklip fillets (1 1/2 to 2 pounds total) in the mixture for about 30 minutes. Prepare 4 large squares of heavy-duty aluminum foil: Place 1 fillet onto each square and fold sides up, leaving an opening. Equally distribute the marinade over the fish and close up the packets. Bake at 400°F for 10 minutes, or until the liquid is bubbling and the fish flakes.

Flavor Affinities:

Almond, avocado, bay leaf, chili powder, curry, dill, garlic, ginger, grapefruit, kiwi, lemon, lentils, mango, mushroom, olive oil, paprika, thyme, tomato.

LAKE PERCH

Other Names:

Amerikanisher flussbarsch (German); *perca americana* (Portuguese); *perca canadiense* (Spanish); *perche canadienne* (French); *persico dorato* (Italian); yellow perch; *zhelty okun* (Russian). **Percidae.**

General Description:

Lake perch (Perca flavescens) *are the best known of various spiny-finned freshwater fish found in North America and Europe, often called yellow perch.* Perch support commercial fishery in Lake Michigan, Lake Erie, and Lake Huron and are a popular sport fish. In Europe, river perch (*P. fluviatilis*) are highly favored for their mild, delicate flavor and lean, firm flesh. The yellow perch is considered by many to be one of the finest eating freshwater fish.

Locale and
Season:

In America, yellow perch are found in freshwater mainly on the East Coast and in the Great Lakes.

Characteristics:

Perch range in size from 1/2 to 3 pounds and are sold fresh and frozen, whole and filleted. Adult yellow perch are usually golden yellow; young fish are lighter with white, flaky flesh.

How to Choose:

Choose small fish for broiling or sautéing; choose larger fish for baking, steaming, or poaching.

Storage:

Store whole fish up to 2 days refrigerated.

x 2

Preparation: •

Pan-fry, poach, steam, bake, or use in soups.

Suggested
Recipe:

Perch with Black Walnuts (serves 4): Pat dry 2 pounds perch fillets, sprinkle with salt and pepper, then dredge in cornmeal. Slowly fry in bacon fat until crisp, about 8 minutes. Remove the fish from the pan and keep warm. Add 2 tablespoons butter to the skillet and 1/2 cup chopped black walnuts. Brown lightly, add the juice of 1 lemon, bring to a boil, and pour over the fish.

Flavor
Affinities:

Bacon, bean sprout, bell pepper, butter, carrot, celery, dill, ginger, lemon, marjoram, mushroom, onion, scallion, sesame, snow pea, soy sauce, thyme, tomato.

LAKE VICTORIA PERCH

Other Names: African snook; *bikutoriakopachi* (Japanese); capitaine; Nile perch; *perca del Lago Victoria* (Spanish); *perche du lac Victoria* (French); *pesce di Lago Victoria* (Italian); *Victoria seebarsch* (German). **Latidae**.

General Description: *Lake Victoria perch* (Lates nilocticus), *formerly known as Nile perch, are freshwater fish found in central Africa's lakes and rivers.* Ancient Egyptians held the fish in high regard; Lake Victoria perch were mummified and even worshipped. Huge, carnivorous fish that dominate their surroundings, Lake Victoria perch support a substantial commercial fishery and have all but taken over Lake Victoria, where they were introduced in the 1960s, decimating some 350 species of fish. They are harvested by small boats working close to shore with gill nets and longlines. Because the flesh is oilier than native fish species and more difficult to dry, increased demand for firewood to dry the catch has contributed to regional deforestation. With its high oil content, this fish stays moist during cooking and is a good candidate for smoking.

Locale and Season:

Lake Victoria perch are almost always from Lake Victoria in Kenya, Tanzania, and Uganda. They are available year-round.

Characteristics: These silver fish with a blue tint have a distinctive dark black eye with a bright yellow outer ring. They can weigh up to 300 pounds, though market average is 6 to 14 pounds. The fillets are large with meaty texture, similar to grouper. The raw meat has a pink-ish color but cooks up to snow white; the meat is mild with moist, medium-firm flake when cooked.

How to Choose: Choose Lake Victoria perch that have been deep-skinned, leaving no layer of fat, or the fish will spoil faster. Red flesh is a sign that the skinning wasn't deep enough; yellowing is an indication of spoilage. Choose small fish for milder flavor.

Storage: Store refrigerated for up to 2 days.

x 2

Preparation: 1.   **Pull out the easily removed small pin bones. If any red flesh remains, trim it away.**

 2.   **Bake, broil, grill, sauté, or hot-smoke.**

Suggested   **Congolese Perch** (serves 4): Heat $1/4$ cup dendé
Recipe: (African palm oil) or vegetable oil in a large skillet. Sauté 1 finely chopped onion and 1 minced hot chile pepper. Add 2 pounds fillet of perch to the oil, and cook on both sides 3 to 4 minutes. Add 1 cup chopped tomatoes, 1 cup sliced okra, 1 chopped green bell pepper, and 2 teaspoons chopped garlic, and cook about 5 minutes until the sauce thickens. Season with salt and serve.

Flavor   Capers, chiles, garlic, lemon, marjoram, mustard,
Affinities: okra, onion, parsley, tarragon, thyme, white wine.

LAMPREY

Other Names:
Lámbrena (Greek); lampers; *lamprea* (Spanish); *lampreda* (Italian); *lamproie, sept trous* (French); *neunauge* (German); *niøeje* (Danish); *rivierprik* (Dutch); stonesucker; *xuclador* (Balearic Islands); *yatsumeunagi* (Japanese). **Petromyzontidae.**

General Description:
The sea lamprey (Petromyzon marinus) *is a primitive creature, with no bones and no true jaws, that evolved 250 million years ago.* Though not true fish, lampreys resemble and are generally referred to as fish. They are highly prized in certain regions of Portugal, Spain, and France. They were harvested for ceremonial and medicinal purposes as well as for food by Native American tribes of the Pacific Northwest. Lampreys are prepared like the eels they resemble, though they have finer flesh. Small to medium lampreys are most commonly braised in a rich red wine sauce.

Locale and Season:
Lampreys are found in saltwater from Greenland to Florida and from Norway to the Mediterranean, with some in landlocked lakes. The Pacific lamprey (*Entosphenus tridentatus*) is found from Baja California to the Bering Sea. They are in season in spring and early summer.

Characteristics:
Lampreys are usually about 1¼ feet long and are greenish-gray to olive-brown with black marbling above and grayish-white skin below. They have a long, thin, tubelike body with a large, round, tooth-filled mouth. Behind each eye is a row of seven small orifices,

called *yeux* ("eyes") in French. Lamprey has mild but extremely fatty flesh, which makes it difficult for many people to digest.

How to Choose: Choose the smallest lampreys for mildest flavor, and have the fishmonger clean and skin them, saving the blood if desired to thicken the sauce.

Storage: Lampreys should be cooked the same day they are obtained.

Preparation: 1. **Cut off the tail, tie a string around the head, and suspend the fish over a bowl with a tablespoon of vinegar added. Open the holes on the side of the fish and allow the blood to drain in the bowl. Rinse the lamprey. (To use the blood, mix it with 1 cup red wine to keep it from coagulating.)**

 2. **Scald the lamprey in boiling water for a few seconds. Scrape off the skin.**

3. **Cut around the neck just below the gills, then pull out the long, inedible dorsal nerve through this opening.**

Suggested Recipe:

Lamprey and Red Wine Stew (serves 6): Cut 2 pounds cleaned, skinned lamprey into sections. Arrange with a bouquet garni (sprigs of parsley, thyme, and 2 bay leaves) and 3 cloves garlic on a bed of thinly sliced onion and carrot in a buttered pan. Add red wine to cover, and boil for 5 minutes. Remove the fish, strain the cooking liquid, and thicken with beurre manié (butter mixed with flour to make a crumbly paste).

Cook the sauce for 15 minutes or until thickened, then add the fish sections back into the pan with 2 leeks sautéed in butter. Cook together 15 minutes or until the sauce is thick and the meat is tender. If desired, thicken the sauce further by whisking in the reserved lamprey blood.

Flavor
Affinities:

Bay leaf, butter, carrot, celery, clove, dried ginger, garlic, leek, mushroom, potato, red wine, red wine vinegar, shallot, thyme, veal stock.

24.

LINGCOD

Other Names:

Ainame (Japanese); *bacalao largo, lorcha* (Spanish); blue, buffalo, cultus, green, or white cod; *grönfish* (Swedish); *langer grünling* (German); *lorcha* (Portuguese); *ofiodonte* (Italian); *terpuga buffalo* (French); *zmeezub* (Russian). **Hexagrammidae.**

General
Description:

Lingcod (Ophiodon elongatus) is unique to the North American West Coast, and rather than true cod, they are greenlings, one of the least attractive but best tasting fish in Pacific waters. They typically inhabit nearshore rocky reefs and have giant heads. Lingcods are extremely aggressive fighters, so they are sought by recreational anglers and are also targeted by commercial fishers, leading to overfishing. Lingcod is a favorite for upscale fish and chips in the Pacific Northwest, works well on the grill, and is especially good prepared on a cedar plank as done by Northwest Coastal Indians.

Although the meat is dense and takes longer to cook than other white-meat fish, be careful not to overcook or it will dry out.

Locale and Season:

Lingcods are found from the Alaska Peninsula south to Baja California. Peak season is April through August. In Alaska, they are protected by a limited season with many restrictions that starts July 1.

Characteristics:

Lingcods can weigh more than 80 pounds. The lean meat has a blue-green tint when raw but turns snow white when cooked. The meat is tender with large, soft, moist flakes. Yield is 40 percent.

How to Choose:

Lingcods range from 3 to 20 pounds and are available whole or as steaks or fillets, especially on the West Coast. The best lingcod is landed by hook-and-line boats that bleed and ice the fish immediately. Cheap lingcod is usually trawl-caught.

Storage:
x 2

Store lingcod up to 2 days refrigerated.

Preparation:

• **Stuff and bake large lingcods.**

• **Bake, broil, fry, grill, or use for soups and stews.**

Suggested Recipe:

Planked Lingcod (serves 4): Buy untreated cedar planks, fully submerge in water, and soak at least 4 hours or overnight. Remove from water, drain, and brush one side of the plank with oil to prevent sticking. Place 2 pounds fillet of lingcod in the center of the plank and place on a preheated grill. Close lid and cook until fish flakes, about 10 minutes, brushing often with a mixture of 1/4 cup each lemon juice and olive oil, 1 tablespoon chopped dill, salt, and pepper. Allow the fish to cool to firm up before removing from the plank.

Flavor
Affinities: Basil, dill, garlic, lemon, mint, mustard, olive oil, oregano, potato, shallot, thyme, tomato.

25.   **MACKEREL**

Other Names: **Atlantic mackerel:** Boston mackerel; *caballa* (Spanish); *hirasaba, marusaba, saba* (Japanese); *makreel* (Dutch); *makrele* (German); *maquereau* (French); *ronnach* (Irish); *sarda* (Portuguese); *scombro* (Italian); *skumbriya* (Russian); *skoumbri* (Greek); *uskumru* (Turkish). **King mackerel:** *A'u* (Hawaiian); *carite lucio* (Spanish); kingfish; *königsmakrele* (German); *maccarello reale* (Italian); *serra azul* (Portuguese); *tai-seiyo saba* (Japanese); *thazard barré* (French); *vasilikó skoumbri* (Greece). **Spanish mackerel:** *Thazard* (German); *sierra* (Spanish); *maccarello reale maculato* (Italian). **Scombridae**.

General
Description: *Though handsome, mackerel are often underrated, especially in America, because of their dark, full-bodied meat.* Mackerel travel in large schools and are rich in beneficial omega-3 fatty acids. Atlantic mackerel (*Scomber scombrus*) is a highly migratory fish found in the icy waters of the Atlantic. Because mackerel spoil

quickly, vendors in London were permitted as early as 1698 to sell them on Sundays, when all trade was otherwise prohibited. In Europe, mackerel is served with sharp fruit sauces. Hot-smoked mackerel is quite popular in Europe.

King mackerel (*Scomberomorus cavalla*), the largest mackerel, are an important commercial and recreational fish. Spanish mackerel (*S. maculatus*) are dark blue or blue-green on the back with orange or yellowish oval spots on the sides. Related species are sought after in Southeast Asia for curries, to which their firm, rich flesh is well suited.

Locale and
Season:

Atlantic mackerel range from the Mediterranean to Iceland and Norway and from Cape Hatteras to Labrador. King mackerel is a subtropical species found from North Carolina to Brazil. Spanish mackerel are found from Cape Cod to Yucatan and Bermuda. Though caught year-round, mackerel are best in fall and early winter, when they have fattened up.

Characteristics:

Atlantic mackerel are slender, slightly flattened from side to side, and covered with very small, hardly visible, loosely attached scales. The fish resemble their cousin the tuna but are much smaller, $1^{1}/2$ to $2^{1}/2$ pounds. King mackerel may weigh almost 100 pounds; Spanish mackerel weigh up to 12 pounds. Mackerel flesh is gray when raw but turns off-white when cooked. The flavor is assertive. The oily flesh spoils quickly, but the meat is firm and free of small bones. Mackerel are susceptible to scombroid poisoning if not stored or handled properly. The

fish may be used for sushi and sashimi. Yield is
45 percent.

How to Choose:
    Mackerel is available fresh or frozen, whole, smoked,
pickled, and salted, and can be filleted, butterfly-
filleted (cut through the belly with both sides
attached at the back), or cut into chunks. It is most
commonly found in Asian or other ethnic markets.
Choose mackerel that are stiff and shiny with clear,
protruding eyes and a clean, briny smell. Young
mackerel weigh less than 1 pound and are more
delicate; they are available in the spring.

Storage:
 x 1
    Store fresh mackerel in the refrigerator up to 1 day
before cooking.

Preparation: **1.** **Cut along either side of the dark, central blood line
and discard.**

2. **Marinate briefly in lime or other citrus juice or
vinegar to whiten and firm the flesh before cooking.**

3. **Grill, barbecue, hot-smoke, broil, or roast.**

Suggested
Recipe:

    Spanish Mackerel Escabeche (serves 6): Rub 6
(1-inch-thick) Spanish mackerel steaks with olive oil
and season with salt and pepper. Grill or broil 10
minutes or until the fish is well browned on the outside. Cook 2 cups sliced onions in 4 tablespoons olive
oil until soft. Stir in 1 tablespoon each curry powder
and ground cumin, and cook briefly. Add 8 cloves
thinly sliced garlic, 2 thinly sliced serrano chiles,

6 bay leaves, 1¹/2 cups sherry vinegar, 1 tablespoon dried oregano, 2 teaspoons turmeric, 2 whole cloves, 1 cinnamon stick, 1 teaspoon allspice berries, and salt to taste. Bring to a simmer, then add the mackerel steaks and 2 cups diced red, yellow, and green bell peppers. Bake at 350°F for 20 minutes, turn the fish, and bake 10 minutes longer, until the fish flakes. Cool and refrigerate 2 days. Toss with lime juice, sliced scallions, and chopped parsley and serve at room temperature.

Flavor
Affinities:

Allspice, bay leaf, chiles, cinnamon, clove, cranberry, curry, garlic, gooseberry, lime, onion, oregano, potato, red wine vinegar, rhubarb, sherry vinegar, thyme.

26a–b.   **MAHIMAHI**

Other Names:

Coryphène, dorade coryphène (French); *corifena, lampuga* (Italian); *doirado* (Portuguese); *dorado, llampuga, perico* (Spanish); *goldmakrele* (German); *keta* (Russian); *shiira* (Japanese). **Coryphaenidae**.

General
Description:

Mahimahi (Coryphaena hippurus) *were long known as dolphin fish because they swim alongside boats as dolphins do.* To make the fish more acceptable to consumers, they are now known by their Hawaiian name, mahimahi, literally meaning "strong-strong," because of their great strength. The best and most expensive mahimahi come from troll fishery in Hawaii, which has less environmental impact than hook-and-line fisheries; significant amounts are caught as bycatch of tuna longlining. This is an exceptionally versatile fish with abundant supplies due to its fast growth rate.

Locale and Season:

Mahimahi are found mostly in the southern Atlantic and the Caribbean. Caribbean and Gulf of Mexico mahimahi are most plentiful from April through August, with peak season in May. Central and South American season is November through March. Hawaiian troll fishery runs from March to May and September to November.

Characteristics:

The strikingly beautiful mahimahi are brilliant iridescent blue-green and gold. They may reach 70 pounds, though 3 to 6 pounds is average. The pinkish raw flesh is darker along the centerline and toward the tail; larger fish may have darker flesh. The lean meat is sweet with a mildly assertive flavor, firm texture, and large, moist flakes. If handled poorly, mahimahi is subject to scombroid poisoning. Due to high mercury levels, children should limit mahimahi to three meals a month. Yield is 35 percent.

How to Choose:

Clipper-grade mahimahi is top-quality mahimahi, frozen at sea. Choose fish with brightly colored skin; fish with faded skin are past their prime. Normally found filleted, the meat should be firm and pink to light beige with a clear red (not brownish) central blood line. The older and larger the fish, the darker the meat and stronger the taste. It's best to buy headed and gutted mahimahi for better shelf life.

Storage:	Keep mahimahi fillets refrigerated for up to 2 days before cooking.
Preparation: 1.	**Trim darker portions of the meat for milder flavor.**
2.	**Remove the thick skin before cooking; if grilling or broiling, remove after cooking.**
3.	**Grill, blacken, bake, broil, sauté, or hot-smoke.**
Suggested Recipe:	**Maui Mahimahi** (serves 6): Melt 2 tablespoons butter over medium heat, add 2 teaspoons chopped garlic, and sauté briefly. Stir in 2 tablespoons teriyaki sauce, the juice of 1 lime, 2 teaspoons honey, and 2 tablespoons sesame seeds. Cool to room temperature, pour over 6 mahimahi fillets, and marinate for 30 minutes. Drain and sauté the fish in 2 tablespoons butter, basting with the reserved marinade.
Flavor Affinities:	Avocado, butter, garlic, ginger, honey, kiwi, lemon, lime, mango, mustard, onion, oregano, rum, scallion, sesame, shallot, soy sauce, teriyaki, thyme, tomato.

---

 27. **MARLIN**

Other Names:	**Blue marlin**: *Aguja azul* (Spanish); *blauer marlin* (German); *espadim azul* (Portuguese); *kurokajiki kurokawa* (Japanese); *makaire bleu* (French); *marlin azzurro* (Italian); *taketonga* (Maori, New Zealand); spikefish. **Istiophoridae.**

General Description:	*Marlin is a huge fish in the billfish family.* In America, it is illegal to commercially sell marlin in many states. Catches are limited to sportsmen, though commercial fishing does take place in Hawaii. Marlin are highly prized for sashimi, and many are shipped to Japan for that purpose. Often referred to as the beefsteak of fish, marlin make for hearty eating and are rich in beneficial omega-3 fatty acids.

Marlins resemble swordfish with their long bills, but their flesh is leaner and more like tuna. They have slender bodies with smooth, iridescent skin and a high dorsal fin that they fold down for speed. Marlin are captured mainly by longlines, although some are taken by gill nets, and a small percentage are harpooned. The best known are the blue marlin (*Makaira mazara*), prized as a sport fish and weighing 150 to 350 pounds and found in tropical waters worldwide; black marlin (*M. indicus*), the largest species, found in the Indian and Pacific Oceans; white marlin (*Tetrapterus albidus*), found in the western Mediterranean and the Caribbean; and the huge striped marlin (*T. audax*), found in the Indian and Pacific Oceans.

Locale and Season:

Marlin are found in all but the coldest waters of the world and are fished by fleets from more than 20 countries. Fresh marlin is available year-round.

Characteristics: Marlin are large fish, up to 8 feet long, and may reach up to 1,000 pounds; market average is 50 pounds. They have the substantiality of beef and are rich in fat. Marlin is almost always sold in steaks.

How to Choose:
Marlin varies according to diet; those from the East Coast are pinkish, while California marlin are creamy white. Choose marlin that are slightly translucent with a bright sheen. The lighter flesh should never be gray; the darker flesh and blood vessels should be red, not brown. Fresh or frozen marlin are sold as skin-on boneless steaks, ranging from 6 ounces to 1 pound. Choose steaks at least 1 inch thick. In the United States, better handling methods raise the price of domestic marlin, always sold fresh.

Storage:
Store marlin refrigerated up to 2 days.

☐ x 2

Preparation: • **Marinate and broil or grill steaks, or cube for kebobs.**

🥣🗡🔥🥘🗡

NOTE:
Allow 10 minutes cooking time per inch of thickness for steaks. Take the fish from the heat shortly before it is fully cooked to allow for carryover heat.

Suggested Recipe:
Marlin and Pineapple Kebobs (serves 4): Cut 1 small gold pineapple into large cubes. Puree half the pineapple with 1/2 cup orange juice and 2 tablespoons peeled, chopped ginger. Cut 1 1/2 pounds marlin into 1-inch cubes and marinate in half the puree with salt and pepper to taste for 1 hour refrigerated. Drain. Alternate marlin and pineapple cubes on skewers and grill or broil on all sides. Boil the remaining marinade until thickened, about 10 minutes, and mix with 1/2 cup mayonnaise. Season with the juice of 1 lime, salt, and pepper, and serve with the kebobs.

| Flavor Affinities: | Curry, fennel, garlic, ginger, hot chiles, lemon, lime, key lime, mustard, olive oil, orange, pineapple, rosemary, saffron, sage, tomato, white peppercorn. |

MOI

| Other Names: | *Barbudo seis barbas*, *pez barbita del pacifico* (Spanish); *barbure ou capitaine* (French); *fingerfisch* (German); Hawaiian moi; *nanyo-agonashi*, *tsubamekonoshiro* (Japanese); Pacific threadfish. **Polynemidae**. |

| General Description: | *Moi* (Polydactylus sexfillis) *was once a delicacy reserved for Hawaii's male royalty; commoners caught eating the fish faced severe penalties.* Stocks of wild moi were depleted by the mid-1990s because of high demand; enhancement programs have rebuilt supplies for sport fishing, but there is practically no commercial fishery. Aquaculture operations in Hawaii now farm moi in open-ocean submerged cages. These fish are harvested, iced, and delivered quickly to market. Luxury restaurants in Hawaii make it a point to include moi on the menu. |

| Locale and Season: | As a farmed fish, moi is available year-round. |

| Characteristics: | Moi is a small, silvery, rounded fish shaped like a flat-fish with dark horizontal striping. It has a moderately high oil content but can turn dry and rubbery when fully cooked, so it is often quick-seared to rare or medium-rare. Its flesh is white to light gray, cooks up |

white, and is silky, rich, and mild in flavor with tender, flaky texture.

How to Choose: Aquafarmed moi are marketed at 3/4 to 1 1/2 pounds.

Storage: Refrigerate moi topped with crushed ice in a perforated pan over another pan to catch the drips for up to 2 days.

Preparation: 1. **Pull out pin bones with fish pliers or needlenose pliers. Leave skin on fillets.**

2. **Steam or bake whole fish, sear fillets skin-side down, grill, broil pan-fry, hot-smoke, or serve raw in sushi and sashimi.**

Suggested Recipe: **Hawaiian Moi Fish and Chips** (serves 6): Bake 4 Hawaiian purple sweet potatoes (molokai), cool, peel, and cut into strips. Cut 2 pounds moi fillet into 1-inch wide strips. Season with salt and pepper, dust with flour, dip in beaten egg, and then dip in panko crumbs. Fry in vegetable oil until golden, about 5 minutes. Separately, fry the sweet potato strips in oil. Serve together with Hawaiian chile pepper water for dipping: Combine 2 cups water with 1 1/2 teaspoons Hawaiian sea salt, 2 teaspoons chopped garlic, 2 tablespoons white vinegar, 1/4 cup minced fresh red chile peppers, 1/4 cup chopped sweet red bell pepper, and 1 1/2 teaspoons hot red pepper flakes.

Flavor Affinities: Garlic, red bell pepper, red chiles, rice wine vinegar, shimeji mushroom, taro, tomato.

28a–b.

MONKFISH AND ANGEL FISH

Other Names:

Monkfish: Anglerfish; *anko, ankimo* (monkfish liver) (Japanese); *baudroie, lotte* (French); bellyfish; *fener baligi* (Turkish); goosefish; *havtaske* (Danish); *rana pescadora, rape, sapo* (Spanish); *rana pescatrice, rospo* (Italian); *seeteufel* (German); *tamboril* (Portuguese); *vatrochópsaro* (Greek). **Lophiidae**. **Angel fish:** Allmouth; *ange de mer* (French); angel shark; *angelote* (Spanish); *ánghelos* (Greek); bellows fish; *havengel* (Danish); *kasuzame* (Japanese); *keler* (Turkish); *láimhineach* (Irish); *meerengel* (German); Molly Gowan (Scotland); *peixe anjo* (Portuguese); *pesce angelo, squadro* (Italian); *sfinn, wagess* (Tunisia). **Squatanidae**.

General
Description:

Monkfish (Lophius americanus) *are large, deepwater, bottom-dwelling primitive fish with huge, gaping mouths.* They are the best known of more than 150 anglerfish species, all with spines that end in a flexible, extended cord that they dangle like a fishing lure. Often known as "poor man's lobster," restaurants sometimes substitute monkfish for lobster in salads and bisques. Mediterranean monkfish (*L. piscatorius*), from European waters, are popular throughout southern Europe. Whole monkfish are broken down at sea with the tail and the delicious liver saved and the rest discarded. The tail is firm and highly versatile and takes well to bold seasonings, marinades, and sauces. Most of the prized livers are exported to Japan for soup and sashimi; American chefs serve them foie-gras style.

Though similar in appearance and use, monkfish and angel fish (*Squatina squatina*) are unrelated;

monkfish are true cartilaginous fish, while angel fish are related to shark and ray. Their rough skin is used to polish wood and ivory and to line sword sheaths. Weights, yields, and cooking methods for angel fish are similar to monkfish.

Locale and
Season:

Monkfish are found worldwide, but the main harvesting areas are in the North Atlantic. On the American East Coast, monkfish are often a bycatch of scalloping. Though available year-round in America, the fish are a winter delicacy in Japan. Angel fish range from the Mediterranean to Scotland and Denmark, with another species found in the western Atlantic. Once common, they have been declared extinct in the North Sea and are scarce in the Mediterranean.

Characteristics:

Monkfish tails weigh from 1 to 4 pounds and are off-white to pale gray and covered with a blue-gray membrane. When cooked, the meat is mild and slightly sweet with firm, dense texture. Monkfish has similar taste and texture to scallops or lobster (which it eats). The skin is not eaten. A monkfish liver weighs more than 1 pound. Yield is 35 percent from whole fish, 60 percent from skinless tail. Angel fish flesh is pleasant in flavor and texture and has no bones.

How to Choose:

Monkfish with red blood at their cut end have been freshly trimmed. Dried-up brownish blood is an indication of age. Avoid monkfish or angel fish that are discolored at the edges or have a strong odor. Allow for significant shrinkage when cooking. The main fishing method used to catch monkfish, trawling, has been shown to damage floor habitat, so some organizations recommend that it be avoided.

Storage:

 x 2

Refrigerate monkfish and angel fish 2 to 3 days on ice.

Preparation:

- **Remove the blue-gray membrane covering monkfish tail. If left on, the membrane will shrink and the meat will toughen.**

- **Grill, broil, sauté, or cook monkfish tail in chowder and stew.**

- **Steam monkfish liver and serve with scallions and grated daikon mixed with Japanese red pepper sauce and ponzu sauce.**

- **Angel fish is best poached, but chunks may also be fried or baked.**

Suggested Recipe:

Tunisian Baked Monkfish (serves 6): Season 6 monkfish steaks with salt and pepper and arrange in a buttered baking dish. Dot with 3 tablespoons butter and cover with 3 sliced tomatoes and 2 sliced green bell peppers. Pour the juice of 1 lemon over and bake at 350°F for 20 minutes or until the fish is mostly cooked. Beat 2 eggs with 1 tablespoon flour, pour over the fish, and bake 10 minutes longer, or until the fish flakes.

Flavor Affinities:

Bell pepper, butter, celery, chiles, cilantro, corn, daikon, fennel, lemon, lime, olive oil, onion, orange, oregano, ponzu, scallion, shallot, tomato, white wine.

29. **MULLET**

Other Names: | Black, flathead, gray, jumping, or striped mullet; *bora* (Japanese); *cefalo mazzone, muggine* (Italian); *grosskopf-meeräsche* (German); *haskefal baligi* (Turkish); *kéfalos* (Greek); *lisa pardete, mújol* (Spanish); *mulet cabot* (French); *multe* (Norwegian). **Mugilidae**.

General Description: | *More than 100 species of mullet are found worldwide in estuaries and the open ocean, but gray or striped mullet (Mugil cephalus) are considered to be the most delicious.* Though quite popular and low-priced in the American South, mullet is practically unknown in the rest of the United States. The delicious orange-yellow roe is a valuable American export to Japan and Taiwan. Due to a net ban enacted in 1995, mullet landings have greatly decreased, raising the once low price. Smoked mullet and mullet roe are traditional in Florida fish houses. European red mullet (p. 129) is an unrelated species.

Locale and Season: | Gray mullet are found in tropical and subtropical coastal waters worldwide. Peak season is November and December, when the fish is heavy with roe. Fish frozen after the roe has been removed can be found in spring and summer.

Characteristics: | Mullet average 3 to 6 pounds. The raw flesh is white and cooks up white, firm, and juicy. The male milt, golden yellow female roe, and gizzards are also eaten; see page 285 for bottarga (salted mullet roe). Yield is 45 percent.

How to Choose:	Mullet are best in fall, just before spawning. Because mullet deteriorate quickly, they are usually sold close to where they have been caught. Choose mullet with bright, clear eyes, red gills, and shiny, unfaded skin with no "fishy" odor.

Storage:

Mullet is best right out of the water but may be refrigerated for up to 2 days, covered in crushed ice, in a perforated pan above another pan. Smoked mullet should be refrigerated and used within 4 days. Mullet can be frozen but lasts only 90 days.

Preparation: 1.

Cut away the oily, strong-flavored skin and remove the dark line of fatty flesh that runs through the meat. It has an overly strong flavor.

 2.

Barbecue, bake, broil, deep-fry, pan-fry, or hot-smoke.

Suggested Recipe:

Florida Broiled Mullet (serves 6): Place 2 pounds skinless mullet fillets in a single layer, skin-side down, on an oiled broiling pan. Combine 2 tablespoons each Worcestershire sauce, soy sauce, and vegetable oil; 2 teaspoons paprika; 1 teaspoon each chili powder and garlic powder; and hot sauce to taste and pour over fish. Broil 8 minutes or until fillets flake, basting once. Serve with lemon wedges.

Flavor Affinities:

Bacon, bell pepper, Cajun seasoning, celery, chili powder, cornmeal, garlic, ginger, hot sauce, onion, paprika, pickling spice, scallion, soy sauce, vinegar.

OCEAN PERCH

Other Names:

Arasuka sake, menuke (Japanese); *gallineta nórdica* (Spanish); *grand sébaste, perche rose, rascasse du nord* (French); *karfi* (Icelandic); Norway haddock; *peixe vermelho* (Portuguese); redbream; redfish; *rodfisk* (Danish, Norwegian, Swedish); *rosefisch, rotbarsch* (German); *scorfano di norvegia* (Italian); sea perch. **Percidae**.

General Description:

The Atlantic ocean perch is closely related to the Pacific rockfish (p. 114). Once commonly known as redfish, the name was changed in America by fish marketers in the 1930s. Three species are known as ocean perch: *Sebastes marinus*, the largest of the three, found in shallower water; *S. mentella*, most common in Canada; and *S. fasciatus*, a small, deepwater species. All are slow-growing, slow-moving, schooling fish that are easily caught. In Japan, whole ocean perch are deep-fried and served with the colorful spines and fins extending over the plate. The bones and head make excellent stock.

Locale and Season:

Fresh-caught fish are immediately iced on board and are occasionally available, but the majority of the catch is processed into frozen, skin-on fillets for sale, defrosted, in American supermarkets.

Characteristics:

Ocean perch have beautiful pink-red skin and delicately flavored, white, moist flesh and typically weigh 1 1/2 to 2 pounds. Relatively inexpensive, they are available head-off and gutted, and as skinless or skin-on fillets. Though the skin is edible, because of the fish's high oil content, shelf life is diminished if the skin is left on. Frozen, they keep 4 to 6 months; fresh about 10 days from processing. Yield is 40 percent.

How to Choose:
Ocean perch are a small fish yielding small fillets. Choose firm fish with bright lustrous skin and a briny smell. The gills of whole fish should be clear pink-red.

Storage:
🗄 x 2
Store fresh ocean perch refrigerated no more than 2 days after purchase.

Preparation: 1.
🚰
Thoroughly rinse the belly cavity and rub away any black lining.

🔪 2.
Trim fins and score the fish crosswise 2 to 3 times in the thick flesh at the head end for even cooking. Cook fillets with the skin on, if present. Any bones can be easily removed.

NOTE:
Ocean perch have small spines on top of the head and sharp fins on the upper body, so care must be taken when cleaning and gutting whole fish.

Suggested Recipe:
🧂🔪🥣
Chinese Steamed Ocean Perch (serves 4): Season a whole trimmed (1 1/2- to 2-pound) ocean perch with salt and pepper. Make 3 shallow cuts into both sides of the fish from the head end. Place in a bamboo steamer, sprinkle with 1/4 cup sliced scallions, 1 tablespoon minced ginger, and 1 tablespoon sesame oil. Cover and steam over 1 to 2 inches of water for 15

minutes, or until the flesh flakes. Mix together 1/4 cup
each soy sauce and rice wine, 1/4 cup sliced scallions,
2 tablespoons each minced ginger and chopped
cilantro, and 1 tablespoon minced garlic, and pour
over the fish just before serving.

Flavor
Affinities:

Avocado, basil, butter, chives, cilantro, dill, garlic,
ginger, lemon, mushroom, onions, orange, rice wine,
scallion, shallot, sesame, soy sauce, tarragon, tomato.

OPAH

Other Names:

Akamanbô, mandai (Japanese); *chrysostome, lampris*
(French); *fengarósparo* (Greek); *glansfisk* (Danish,
Swedish); *gotteslachs* (German); Hawaiian moonfish;
luna real, opa (Spanish); moonfish; *peixe cravo*
(Portuguese); *pesce ré* (Italian); sunfish. **Lampridae.**

General
Description:

The opah (Lampris guttatus)*, which can weigh 100
pounds or more, has long been regarded as good luck fish.*
Once Hawaiian fishers would give them away, but
after Hawaii started to promote its native fish in the
late 1980s, this practice stopped. Opah's firm, large-
grained, fatty flesh works well with strong seasonings.

Locale and
Season:

Opahs are found worldwide in tropical and temperate
waters. Opahs are not consistently available because
they don't swim in schools and aren't easily harvested
in commercial quantities. They are often taken as
bycatch by Pacific tuna longliners. Opahs may be

found year-round from longline fisheries, but are most abundant from April to August.

Characteristics:
Opahs have four different types of flesh, each a different color. The loin, from along the backbone, is light orange and tender. The side flesh tends to be stringy and tough and is the same color as the loin at the top but fades toward the bottom. The dense, luscious cheek meat is dark red, while the breast meat is bright red. Opah's rich, creamy texture and firm, fatty flesh make it a favorite for sushi.

How to Choose:
Opahs from Hawaii are larger with firmer, more lively meat, averaging 45 pounds. Those from New Zealand average 30 pounds and have softer, duller meat.

Storage:
Store opah up to 2 days refrigerated.

x 2

Preparation: •
Use the steaklike loin fillets for grilling, broiling, or pan-searing like a beefsteak and for sashimi and sushi. Other cuts are too stringy to be good raw but are tender when cooked.

Suggested Recipe:
Macadamia-Crusted Opah with Citrus (serves 4): Beat 1 egg with 1 cup milk. Season 4 opah fillets with salt and pepper and then dip in the mixture. Roll in 1/2 cup crushed macadamia nuts, then dust with flour. Sauté in olive oil 4 minutes per side, until browned. Combine 1/4 cup olive oil with 1 teaspoon each lime, lemon, and orange zest and the juice of 1 lime, 1 lemon, and 1 orange, and ladle over the fish to serve.

Flavor
Affinities:

Brown sugar, cilantro, dill, garlic, ginger, key lime, lemon, lime, macadamia, olive oil, orange, oyster sauce, pineapple, rosemary, shiitake mushroom, soy sauce.

ORANGE ROUGHY

Other Names:

Atlantischer sägebauch (German); *empereur, hoplostète orange* (French); *islandsky beriks* (Russian); *olho de vidro laranja* (Portuguese); *orenzi-raffi* (Japanese); *pesce specchio atlantico* (Italian); *reloj anaranjado* (Spanish); slimehead; *soldatfisk* (Danish). **Trachichthyidae**.

General
Description:

The orange roughy (Hoplostethus atlanticus) *has bright orange skin, spiky fins, and a large, bony head.* They were first fished off New Zealand and later Australia under their unappetizing original name, slimehead. Because orange roughies live in such cold and highly pressurized water, they reproduce slowly and are highly susceptible to overfishing. With their moderate oil content, they resist drying out when cooked and are suited to most cooking methods except deep-frying and grilling. Though orange roughies are usually frozen twice (once on board when caught and a second time after being skinned and filleted), they maintain quality if handled with care.

Locale and
Season:

Orange roughies are found in deep water off the coasts of Australia and New Zealand. The fresh season is November through March.

Characteristics:	Orange roughy is mild and delicate in flavor with moist, large-flaked flesh that holds together well when cooked. Raw, the flesh is pearly white; cooked it is opaque white. It should be sold as skinless fillets. Directly beneath the skin lies a brownish-orange band of color that contains wax ester, a substance that is only partly digestible and must be removed.
How to Choose:	A whole orange roughy averages 3 1/2 pounds. Fillet size ranges from 6 to 8 ounces. The darker the flesh, the lower the quality.
Storage:	Orange roughy fillets for sale in the American market have been frozen and defrosted, so cook within 1 or 2 days of purchase. Store refrigerated on ice.
Preparation:	• **Bake, broil, poach, sauté, or steam.**
Suggested Recipe:	**Broiled Orange Roughy with Papaya-Kiwi Salsa** (serves 4): Combine 2 diced papayas, 3 diced kiwis, 1 diced red bell pepper, 1 diced red onion, 2 minced and seeded jalapeños, and the juice of 2 limes and 1 lemon. Sprinkle 4 (6-ounce) fillets of orange roughy with salt, pepper, and lemon juice. Brush with melted butter and broil 3 to 4 minutes on each side, or until the fish flakes. Top with the salsa and serve.
Flavor Affinities:	Basil, bell pepper, butter, chiles, chives, curry, ginger, kiwi, lemon, lime, mango, orange, papaya, pineapple, rice wine, sesame, shallot, soy sauce, tomato.

30. **PACIFIC ROCKFISH**

Other Names: Canary rockfish; chilipepper; *gallineta* (Spanish); *menuke* (Japanese); Pacific ocean perch; Pacific red snapper; pygmy; quillback; *rascasse du nor* (French); redfish; rock cod; *rotbarsc* (German); scorpionfish; *sebaste* (Italian); shortbelly; thornyhead; widow rockfish; yelloweye rockfish. **Sebastes**.

General
Description: *There are more than 70 species of wild rockfish along the American Pacific coast.* Unrelated to the striped bass (p. 161), also known as rockfish, these deep-water fish weigh up to 20 pounds. Rockfish's firm texture suits them to stews, soups, and chowders. In Asian restaurants, rockfish are often served whole, either steamed or deep-fried. Pacific Ocean perch (*Sebastes alutus*) is the most important commercial species. The tasty chilipepper (*S. goodei*) is small and pink and white. Vermilion rockfish (*S. miniatus*) are bright red with large black eyes and moderately firm flesh. Canary rockfish (*S. pinninger*) are yellow-orange with three dark orange stripes across their head. Copper rockfish (*S. caurinus*) have a wide stripe on their lateral lines and coppery stripes radiating back from their eyes. They range from Alaska to California and are popular for sport and eating.

Locale and
Season: Rockfish are found in the Pacific from the Bering Strait to Baja California. They are harvested year-round by almost all methods and also as bycatch.

Characteristics:	Rockfish meat is lean and medium-firm with a delicate, nutty flavor. Market average is 2 to 5 pounds. Rockfish are red-fleshed or brown-fleshed: the preferable red are leaner, and the brown are stronger and more perishable. Because rockfish are slow-growing, they are highly susceptible to overfishing. Yield is 30 to 40 percent.
How to Choose:	Choose rockfish with bright, shiny skin. Those with thick bodies usually have firm flesh. Whole rockfish may have bulging eyes if they are brought up from great depths, but this does not affect their quality. They are often sold as skin-on fillets.
Storage:	Store whole fish up to 2 days refrigerated; store fillets up to 1 day refrigerated.

Storage:
 x 2

Preparation: **1.** When serving whole rockfish, trim off the sharp spiny fins before cooking or cutting up.

2. Remove the fat layer under the skin of rockfish fillets.

 3. Bake, fry, poach, sauté, or steam, whole or in fillets.

Suggested Recipe: **Steamed Rockfish with Hoisin and Spinach** (serves 4): Combine 3 tablespoons hoisin sauce, 1 tablespoon sesame oil, and 2 teaspoons grated orange zest. Spread on 4 (6- to 8-ounce) rockfish fillets. Steam 1/2 pound baby spinach briefly to wilt; reserve. Steam the fish for 12 minutes or until it flakes. Serve over the spinach.

Flavor
Affinities: Brown butter, chiles, coconut, ginger, guava, kiwi,
lemon, lime, mango, olive oil, orange, papaya, passion
fruit, scallion, soy sauce, spinach, white wine.

PICAREL

Other Names: *Asineddu* (Sicily); *caramel, chucla* (Spanish); *izmarit*
(Turkish); *jarret* (Marseille); *laxierfisch* (German);
marída (Greek); *mendole* (French); *menola, zerro*
(Italian); smare (Great Britain); *tromberio choupa*
(Portuguese); *zmeimra* (Tunisia). **Centracanthidae**.

General
Description: *Picarels are the largest member of the sea bream family
and are unrelated to the North American pickerel.* In
Venice, it was an insult to call someone a picarel-
eater, because the fish were considered lowly. But
along the Adriatic coast in Italy, Dalmatia, and
Greece, they are esteemed. One picarel, *Spicara
smaris*, is gray-brown to slate on its back with rows
of blue spots, brighter on the males, along its sides.
S. maena is slightly larger with a brownish or slate
back. Both species have a characteristic black splotch
on their sides.

Locale and
Season: Picarels are common in the Mediterranean, especially
in the Adriatic, and are in season in fall and winter.

Characteristics: Large picarels are strongly flavored with oily flesh;
smaller fish are less oily and more delicate.

How to Choose:	Choose small picarels, with bright eyes and shiny skin, weighing less than 1/4 pound for more delicate flavor.

Storage:

Because this oily fish deteriorates quickly, cook within 1 day of purchase. Store refrigerated on ice.

Preparation: • **Deep-fry, broil, grill, or use for escabeche.**

Suggested
Recipe:

Greek Fried and Marinated Picarel (serves 4):
Marinate 2 pounds small cleaned whole picarel in salt, pepper, and lemon juice for 1 hour. Drain, pat dry, and dust with flour. Pan-fry in 1/2 cup hot olive oil until crisp, about 2 minutes per side. Set aside. Pour off the oil, add 1 tablespoon each fresh olive oil and flour and brown lightly. Stir in 1 tablespoon each chopped garlic, chopped rosemary, and dried currants; 1 cup white wine; 1/4 cup red wine vinegar; a large pinch of sugar; and salt to taste. Bring to a boil, then stir in 1/4 cup olive oil, the grated pulp of 1 tomato, and 2 tablespoons chopped Italian parsley and bring back to a boil. Pour over the fish, cool, and then refrigerate for at least 2 days before serving at room temperature.

Flavor
Affinities:

Coriander seed, currant, garlic, lemon, marjoram, olive oil, oregano, parsley, pine nut, red wine vinegar, rosemary, thyme, tomato, white wine.

PIKE

Other Names:	*Brochet* (French); *flusshecht*, *hecht* (German); *gädda* (Swedish); ged (Scotland and northern England); *gjedde* (Norwegian); jackfish; *kinoje* (Ojibwe); *luccio* (Italian); *lucio* (Portuguese); *lúcio* (Spanish); pike-fish; *snoek* (Dutch); *toúrna* (Greek). **Esocidae**.
General Description:	*Northern pike* (Esox lucius) *are the largest and most voracious predator of northern freshwaters.* The pointy-headed pike is the most widely distributed freshwater fish in the world. *Pike* originally referred to adult fish, while *pickerel* referred to young fish (this term is now used for some smaller pike). All pike are lean with lots of tiny bones, so the French puree it for quenelles and fish terrines and Ashkenazi Jews grind it for gefilte fish. The northern pike's pointed mouth resembles a duck's bill, though filled with sharp teeth. The uncommon silver pike is dark silver or greenish gray.
Locale and Season:	Pike range across northern North America and from western Europe to Siberia. In American fish markets, they are most commonly found in the Great Lakes region, close to where they're caught.
Characteristics:	Pike have fine flesh that is notoriously bony. The fish are covered by a layer of slime, a sign of freshness. Yield is 30 percent.
How to Choose:	Choose pike with bright silver scales. Avoid brownish fish, which may have been in stagnant water too long, developing a muddy taste. Whole pike average 2 to

5 pounds; fillets are also sold. Look for firm fillets with a translucent quality and a clean, sweet aroma.

Storage: Store refrigerated on ice up to 1 day.

Preparation: 1. **Wash the fish inside and out and pat dry.**

2. **To remove the slime, poach the pike whole with scales on, then rub off the scales and skin at the same time. Or pour boiling water over a whole pike, coagulating the slime and making it easier to rub off.**

3. **Poach or bake whole fish; pan-fry steaks; grind fillets for mousse, quenelles, and gefilte fish.**

Suggested Recipe: **Baked Stuffed Pike** (serves 6): Remove the backbone of a 3-pound pike. Cook 1/2 cup chopped onions in 2 tablespoons butter until soft. Add 2 chopped hard-cooked eggs, 2 cups mostly cooked rice, 1/2 cup chopped Italian parsley, and 1/4 cup each sliced chives and heavy cream. Season with salt and pepper and let cool. Stuff this mixture into the fish and tie closed. In an ovenproof pan, brown the fish in butter on both sides, then sprinkle bread crumbs on both sides. Pour 1/2 cup white wine around the fish, bring to a boil, and then bake, uncovered, in a 350°F oven for 30 minutes or until the fish flakes.

Flavor Affinities: Anchovy, butter, celery, chives, crayfish, cream, cucumber, dill, ginger, horseradish, lemon, lobster, mace, marjoram, red wine, sorrel, thyme, truffle, white wine.

PLAICE

Other Names:

European plaice: *Bladijs* (Flemish); *carrelet, plie* (French); *glossa* (Greek); *gullflyndre, rødspette* (Norwegian); *leathóg* (Irish); *lleden* (Welsh); *passera di mare* (Italian); *platija* (Spanish); *rødspaette* (Danish); *scholle* (German); *skarkoli* (Icelandic); *solha* (Portuguese). **American plaice:** *Balai* (French); Canadian plaice; dab; *hirame* (Japanese); *lerskadda* (Swedish); *rauhe scharbe* (German); roughback; sand dab. **Pleuronectidae.**

General Description:

Plaice, a right-eyed member of the flounder family, have a distinctive flat body. European plaice (*Pleuronectes platessa*) are the most common and abundant flatfish in Europe. This inexpensive fish is most popular in Denmark and Sweden; fried fillets of plaice are common in fish and chips in Great Britain. American plaice (*Hippoglossoides platessoides*) are the most common of the flounders off Canada's Atlantic coast. They are harvested largely by trawls, seine nets, and longlines. Plaice makes a good alternative to high-priced sole (pp. 47, 57).

Locale and Season:

Plaice range from the western Mediterranean to north of Norway. American plaice, found southward from the Grand Banks in Canada, are available year-round with peak season in summer.

Characteristics:

Plaice average 2 pounds and have moderately firm meat that is pure white, lean, boneless, and flaky with a mild flavor. Yield is 30 to 40 percent.

How to Choose:	European plaice may be sold in fillet form in the United States. American plaice are sold fresh and frozen as whole fish, fillets, and blocks.
Storage:	Store whole plaice up to 3 days refrigerated on ice; store plaice fillets up to 1 day refrigerated on ice.
Preparation: •	**Pan-fry or grill whole fish or fillets; poach whole fish only; sauté fillets.**
Suggested Recipe:	**Fried Plaice in Beer Batter** (serves 4 to 6): Whisk 3 cups dark beer, 4 egg yolks, 1/4 cup sliced chives, 1/2 teaspoon cayenne, and salt to taste. Separately stir together 1 cup all-purpose flour and 2 teaspoons baking powder, and fold into the batter. Chill until ready to use. Just before cooking, beat 4 egg whites until firm and fold into the batter. Heat 1 quart canola oil until shimmering. Dust 2 pounds plaice fillets cut into chunks in flour and then dip in batter. Fry until well-browned, about 5 minutes. Drain and season with salt. Serve with tartar sauce.
Flavor Affinities:	Bacon, beer, cayenne, coriander seed, cranberry, dill, fennel, lemon, malt vinegar, mayonnaise, parsley, potato, sorrel, tarragon, tartar sauce, white wine.

---

31. **POLLOCK**

Other Names:	**Alaska pollock:** *Abadejo* (Spanish); *alaskasej* (Danish); bigeye or walleye cod; *colin, lieu de l'Alaska* (French);

escamudo do Alasca (Portuguese); *merluzzo dell'Alasca* (Italian); *mintai* (Russian); Pacific tomcod; *suketôdara* (Japanese). **Atlantic pollock:** *Blaase* (Danish); Boston bluefish; coalfish, coley, saithe (Great Britain); *colin*, *lieu jaune* (French); *goberge* (French Canadian); *gråsej*, *sej* (Swedish); *juliana* (Portuguese); *lyr* (Norwegian, Icelandic); *lyur* (Russian); *merluzzo giallo* (Italian); *seelachs* (German). **Gadidae**.

General
Description:

Alaska pollock (Theragra chalcogramma) *are served at chain restaurants around the world because of good availability, mild flavor, and flaky white flesh.* Pollock are the most important fish in American waters and represent nearly 10 percent of world fish harvest by weight. In the United States, pollock are harvested by factory trawlers that process on board and by smaller boats that deliver directly to restaurants. Large operations produce blocks of frozen fillet and surimi (p. 293) from pollock. Because of their high oil content, pollock are a bit more pronounced in flavor and take longer to cook than leaner fish of similar size.

Atlantic pollock (*Pollachius pollachius*), a distant cousin of Alaska pollock, are found in the cold North Atlantic waters of Great Britain, Iceland, and Scandinavia. They are large fish, greenish brown to charcoal color. They are especially important in the Shetland and Orkney Islands and Ireland.

Locale and
Season:

Alaska pollock range from California to Japan and are in season from July through September and from December through April. They are found year-round at supermarkets, often frozen and defrosted. Atlantic pollock are in season in spring.

Characteristics:
Both types of pollock are mild and delicate in flavor with somewhat coarse texture. Boneless fillets are creamy tan in color. Cooked, the lean meat is white and firm with good flake. Full-grown Atlantic pollock meat is grayish in color.

How to Choose:
Alaska pollock weigh 1 1/2 to 2 pounds, with small fillets (2 to 3 ounces). Fish that have been frozen twice (once whole aboard ship, and a second time after filleting) are apt to be gray. Choose deep-filleted pollock with the dark fat line removed; they will be milder in flavor and whiter in color. Atlantic pollock usually weigh 10 to 20 pounds and must be extremely fresh or they will be unpleasantly wooly in texture.

Storage:

Store whole pollock up to 2 days refrigerated on ice; store pollock fillets up to 1 day refrigerated on ice.

Preparation: 1.
Remove the dark, strong-tasting fat line in the center, if not done by the fishmonger.

2.
Bake, broil, pan-fry, deep-fry, sauté, or steam.

Suggested Recipe:
Tequila-Broiled Pollock (serves 4): Marinate 2 pounds of pollock fillets in 1/2 cup tequila, the juice of 2 limes, 2 teaspoons chopped garlic, 1/4 cup olive oil, and salt and pepper to taste for 1 hour, refrigerated. Broil for 8 minutes or until the fish flakes. Serve with Pepper Salsa: Combine 1 each roasted, peeled, and diced red

and green bell pepper; 1 minced jalapeño; 3 chopped tomatillos; 2 sliced scallions; 1 tablespoon chopped cilantro; the juice of 1 lime; 2 tablespoons olive oil; and salt to taste.

Flavor
Affinities:

Bell pepper, butter, cilantro, coriander seed, cumin, garlic, jalapeño, lemon, lime, onion, scallion, shallot, sour cream, tarragon, tequila, tomatillo, tomato.

32.   **POMFRET AND BUTTERFISH**

Other Names:

White pomfret: *Achopito* (Pakistan); *aileron argenté* (French); *alumbeberas* (Filipino); *bai chang* (Taiwanese); *bawal puteh* (Malaysian); *cá chim trang* (Vietnamese); *managatsuo* (Japanese); *pak cheong* (Hong Kong); *palometa plateada* (Spanish); *pla jara met khao* (Thai); *vella vavel* (Tamil); *yin chang* (Chinese). **Black pomfret:** *Bawa hitam* (Malaysia, Indonesia); *cá chim den* (Vietnamese); *duhay* (Filipino); *hak chong* (Hong Kong); *karuvaval* (Tamil); *kuroaji-modoki* (Japanese); *pla jara met dum* (Thai). **Butterfish:** Dollarfish; *fieto americano* (Italian); *ibodai* (Japanese); *pez mantequilla americano* (Spanish); pumpkin-seed; shiner; *stromatée à fossettes* (French). **Stromateidae.**

General
Description:

Pomfret is the name for two deep-bodied narrow fish resembling pompano (p. 126) that are found in Asian coastal waters. White pomfrets (*Pampus argenteus*) grow to 20 inches long, larger than black pomfret (*Parastromateus niger*), which only reach 12 inches.

Pomfrets follow each other like sheep, a trait exploited by fishermen. Be sure to eat the lower soft fin and the tail of fried pomfret, which are considered delicacies.

Adult pomfrets have no pelvic fins, a trait they share with the similar and related American butterfish (*Peprilus triacanthus*), a rare and delicious small fish. In Cape Cod, baby butterfish are dusted in flour and deep-fried whole. Pacific butterfish (*P. simillimus*) are also called Pacific pompano. Look for butterfish at good prices in Caribbean and Asian markets.

Locale and Season:

White pomfrets are found from the Persian Gulf east to Indonesia and north to Hokkaido, Japan. Black pomfrets are found from eastern Africa to southern Japan and Australia and are more common in Indonesia and the Philippines. Butterfish are found on the American Atlantic and Pacific coasts.

Characteristics:

Pomfrets and butterfish have delicious, succulent flesh that is easily separated from the bones. When cooked, the mild meat is fine and flaky with moderate fat and soft, buttery texture. Yield is about 35 percent.

How to Choose:

Choose the largest fish because they tend to be small.

Storage:

Store whole fish up to 2 days refrigerated on ice.

Preparation: •

For whole pomfret, cut shallow slits crosswise into the flesh starting at the head end.

• **Grill, pan-fry, steam, or poach whole.**

• **For butterfish, pan-fry, grill, broil, or use for sushi.**

Suggested
Recipe:

 Malaysian Grilled Pomfret (serves 4): Trim and slit 2 cleaned and scaled pomfret. Finely chop 2 shallots, 4 cloves garlic, and 4 seeded small hot red chiles. Mix with 1 cup unsweetened coconut cream, then pour over the fish and marinate for 1 hour. Drain, then grill or broil, about 10 minutes, brushing with the marinade. Serve with lime wedges.

Flavor
Affinities:

Banana leaf, brown sugar, chiles, coconut, garlic, ginger, lemon, lemongrass, lime, red onion, shallot, shrimp paste, soy sauce, tamarind, turmeric, wild lime.

33. 📷 **POMPANO AND AMBERJACK**

Other Names:

Pompano: American, Atlantic, or Florida pompano; butterfish; *gabelmakrele* (German); *kobanaji* (Japanese); *leccia stella* (Italian); *palometa* (Spanish); sunfish; trevally. **Amberjack:** *Bernsteinfisch* (German); *kanpachi* (Japanese); *medregal coronado* (Spanish); *ricciola* (Italian) *sériole* (French). **Carangidae.**

General
Description:

Pompano (Trachinotus carolinus) are one of the best-tasting fish, with their firm, rich flesh and mild, sweet, distinctive, full-bodied flavor. Commercial harvests are small, and prices for this prized fish are always high. They are often simply broiled, though their most famous preparation is *en papillote* (in parchment). Palometa (*T. goodei*) are thinner than pompano, with two long fins reaching almost to the tail and dark vertical bars halfway down the body. Not as desirable as pompano, palometa are oilier and coarser. The permit (*T. falcatus*), nearly identical in appearance to pompano, is larger and less delicate. The greater amberjack (*Seriola dumerili*) is the largest and most important amberjack in the temperate and tropical waters of the Atlantic.

Locale and
Season:

Pompano are harvested in the United States primarily off Florida's Gulf coast and in warm waters of the Indian and Pacific Oceans. Palometa are found off the coast of Florida and South America. Pompano and permit are in season sporadically throughout the year, with peak season spring through fall. Amberjacks are found year-round in warm seas worldwide.

Characteristics:

Pompano are usually sold whole and are rarely frozen. They have moderately oily, pearly white raw flesh, cooking up white with fine flake, succulent texture, and mild, sweet, appealing flavor. The meat is quite dense, so even though the fish is thin, it requires more time to cook through. The skin is edible, and it has no scales. Amberjacks can grow to more than 100 pounds and have brown skin with an amber-colored band from head to tail. Yield is less than 40 percent for pompano, more for amberjacks.

How to Choose:

Beware of pompano substitutions, which are usually the similar-looking permit and palometa. True pompano are sold whole fresh; they average 2 pounds. Any significantly larger fish sold as pompano are apt to be fakes. Large amberjacks should be avoided, because they will be overly strong in flavor, often harbor parasites, and may contain ciguatera toxins.

Storage:
 x 3

Once purchased or caught, pompano freeze well. Store whole pompano on ice for up to 3 days; store fillets on ice up to 1 day.

Preparation:

- **For whole fish, cut shallow slits crosswise into the flesh starting at the head end.**

- **Bake, broil, fry, grill, or sauté whole. Sauté or broil fillets. Use pompano and amberjack for sushi.**

Suggested Recipe:

Florida Grilled or Broiled Pompano (serves 2): Whisk together the juice of 2 limes, 2 tablespoons olive oil, 1 teaspoon chopped garlic, 1 tablespoon each soy sauce and Dijon mustard, 1 teaspoon each grated ginger and hot sauce, and season to taste with salt and pepper. Brush most of the marinade over 2 whole pompano. Grill or broil over moderate heat for 10 to 15 minutes, or until the fish flakes, basting with the marinade and serving with the remainder.

Flavor Affinities:

Avocado, bell pepper, coconut, grapefruit, key lime, lemon, lime, lobster, mustard, orange, pineapple, scallion, star fruit, soy sauce, tomato, white wine.

34. 📷 **RED MULLET**

Other Names:
Red mullet: *Barbunya baligi* (Turkish); *gewöhnliche meerbarbe* (German); *himeji* (Japanese); *koutsomoúra* (Greek); *rouget-barbet de vase* (French); *salmonete de fango* (Spanish); *Sultan Ibrahim ramleh* (Lebanese); *triglia di fango* (Italian); *trilia hajar* (Tunisian).
Striped mullet: *Barboúni* (Greek); *bouqit, melou* (Tunisian); *gestreifte meerbarbe* (German); *himeji* (Japanese); *rouget-barbet de roche* (French); *salmonete de roca* (Spanish); *salmonete legítimo* (Portuguese); *Sultan Ibrahim sahkri* (Lebanese); surmullet; *tekir* (Turkish); *triglia di scoglio* (Italian). **Mullidae.**

General Description:
Two main species of the beautiful and succulent red mullet are found in the Mediterranean. Red mullet (*Mullus barbatus*) are rosy with gold iridescence and a straight-fronted head. The ancient Greeks regarded them as sacred to Hecate, and wealthy first-century Romans paid astronomical prices to watch its color change from red to gold, pale pink, vermilion, and blue as the fish died. Highly prized, striped red mullet (*M. surmuletus*) have a sloping head, stripes on their first dorsal fin, and sometimes horizontal yellow stripes on the sides, though coloring varies with surroundings. The livers are also eaten, often cooked in butter and then stuffed into the fish before baking whole. Spotted goatfish (*Pseudupeneus maculatus*) are related western Atlantic fish with pink to orange speckled coloring that also make for delicious eating.

Locale and Season:	Red mullet are found throughout the Mediterranean. They are sporadically available in American fish markets, sometimes at good prices in ethnic markets. Striped red mullet are found in the Mediterranean, the Black Sea, and the eastern Atlantic. Both are in peak season in fall. Spotted goatfish are commonly found off the coast of Florida but range from New Jersey to Brazil.
Characteristics:	Though they have tiny bones, mullet's delicate and unique flavor and firm, buttery texture make them highly desirable, especially for pan-frying and grilling whole. Red mullet weigh up to 4 pounds; striped mullet weigh up to 2 pounds. Scaling a fresh-caught mullet will make it even redder. Yield is 45 percent.
How to Choose:	Look for fish with shiny, brightly colored skin and clear eyes. Choose smaller fish for frying whole; larger fish for grilling, baking, and pan-frying fillets.
Storage:	Store whole fish 2 day refrigerated on ice. Store fillets 1 day refrigerated on ice.
Preparation:	• **When very fresh, red mullet is often cooked whole on the grill without gutting or scaling, or it may be gutted through the gills. The scales and skin are then peeled off just before serving.**
	• **Grill, pan-fry, deep-fry, bake, stew, or stuff and bake.**
Suggested Recipe:	**Triglia Livornese** (serves 4): Season 2 pounds whole, cleaned, scaled red mullet with salt and pepper and dust with flour. In a large skillet, brown the fish in

olive oil, about 3 minutes a side. Just before they're brown, add 2 teaspoons chopped garlic, 1 teaspoon chopped thyme, 2 bay leaves, 1/4 cup chopped Italian parsley, and a pinch of hot red pepper flakes, cook briefly, then add 2 cups fresh tomato puree and 2 bay leaves. Cover and simmer about 10 minutes or until the fish flakes.

Flavor Affinities: Almond, anchovy, bay leaf, capers, chervil, cured olive, fennel, garlic, lemon, mint, olive oil, onion, orange, Pernod, prosciutto, rosemary, shallot, tarragon, thyme, tomato, white wine.

RED SNAPPER AND OTHER SNAPPERS

Other Names: *Huachinango* (Mexico); *kókkinos louti nos* (Greek); *lutiano rosso* (Italian); *nordlig snapper* (Danish); *pargo del Golfo* (Spanish); *roter schnapper* (German); *tarumi feudai* (Japanese); *vivaneau campèche* (French). **Hawaiian red snapper:** *Onaga* (Japanese); ruby snapper; *ula'ula* (Hawaiian). **Jobfish:** Gray snapper; *uku* (Hawaiian). **Kawago snapper:** Spangled emperor. **Pink snapper:** Crimson or rose jobfish; *opakapaka* (Hawaiian). **Vermilion snapper:** B-line snapper. **Lutjanidae**.

General Description: *Hundreds of species of snappers, named after their snapping teeth, are found in the western Atlantic, with closely related fish in the eastern Pacific.* Magnificent true American red snapper (*Lutjanus campechanus*) are much sought after in the Caribbean and along the American mid-Atlantic coast for their fine texture and delicate flavor. Narrower vermilion snapper (*Rhomboplites aurorubens*) are the most common member of this family in American waters and often sold as red snapper. Yellowtail snapper (*Ocyurus chyrsurus*) are gray with a yellow stripe that runs from head to tail. Much appreciated in Florida, they are quite perishable.

Lane snapper (*L. synagris*) are small and pale pink with bright yellow stripes from head to tail; they are best cooked whole. Pacific red snapper (*L. peru*), found off the Pacific coast of Mexico and Baja California, are more elongated than the American red snapper from the Gulf of Mexico. Pacific rockfish, also called red snapper, are a different fish (p. 114). Hawaiian red or ruby snapper (*Etelis coruscans*) are bright red with a long tail and clear, light pink flesh. Those caught in winter are higher in fat, so they make the best sashimi, served to celebrate the New Year in Hawaii. Pink snapper (*Pristipomoides filamentosus*) are highly prized in Hawaii, especially for sashimi. Jobfish (*Aprion virescens*), though not snapper, are similar. They are gray with a greenish hue and are sought after in Hawaii for sashimi and for cooking. Kawago snapper (*Lethrinus nebulosus*) are a prestige fish found in the waters off Hawaii and the Indo-Pacific region. They are a tropical species in the Lethrinidae family, related to the snapper, with excellent flavor.

Locale and
Season:

Most American red snappers come from the Gulf Coast, caught near the reefs where they gather. The spring commercial red snapper fishing season begins on February 1; the fall season begins on October 1. Fishing is allowed from the first to the tenth of the month, until the quota is reached. Red snapper and their close relatives are found from North Carolina and Florida's "snapper banks" to Louisiana, Texas, and the Gulf coast of Mexico. Peak season for ruby snapper is December. Pink snapper are best in winter, when fat content is highest. Jobfish are best and most available in summer.

Characteristics:

Red snapper average 4 to 6 pounds with brilliant red skin, though small fish will be metallic pink. The meat is soft, tender, and semitransparent with a pinkish tone when fresh. Cooked, the meat is pink-white. American snapper are almost always sold with their beautiful (and edible) skin to prevent substitutions. Vermilion snapper are small, at $1^1/2$ to 2 pounds, with bright red color and broken yellow stripes. Market weight for ruby snapper is 1 pound. Pink snapper average 3 to 5 pounds. Yield for snappers is 45 percent.

How to Choose:

Choose fish with clear, bright red eyes; buy fillets with the skin on, because it helps to hold the delicate flesh together and ensures that you're buying the real thing. Note that snappers are reef fish, and if caught in an area with ciguatera, especially in the Caribbean, they may contain this poison. This is unlikely, however, because known areas are avoided.

Storage: Red snapper have delicate flesh and should be handled gently. Store whole red snapper up to 2 days
refrigerated covered with crushed ice; store fillets
1 day refrigerated covered with crushed ice.

Preparation: • **To cook whole red snapper, score crosswise in 2 or
3 places through the thickest flesh near the head.**

• **Broil or grill whole, pan-fry whole or fillets, steam
whole or fillets, bake or deep-fry whole.**

Suggested
Recipe:

Huachinango Veracruzana (serves 4): Marinate a
2- to 3-pound cleaned, scored, whole red snapper in
a mixture of 1 tablespoon chopped garlic, the juice of
2 limes, and a pinch of ground cloves and black pepper for 30 minutes. Drain and, in a large skillet,
brown the fish on both sides in 4 tablespoons hot
vegetable oil and then add 1 sliced white onion,
2 bay leaves, 2 cups diced, peeled plum tomatoes,
2 sliced jalapeño or serrano chiles, 1/2 cup sliced
pitted green olives, 1 tablespoon capers, 2 teaspoons
dried oregano, and salt to taste. Simmer 15 minutes
or until the fish flakes. Sprinkle with chopped
cilantro and serve.

Flavor
Affinities:

Capers, chervil, chiles, chives, cilantro, grapefruit,
guava, key lime, lemon, lime, mango, marjoram,
mint, olive oil, orange, oregano, passion fruit, pineapple, star fruit, tarragon, tomato, white wine.

36. SABLEFISH (BLACK COD)

Other Names:	Alaska blackcod or cod; *anoplopoma* (Russian); *bacalao negro* (Spanish); butterfish; coalfish; *gindara* (Japanese); *kohlenfisch* (German); *merluzzo dell'Alasca* (Italian); *morue charbonnière, rascasse noire* (French); sable; skilfish. **Anaplapomatadae.**
General Description:	*Sablefish* (Anoplopoma fimbria), *long slender fish with black skin, come from the cold-water Pacific.* Highly prized by the Japanese, they have firm, pearly white meat with deep, rich flavor that is very juicy when cooked and high in omega-3 fatty acids. In a practice started by Makah Indians in the Pacific Northwest, sablefish are smoked for sale at Jewish delis.
Locale and Season:	Sablefish is found in deep water on the Pacific coast and is most abundant off northern British Columbia and the Gulf of Alaska. They are in season from March 15 through November 15 in Alaska and from January through September in California.
Characteristics:	Sablefish have a rich, mild, and distinctive flavor with soft, velvety texture and large, moist white flakes. They average 3 to 10 pounds. Yield is 40 percent.
How to Choose:	Generally, the larger the fish, the better the quality, with the largest fish coming from the north. Longline and trap-caught fish are considered to be of superior quality. Fresh sablefish are available as fillets, J-cut fillets (with the head and collar removed), or as steaks.

Storage:

Because they are high in oil, sablefish are quite perishable and must be handled with extra care. Store surrounded by crushed ice.

Preparation:

• **Grill, sauté, pan-fry, hot-smoke, steam, poach, braise, or roast.**

Suggested Recipe:

Black Cod with Miso (serves 4): Bring 3/4 cup mirin and 1/2 cup sake to a boil over high heat. Boil briefly to evaporate the alcohol, then reduce the heat and mix in 2 cups white miso until it dissolves. Turn heat to high, add 1 cup sugar, and boil, stirring until the sugar dissolves. Let cool. Pat 4 black cod fillets dry and cover with the miso mixture. Cover and refrigerate 2 days. Wipe off excess miso mixture, grill or broil until brown, then bake at 400°F for 10 additional minutes or until the fish flakes.

Flavor Affinities:

Chinese five-spice powder, dashi, garlic, ginger, honey, jicama, miso, mustard, napa cabbage, oyster mushroom, sake, scallion, sesame oil, soy sauce, sugar, tea-smoke.

37a–d. **SALMON**

Other Names:

Atlantic salmon: *Echter lachs* (German); *laks* (Danish, Norwegian); *lax* (Icelandic, Swedish); *lohi* (Finnish); *losos, syemga* (Russian); *sake masu-rui* (Japanese); *salmão do Atlântico* (Portuguese); *salmón* (Spanish); *salmone atlantico* (Italian); *saumon atlantique* (French); *solomós tou Atlantikoú* (Greek); *som baligi* (Turkish);

zalm (Dutch). **Chinook salmon:** Blackmouth; king or spring salmon; *konigslachs* (German); *salmone reale* (Italian); *saumon royal* (French); tyee. **Chum salmon:** Calico, dog, or keta salmon; chub. **Coho salmon:** Blush, silver, or white salmon; *ginzake* (Japanese); hoopid salmon; *salmone argentato* (Italian); *saumon argenté* (French); *silberlachs* (German); silversides. **Pink salmon:** *Buckellachs* (German); humpback salmon; humpy; *salmon rosado* (Spanish); *salmone rosa* (Italian); *saumon rose* (French); *sepparimasu* (Japanese). **Sockeye salmon:** *Beni-zake* (Japanese); quinaults; *rot-lachs* (German); *saumon rouge* (French); *salmone rosso* (Italian). **Salmonidae**.

General Description:

Salmon all swim in temperate or cold waters of the Northern Hemisphere and are anadromous, spawning in fresh water but spending much of their life at sea. They get their pink to red color from eating krill. Numbers of wild salmon have dropped greatly in the past fifty years because of environmental deterioration, and some traditional runs have tragically disappeared. Wild Atlantic salmon (*Salmo salar*) are silver-skinned with distinct black crosslike spots on the upper half of the body and head. Limited quantities of wild Atlantic salmon are found in the rivers of Europe and North America, though today most is farmed and air-freighted to market. Atlantic salmon are also farm-raised in the Pacific waters of Chile. Farm-raised salmon are one of the great successes of modern aquaculture, though this has led to significant pollution.

Wild Pacific salmon range from Alaska to California, and in America, wild salmon is almost invariably from the Pacific, though these may also be farmed. Chinook or kings (*Onchorhynchus shawytscha*) are the largest species, often served in top restaurants. They are fatty enough to stay moist and mild in flavor. Coho (*O. kisutch*) most resemble Atlantic salmon, with plump bodies and black spots on their fins. They have light to deep pink flesh and are quite succulent. Coho are favored by European cold-smokers. Sockeye salmon (*O. nerka*) have deep red, firm flesh, though the lean meat and pronounced flavor make them less versatile. They show up in premium cans as "red salmon." Chum salmon (*O. keta*) are less prized because of light color and low fat content, though for those reasons, they have a longer shelf life. Humpback or pink salmon (*O. gorbuscha*) are the smallest variety and are more valued in Asia. Sea or salmon trout (*S. trutta*) are a close relation and are the same species as the brown trout of rivers (p. 173).

Locale and Season:

Farmed Atlantic salmon is in season year-round. The Pacific wild salmon season starts in June with chinook, followed by sockeyes through August and smaller cohos into September. Coho are farmed in floating pens in Chile and Japan, and they have been introduced to some lakes and are farm-raised in the United States. Humpback salmon are in season in July and August, with runs heavier in alternate years. Wide-ranging chum, landed in the northeastern Pacific, are in season in August and September.

Characteristics:

Farmed Atlantic salmon may weigh up to 18 pounds, but 4 to 6 pounds is common. The flesh of farmed salmon varies according to diet. In general it is milder and less firm than wild, retains its color when cooked, is moderately oily, and has large, moist flakes. The quality of wild salmon is directly related to the length of its native river. The longer it takes a salmon to reach its spawning grounds, the higher its oil content and the better its flavor. The best salmon are troll-caught, gill-bled, and chilled on board. Note that anisakis, a small roundworm, can be present in wild but not in farmed salmon. Darker salmon are often leaner than paler salmon.

Chinook have dark spots on their fins and back and may reach more than 50 pounds, though average market weight is 11 to 18 pounds. Chinooks develop a high level of fat for their long voyages, so they are buttery rich in flavor with soft meat. Their flesh is red, except for rare and prized white-flesh kings, not to be confused with pale kings, which are sexually mature fish. The highest quality chinooks are troll-caught in the ocean.

Sockeyes range from 4 to 10 pounds. Seine-caught fish fetch a premium price, as do the small amount of troll-caught salmon. Their meat is brilliant red when raw and red and firm when cooked. Sockeyes do well with brief marinating and simple grilling. Coho are large, about 10 pounds, with relatively high fat content and excellent color retention. They have mild flavor, medium-firm flesh, and velvety texture. Those farmed in floating pens in Chile and Japan are smaller, 2 to 3 pounds each.

Chum average 6 to 12 pounds and may be inconsistent in quality; the best are from British Columbia and Alaska. Chum are light in color with low fat content, so they are not suited to grilling or broiling. They are often used in value-added products such as canned and hot-smoked salmon because of low price. Pinks are the smallest salmon, with market weight 2 to 6 pounds. Their mild-flavored meat is relatively lean, so it can be on the dry side. Yield is 60 percent and up for larger fish.

How to Choose:
Choose the freshest, firmest fish possible with bright eyes. Avoid fish with signs of bruising or with flesh that doesn't spring back when pressed. Freezing to -20°F (critical if serving wild salmon raw) or cooking to an internal temperature of 145°F kills parasites.

Storage:
Keep salmon as cold as possible and serve it within 2 days. Store refrigerated topped with crushed (not cubed) ice in a perforated pan set over a second pan.

Preparation: 1.
Remove the pin bones from the salmon using fish pliers or needlenose pliers.

2.
Bake, broil, grill, poach, sauté, hot- or cold-smoke, or steam. Use farm-raised salmon for sushi.

Suggested Recipe:

Pan-Fried Salmon with Lemon and Pine Nuts (serves 4): Soak 1/4 cup dried currants in 1/4 cup brandy. Mash together 2 tablespoons soft butter with 1 tablespoon each lemon juice and zest. Season 4 (6- to 8-ounce) salmon fillets with salt and pepper and dust with flour. Brown in olive oil on both sides. Remove fish from pan and keep warm. Reduce heat,

add ¼ cup pine nuts, and brown lightly in 2 tablespoons butter. Add the currants and brandy; flame
the pan. When the flames die down, add ½ cup
diced tomato to the pan along with the salmon.
Simmer 10 minutes, or until the salmon is medium-
rare, then swirl in the lemon butter.

Flavor
Affinities:
Almond, basil, butter, chervil, cream, cucumber, dill,
lemongrass, lime, mushroom, pine nut, potato, scallion, shallot, spinach, tarragon, white wine, yogurt.

38. **SARDINE**

Other Names:
Célan (larger sardine), *sardine* (French); *haiwash,
iwashi, sappa-rui* (Japanese); *parrocha, sardina europea*
(Spanish); *pelser, sardien* (Dutch); pilchard; *sardalyo*
(Turkish); *sardélla* (Greece); *sardella, sardina* (Italian);
sardin (Danish); *sardinha* (Portuguese). **Clupeidae**.

General
Description:
The small, silvery, rich-fleshed sardine (Sardina pilchardus)
has a green back and yellow sides. In Great Britain,
sardines are young fish and pilchards older fish, but
elsewhere *sardine* is used for both. True sardines
come from Europe; young sardines are important in
Portugal, Spain, and France, and adult pilchards are
most common in northern Europe. Sardines are often
grilled, especially over hardwood charcoal, because
their soft, dark, rather oily flesh takes well to direct
heat. Pacific sardines (*Sardinops sagax*) were abundant
along the Pacific coast until the 1930s, especially near

Monterey's famed Cannery Row, but were so over-fished that they practically disappeared. Today, the Pacific sardine population is recovering. Canned sardines are known worldwide (p. 290).

Locale and Season:

Fresh sardines are seasonal, usually local, and most common in summer. In Portugal, where fresh sardines are hugely popular, the season lasts from the end of May to the end of October. Pacific sardines may be found from Chile to Alaska in spring and summer.

Characteristics:

Sardines have soft, moderately oily flesh and pronounced flavor. They weigh less than 1/2 pound. Pacific sardines weigh more than 1/3 pound. Yield is 45 to 50 percent.

How to Choose:

Choose plump shiny fish, larger if baking, smaller if grilling. "Sardines" harvested in American Atlantic waters are actually young herring (p. 77).

Storage:

Sardines should be cooked the day of purchase.

Preparation: 1.

To gut a whole head-on sardine, pinch the gills on both sides at the base of the head and pull them out. Often the innards will pull out at the same time. If not, slit open underneath and scoop them out from the belly cavity.

2.

Rinse inside and out under cold water while rubbing to remove the scales. Wipe dry. To remove the head, snap it back, breaking the spine, and pull it off.

3. **Sardines can also be gutted and boned through the back, a good method if stuffing and baking.**

 4. **Grill whole, bake, use for escabeche, hot-smoke, broil, or pan-fry. They are too soft and their flavor too strong for soups or stews.**

Suggested Recipe:

Fried Sardines Neapolitan Style (serves 4): Arrange 2 pounds filleted split-open sardines in a baking dish in 1 to 2 layers. Add 1/4 cup olive oil to cover the bottom of the dish, season with salt, pepper, 2 tablespoons chopped parsley, 1 tablespoon chopped garlic, and 1 tablespoon chopped oregano, then dot with 2 cups fresh tomato chunks. Bake at 425°F for 15 to 20 minutes, or until the fish are opaque.

Flavor Affinities:
Bay leaf, currant, fennel, garlic, green olives, lemon, olive oil, oregano, parsley, pine nut, raisin, red onion, rosemary, saffron, sherry vinegar, thyme, tomato.

39. **SAURY AND GARFISH**

Other Names:
Saury: *Agulhão* (Portuguese); *aiguille de mer, balaou* (French); billfish; *costardello, gastaurello* (Italian); *gastadélo* (Provençal); *geirnefur* (Icelandic); *makreelgeep* (Dutch); *makrelenheckte* (German); *m'sella* (Tunisia); needlefish; *paparda* (Spanish); skipper; *zargána* (Greek); *zurna* (Turkish). **Pacific saury:** Mackerel pike; *sanma* (Japanese); *saira* (Finnish, Russian). **Garfish:** *Aguglia* (Italian); *aguja* (Spanish); *aiguile,*

bécassine de mer, orphie (French); *morska bekasa* (Bulgaria); *m'sella* (Tunisia); *sauteur* (Algerian); *zargan* (Romania); *zargana* (Turkish). **Scomberesocidae**.

General
Description:

Sauries (Scomberesox saurus) are long thin fish with a silver band that separates the olive-green to blue back from the gold to silver underside. Sauries are caught in North America using the Japanese technique of attracting them by lights and scoop-netting them. Pacific sauries (*Cololabis saira*) do not have a long beak like saury but share the same dark, rich flesh. The similar garfish (*Belone belone*) are longer and thinner.

Locale and
Season:
☀ ☖ ❄

Sauries are found on both sides of the Atlantic; in summer, they migrate far north to Norway. Garfish are in season in summer and early fall. Pacific sauries are in season in autumn and winter.

Characteristics:

Sauries are small with dark, meaty, rich-flavored flesh that provides bone-free fillets. Garfish are long and narrow with green-tinted flesh when raw that turns white when cooked. Garfish are usually sold whole, but may also be cut into chunks. Both are gelatinous, so they are good for soups and stews.

How to Choose:

Choose firm, shiny, brightly colored fish with bright eyes. These small fish, generally 3 to 6 ounces each, are sold whole. Pacific saury (often marketed as mackerel pike) may be found in Asian markets. Saury may also be found salted. Garfish may be as much as 6 feet long, though 3 feet is more common.

Storage: Cook sauries the day they are purchased.

Preparation: **1.**   **To cut up, scale and cut off the head and tail. Remove the innards and clean the fish by rubbing out the gut cavity with a wedge of lemon.**

2.   **Cut the body into 5 to 6 sections.**

3.   **Fry in oil, cook in court bouillon, use in couscous, or cook in tomato sauce with oregano. Pacific saury can be pan-fried, broiled, or braised.**

Suggested Recipe: **Imsell Mixwi** (from Malta; serves 2). Take the pointed beak of a 1 1/2- to 2-pound garfish and stick it into the tail, making the fish into a ring. Marinate in the juice of 1 lemon, 2 tablespoons olive oil, 2 tablespoons chopped Italian parsley, 1 to 2 crushed cloves garlic, and salt and pepper to taste for 1 hour. Drain, reserving the marinade. Grill over a slow fire for 15 minutes, basting with marinade. Discard any remaining marinade and serve.

Flavor Affinities: Daikon, garlic, lemon, olive oil, onion, orange, oregano, parsley, rice vinegar, sake, scallion, sesame, soy sauce, sugar, thyme, tomato, vinegar, white wine.

SCORPIONFISH AND SCULPIN

Other Names: **Red rascasse:** *Cabracho, rascacio* (Spanish); *chapon* (Provence); *iskorpit, lipsoz* (Turkish); *rascasse rouge*

(French); *rascasso vermelho* (Portuguese); *roter drachenkopf* (German); *scorfano rosso* (Italian); *scórpena* (Greek). **Black rascasse:** *Bou keshesh aghel* (Tunisia); *rascasse noire* or *brune* (French); *scorfano nero* (Italian). **Scorpaenidae** (scorpionfish); **Cottidae** (sculpin).

General Description:

Scorpionfish, or rascasse, are essential for the iconic Provençal seafood stew bouillabaisse. They get their name because many species have venomous spines that can inflict a painful, even deadly, sting. The red (*Scorpaena scrofa*) and the black (*S. porcus*) species are best. Though unrelated, sculpin (*Myoxocephalus scorpius*) resemble and are often termed scorpionfish. They have large spiny or armored heads and short, tapering bodies with no scales. The great sculpin (*M. polyacanthocephalus*) and the cabezon (*Scopaenichthys marmoratus*) are West Coast sculpins. The closely related blue-mouth or black-bellied rosefish (*Helicolenus dactylopterus*) may be sold under the name *scorpina*.

Locale and Season:

Scorpionfish may be found on both sides of the Atlantic. The red rascasse is found in deeper waters all over the Mediterranean and in the eastern Atlantic. Black (sometimes called brown) rascasse are common throughout the Mediterranean in shallow water. Sculpins are found in both salt and fresh water in arctic and northern waters.

Characteristics:

Scorpionfish have small amounts of firm, lobsterlike meat with skin that is too tough to eat. The meat is off-white when cooked, moderately firm and lean, and has mild flavor. Note that the roe of cabezon is poisonous. Sculpins have mild-flavored but firm flesh. Yield is 35 percent.

How to Choose:
Choose the largest rascasse for the most meat, preferably red or black. Smaller black rascasse are considered finer in flavor than the red.

Storage:
Cook rascasse the day they are purchased.

Preparation: •
Grill whole or bake, pan-fry, or use fillets in soups and stews.

Serving
Suggestion:
Use rascasse in bouillabaisse recipes.

Flavor
Affinities:
Almond, butter, fennel, garlic, lemon, olive oil, onion, orange, oregano, Pernod, saffron, shallot, thyme, tomato, white wine.

41a–b.

SEA BREAM AND PORGY

Other Names:
Gilt-head bream: *Daurade royale* (French); *dorada* (Spanish); *goldbrassen* (German); *orata* (Italian). **Red sea bream:** *Besugo* (Spanish); *bishigua* (Basque); black spot bream; *goraz* (Portuguese); *nordischer meerbrassen* (German); *pageot rose* (French); *roode zeebrasen* (Dutch). **Red porgy:** *Pagre commun* (French); *pagro* (Italian); *pargo* (Spanish); pink porgy; *sackbrasse* (German); silver snapper; *yoroppa-madai* (Japanese). **Sheepshead porgy:** *Rondeau mouton* (French); *sarago americano*

(Italian); *sargo chopa* (Spanish); *sargo choupa* (Portuguese); *schafskopf-brassen* (German). **Northern porgy:** Mishcuppauog; paugy; scup; scuppaug. **Sparidae**.

General
Description:

There are about 15 species of porgy found in the western Atlantic and the Caribbean and more than 20 types in the Mediterranean and the eastern Atlantic, where they are known as sea bream. Porgies get their name from a Native American word meaning "fertilizer," for which they were commonly used. The most prized member of this family is the European gilt-head bream (*Sparus aurata*); the Romans considered them sacred to the goddess Aphrodite. Sea bream are male for the first two years of their life and transform into females in their third year. They have firm, succulent flesh with excellent flavor. Red sea bream (*Pagellus bogaraveo*) are the only member of the family common in eastern Atlantic waters. They have good meat suited to poaching, stuffing, and baking.

Red porgy (*Pagrus pagrus*) are found on both sides of the Atlantic, though the western porgy was long treated as a separate species (*P. sedecim*) by Americans. Their flesh is firmer than that of other porgies, and the fish is also a bit larger and not as delicate as the gilt-head bream. It works well as steaks or for stuffing and baking. Sheepshead porgy (*Archosargus probato-cephalus*) are found in the eastern Atlantic and the Caribbean. They have always been highly regarded as food and are pan-fried in the American South.

Northern porgy (*Stenotomus chrysops*) range from Cape Cod to the Carolinas and were amazingly abundant in nineteenth-century New England. The plump, golden-silver jolthead porgy (*Calamus bajonado*) are delicious and beautiful and may be found along the North Carolina coast to Bermuda, the Bahamas, and the Caribbean.

Locale and Season:

Sea bream are found in the Atlantic and the Mediterranean, but commercial harvests are small, so they are increasingly being supplied by aquaculture in Europe and Iceland. They are in season from the summer months until December. Porgies are caught by hook and line and trawls; they're a popular sport fish, with their American East Coast season starting in May or June and running until October. Argentina is the world's most important red porgy producer.

Characteristics: Gilthead bream weigh about 2 pounds and are always sold whole. Porgy range from 1/2 to 20 pounds, though average market weight is 3 pounds. Red sea bream meat is rosy when raw but turns white when cooked; it is moist with rich, sweet flavor and firm but tender texture. Red porgy have white, tender meat with large flake and mild, sweet, but satisfying flavor, though its numerous small bones make it hard to fillet. The fat-bodied northern porgy has firm, flaky flesh, though it is quite bony.

How to Choose: Sea bream are usually found whole. Choose fish with bright, shiny scales. They have a high percentage of waste, so allow at least 1 pound per person. Note that in Europe red bream and red porgy are considered inferior to gilthead bream. Small bones will be easier to remove from the largest porgies.

Storage:

Store whole fish in the refrigerator, surrounded by crushed ice, for 1 to 2 days after purchase or catch.

Preparation:

•

Bake, broil, grill, poach, or sauté porgy. Sea bream are best cooked whole; they are traditionally added to bouillabaisse. Very fresh gilt-head and red bream may be used for sushi and sashimi.

Suggested Recipe:

Niçoise Gilt-Head Bream (serves 4): Season a whole (2-pound) cleaned gilt-head bream (or porgy) with salt and pepper. Place several sprigs of thyme and parsley and 2 bay leaves inside. Place in a baking dish with 1/4 cup olive oil. Arrange sliced lemons on top of the fish and sliced tomatoes around the fish. Bake at 400°F for 20 minutes, basting with the olive oil. Arrange anchovy fillets and halved cured black olives on the fish and add 1/4 cup white wine. Bake about 5 minutes longer and serve.

Flavor Affinities:

Anchovy, basil, bay leaf, celery, chervil, cured black olives, fennel, lemon, onion, parsley, potato, saffron, scallion, shallot, thyme, tomato, white wine.

SHAD

Other Names:

American shad: *Alose savoureuse* (French); poplarback shad; *shyado* (Japanese); white shad. **European shad:** *Alaccia, alosa* (Italian); alewife, allis shad (Great Britain); *alosa, alse, maifisch* (German); *alose vraie* (French); *kepa, sardellomána* (Greek); *maisild* (Dutch,

Color Plates

Icon Key

SEASON

spring

summer

fall

winter

PREPARATION

bowl

blender or
food processor

mortar and pestle

knife

pliers

meat mallet

spatula

scissors

plastic bag

frying pan

roasting pan

pot

broiler

grill

oven

smoke

no light

requires waiting

PREPARATION (continued)

paper towel	tap water	boiling water
ice	lemon	season

MISCELLANEOUS

caution	danger	photograph

STORAGE

x number of days

1. **anchovies:** european

2. **arctic char**

3. **barramundi**

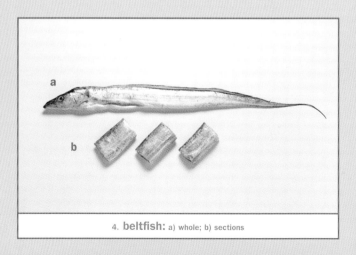

4. **beltfish:** a) whole; b) sections

5. **black sea bass**

6. **bluefish**

7. **bluenose bass**

8. **catfish:** mississippi

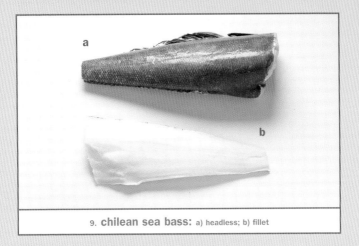

9. **chilean sea bass:** a) headless; b) fillet

10. **cobia**

11. **cod:** atlantic

12a. **croaker:** a) atlantic croaker; b) yellow croaker; c) spot

12b. **suzuki mulloway**

12c. **california white sea bass**

13. **dover sole**

14. **eel:** american

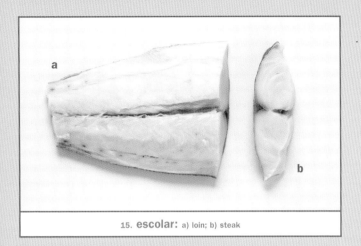

15. **escolar:** a) loin; b) steak

16. **european sea bass**

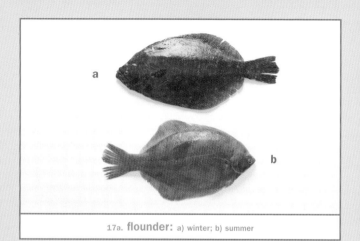

17a. **flounder:** a) winter; b) summer

17b. **gray sole**

17c. **california halibut-fluke**

18a. grouper: red

18b. **giant hawkfish**

19. **haddock**

20. **whiting:** a) atlantic; b) pacific

21a. **halibut:** pacific

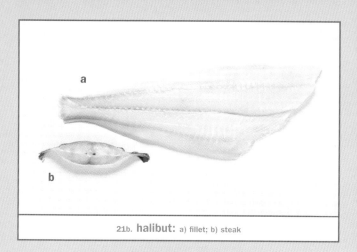

21b. halibut: a) fillet; b) steak

22a. hamachi

22b. **japanese kingfish**

23. **john dory**

24. lingcod

25. mackerel: a) king; b) spanish; c) atlantic

26a. **mahimahi**

26b. **mahimahi:** fillet

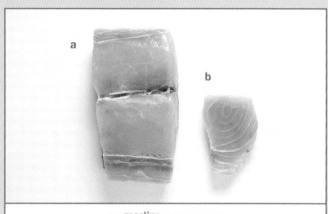

27. marlin: a) fillet, b) steak

28a. monkfish: american

28b. **monkfish:** tail

29. **mullet:** gray

30. **pacific rockfish:** copper rockfish

31. **pollock:** atlantic

32. **american butterfish**

33. **pompano**

34. **red mullet**

35a. **red snapper:** a) vermilion snapper; b) american red snapper

35b. **red snapper:** a) yellowtail snapper; b) lane snapper

36. **sablefish**

37a. **salmon:** a) atlantic; b) king

37b. **salmon:** a) coho; b) sockeye

37c. **salmon:** a) atlantic, fillet; b) atlantic, steak; c) king, fillet

37d. **salmon:** a) coho, fillet; b) sockeye, fillet

38. **sardines**

39. **saury:** pacific

40a. **scorpionfish:** red

40b. **sculpin**

41a. **gilt-head bream**

41b. **porgy:** northern

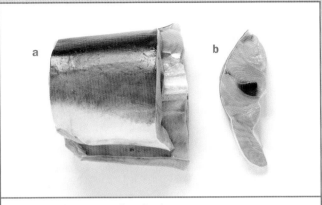

42. mako shark: a) loin; b) steak

43. skate: whole wings

44a. **striped bass:** a) wild striped bass; b) hybrid

44b. **white perch**

45a. swordfish

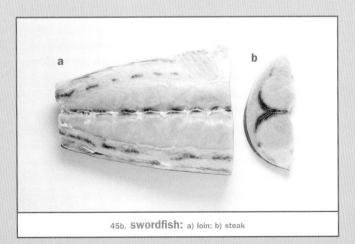

45b. swordfish: a) loin; b) steak

46. **tilapia:** a) red; b) black

47. **tilefish**

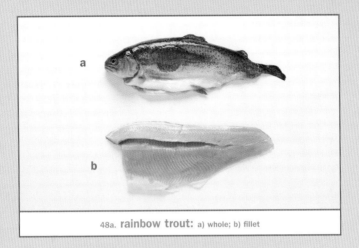

48a. **rainbow trout:** a) whole; b) fillet

48b. **trout: steelhead**

49a. **tuna: bluefin**

49b. **yellowfin tuna:** a) loin; b) steak

50. **turbot**

51. **weakfish**

52. **tautog**

53. **abalone:** red

54a. **clams:** hard-shell

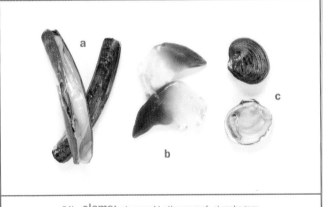

54b. **clams:** a) razor; b) stimson surf; c) mahogany

54c. **clams:** manila

55. **cockle**

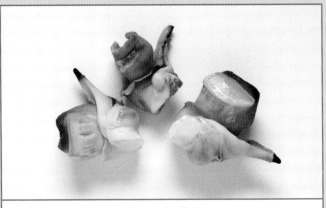

56. **queen conch:** meats

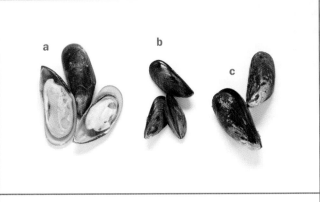

57. **mussels:** a) new zealand green; b) cultivated blue; c) blue

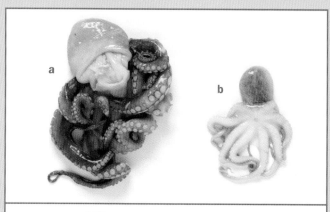

58. octopus: a) medium (spain); b) baby (taiwan)

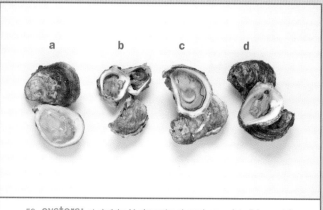

59. oysters: a) virginia; b) gigamoto; c) raspberry point; d) beausoleil

60. **top-shells**

61. **scallop:** a) sea; b) bay

62a. **loligo squid:** a) cleaned tentacles; b) cleaned tube; c) whole

62b. **squid ink**

63a. **blue crab:** a) male; b) female

63b. **blue crab:** a) pasteurized backfin lump; b) fresh jumbo lump; c) claw meat

64. **red swamp crawfish**

65. **dungeness crab:** claw

66. a) **jonah crab:** whole; b) **jonah crab:** claws;
c) **peekytoe crabmeat**

67. a) **king crab:** leg; b) **snow crab:** claw

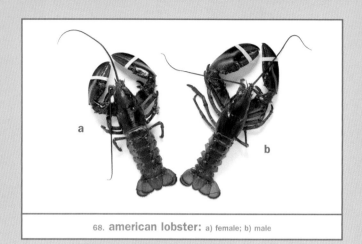

68. **american lobster:** a) female; b) male

69. **lobsterette**

70. **rock shrimp**

71a. **pacific white shrimp:** a) head-on; b) headless

71b. shrimp: santa barbara spot

72a. spiny lobster: a) florida; b) new zealand; c) south african

72b. **spiny lobster:** a) west australian cold-water tail; b) brazilian warm-water tail

73a. **frog legs:** a) saddle off; b) saddle on

73b. frog: live

74. sea urchin: a) purple; b) uni

75. **anchovies:** preserved

76. **asian fish sauce**

77. **bottarga:** a) grated tuna; b) whole mullet

78. **canned tuna:** a) whole tuna in olive oil; b) ventresca; c) light tuna in can

79. **colatura di alici**

80. **dried shrimp**

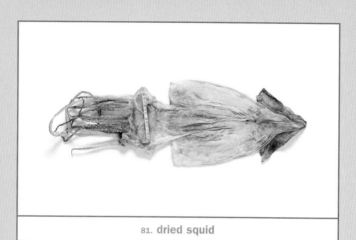

81. **dried squid**

82. **fish roe:** a) paddlefish; b) keta salmon; c) whitefish

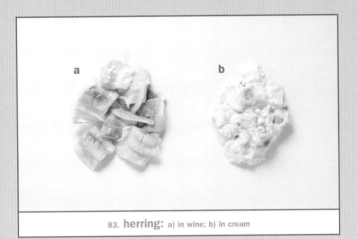

83. **herring:** a) in wine; b) in cream

84. **salt cod:** a) whole; b) fillet

85. sardines

86a. smoked whitefish

86b. **smoked whiting**

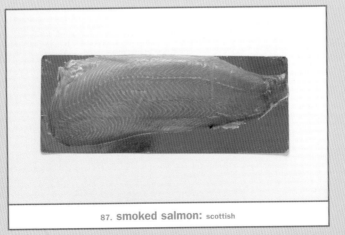

87. **smoked salmon:** scottish

88. **surimi**

89. **tobiko**

90. **unagi**

Norwegian); *sábalo commun, trisa* (Spanish); *sável* (Portuguese); *tirsi* (Turkish). **Clupeidae.**

General Description:

The American shad (Alosa sapidissima) *is an important fish on the Atlantic coast resembling plump silver-green herring.* Shad have sweet, delicate flesh and lots of small bones. A second set of bones perpendicular to the main skeleton makes it a challenge to fillet, and shad-boners get a premium rate. Shad roe is more sought after than the fish in America; in Europe, the opposite is true. According to the Micmac Indians, shad were originally a discontented porcupine that asked the Great Spirit to change them into something else. The Spirit responded by turning them inside out and tossing them in the river.

European shad (*A. alosa*) are traditionally served cooked in or accompanied by sorrel sauce, which is supposed to dissolve the small bones.

Locale and Season:

American shad range northward up the Atlantic coast from Florida to Labrador, starting in spring. On the Pacific Coast, the fish work their way up the Columbia River from May to July. After spawning around the first of June, the fish are not good eating. European shad are rare in northern Europe but are common southward. Shad roe has a firm but delicate texture; the light-colored male milt is also eaten.

Characteristics:

Shad usually weigh 3 to 5 pounds. The pale gray flesh is rich in flavor and soft in texture. Yield is 55 percent.

How to Choose:

Shad fillets are found at upscale fish markets because of the cost of filleting. Look for moist, bright-orange shad roe, removed from the fish while you watch, if possible. Avoid eating shad roe more than once a week, because it has a tendency to accumulate environmental contaminants. Smaller shad sold early in their season are more delicate in flavor; larger shad may be oily and mushy.

Storage: Store shad refrigerated on ice for up to 1 day before cooking.

Preparation: • **Sauté, pan-fry, bake, or stuff and bake shad.**

• **Shad roe is best pan-fried in butter or bacon fat.**

Suggested Recipe: **Pan-Fried Shad Roe** (serves 4): Pull off the outer membrane and fat from 4 pairs of shad roe, leaving the roe sac intact. Fry $1/2$ pound thin strips of bacon until crisp; set aside. Dust the roe sacs in flour, then pan-fry in bacon fat until just firm. Pour off any excess fat, then add 1 bunch sliced scallions to the pan; cook until just wilted, about 2 minutes. Add the juice of 1 lemon, 2 tablespoons butter, and salt and pepper to taste. Swirl to combine into a smooth sauce. Pour over roe and served with crisp bacon. •
Broiled Shad with Herbs and Onion (serves 4):

Season 2 pounds shad fillet with salt and pepper. Arrange skin-side up in a single layer on an oiled baking pan. Brush with a mixture of $1/4$ cup melted butter, the juice of 1 lemon, $1/4$ cup finely diced onion, 2 teaspoons paprika, and 2 teaspoons chopped fresh thyme, and broil 5 minutes. Turn carefully, brush again with the sauce, and broil 6 minutes longer, or until the fish flakes. Sprinkle with 2 table-spoons chopped parsley, spoon any pan juices and remaining sauce over top, and serve.

Flavor
Affinities:

Apple, apple cider, bacon, butter, celery, chervil, chive, cream, lemon, onion, paprika, parsley, potato, scallion, shallot, sorrel, tarragon, thyme, white wine.

42. 📷

SHARK

Other Names:

Dogfish: *Aiguillat commun, chien de mer, saumonette* (French); *kalb bahr* (Tunisia); *mahmuzlu camgöz* (Turkish); *melga* (Portuguese); *pesce cane, spinarola* (Italian); rock salmon (Great Britain); *rosada* (fillet), *galludo mielga, pinchorro* (Spanish); *skylópsaro* (Greek); *tsunozame* (Japanese). **Mako shark:** *Aozame* (Japanese); blue pointer; bonito shark; *dikburun* (Turkish); *kom-brokarcharías* (Greek); *marrajo* (Spanish); *squalo, smeriglio mako* (Italian); *tubarão anequim* (Portuguese). **Blacktip shark:** *Requin bordé* or *blanc* (French); *squalla pinne nere* (Italian); *tiburón macuira* (Spanish); *tubarão de pontas negras* (Portuguese). **Lamnidae** and **Carcharchinidae**.

General
Description:

There are hundreds of species of shark, but the mako, blacktip, sand, and spiny dogfish are most common at the table. Sharks are often used in Great Britain for fish and chips and are sought after in Japan. Dogfish (*Squalus acanthius*) are small sharks now being sold as Cape shark. Mako shark (*Isurus oxyrinchus*) is considered among the best tasting sharks. Their fins are dried for use in Chinese cuisine (p. 291). Blacktip shark (*Carcharhinus limbarus*) is sold as steaks that can be recognized by the ring of red flesh just under the skin.

Locale and Season:

Dogfish are mainly found in northern Atlantic waters with peak season June to September. Makos are harvested from subtropical and temperate waters and are in season from June through December. Blacktip sharks are caught in the Caribbean and other temperate to subtropical regions.

Characteristics:

Because sharks excrete their urea through their skin, they must be gutted, bled, and chilled immediately upon landing or they will quickly develop an ammoniac odor. Dogfish meat is bright white, sweet, and mild with flaky yet firm texture. Dogfish's moderately high oil content prevents it from drying out when cooked. Makos may weigh as much as 1,500 pounds, but market average is 125 pounds. Their full-bodied flavor and firm texture are similar to those of swordfish, though swordfish is drier and sweeter. Cooked mako has a rippled surface and protruding grain without the whorls of swordfish. Blacktip sharks usually weigh 3 to 5 pounds and have excellent flavor. Shark livers are also eaten.

How to Choose:

Shark meat is white with fairly coarse structure; dark meat should be avoided because of its strong taste. Choose shark with a faintly sweet smell. To distinguish mako from swordfish, feel the skin: Swordfish has smooth skin; mako has sandpaper-rough skin.

Storage: x 2	Store shark steaks refrigerated for up to 2 days. Wrap or cover the meat to keep it from drying out.

Preparation:

• **Cut away any reddish outer flesh, because this blood-rich meat can impart a strong, bitter taste.**

• **Marinate and grill, blacken, deep-fry, sauté, hot-smoke, pan-fry, add to soups and stews, or thread on skewers for kebobs.**

Suggested Recipe:

Honey-Mustard Glazed Shark Steaks (serves 4): Combine 1/4 cup honey, 2 tablespoons each Dijon and coarse-grain mustard, 1 tablespoon finely chopped thyme, and salt, black pepper, and cayenne pepper to taste. Spread the mixture over 4 (1-inch thick) shark steaks. Heat a thin layer of oil in a large nonstick skillet and sear the steaks until well-browned on both sides and cooked through and the meat is opaque, about 10 minutes.

Flavor Affinities:

Chiles, cilantro, cumin, garlic, ginger, honey, lemon, lemongrass, lime, mustard, olive oil, oregano, red onion, sesame, soy sauce, thyme, tomato, turmeric.

43. **SKATE AND RAY**

Other Names:

Gangiei (Japanese); *kalkanóvatos* (Greek); *raia* (Portuguese); *raie* (French); rajafish; *raya* (Spanish); *razza* (Italian); *rochen* (German); *skat* (Russian); *vatoz* (Turkish). **Rajidae.**

General
Description:

The bottom-dwelling, kite-shaped skate is found world-wide and is usually brownish gray. Like sharks, skate have the cartilage of primitive fish. In America, all members of the Rajidae family are known as skate; elsewhere, skate are larger with long snouts, and rays are smaller with rounded heads. The thornback ray (*R. clavata*) is most common in Great Britain, while the starry ray or thorny skate (*R. radiata*) is found in northern and arctic Atlantic waters. Skate does well with spices, rubs, and other strong flavors. Flaked, cooked skate may be substituted for crab while circles of cut-out skate wing were legendarily, but not necessarily truly, substituted for sea scallops. Because of its high gelatin content, skate should be eaten piping hot, or it can feel sticky.

Locale and
Season:

Skate harvested in winter are considered the best, but they're most abundant in the market from summer through late fall.

Characteristics:

Skate wings are composed of long strips of flesh separated by strips of cartilage, all coming together in an open fan shape. Skate taste better when they are several days old so any ammonia odor dissipates. The skin is thick and inedible, and it is usually removed before sale. The raw meat is pinkish to light tan in color, cooking up to off-white with firm, gelatin-rich meat that is moderately pronounced in flavor. The livers are also eaten.

How to Choose:

Choose shiny skate wings with no ammonia odor.

Storage:	Store skate up to 2 days refrigerated. Store poached skate up to 2 days longer before finishing.
Preparation: 1.	**To remove the skin, poach the wings briefly in salted water, about 2 minutes, just long enough to firm them up. Remove from the water, rinse, and then peel off the skin. After cooking, the flesh can be separated from the cartilage. Skate may also be filleted and skinned like a common fish.**
2.	**Bake, pan-fry, deep-fry, poach, or sauté.**
Suggested Recipe:	**Skate in Black Butter** (serves 4): Poach 3 pounds skate wings in a court bouillon for 6 minutes, drain, cool, and trim. Flour the wings and brown well in a little oil in a hot skillet. Remove from the pan, pour off the excess oil, and add 4 tablespoons butter. Brown the butter until rich, deep brown, add 4 tablespoons capers, the juice of 1 lemon, and boil until syrupy, about 5 minutes. Stir in chopped parsley and pour over the skate and serve very hot.
Flavor Affinities:	Bacon, bay leaf, capers, fennel, leek, lemon, mustard, nutmeg, onion, red wine, sherry, tomato, vinegar.

SMELT

Other Names:	Candlefish; capelin; cucumber fish; *éperlan* (French); *eperlano* (Spanish); eulachon; grunion; jacksmelt; *korjuszka* (Russian); *kyûrino* (Japanese); *nors* (Swedish);

sperlano (Italian); *spiering* (Dutch); *stint* (German); whitebait. **Ammotidytidae**.

General
Description:

Smelt (Osmerus mordax) live most of their life in salt water but migrate to lakes and streams to spawn. These small, silvery fish get their name from an Anglo-Saxon word meaning "shiny." Smelt are much appreciated for their fresh, clean aroma reminiscent of fresh-mowed grass or sliced cucumber. They are well-known in parts of France, especially Normandy, and are also found in the Baltic, around the British Isles, and the Bay of Biscay. In America, rainbow smelt (*O. mordax*) are most common. The larger and more oily Pacific or Columbia River smelt (*Thleichthys pacificus*), also called the eulachon, are popular. Larger smelts can be butterflied or filleted for broiling or grilling (using a wire fish cage). Smaller whole smelts are often dipped in batter and deep-fried.

Locale and
Season:

Smelt catches are greatest in spring; they are also ice-fished in frozen lakes. They are usually sold fresh but may be found frozen. Pacific smelts are in season in late winter and spring.

Characteristics:

Smelt have lean, white flesh with fine, soft bones. Their cooked flesh is soft and very finely flaked. If small enough, they may be eaten bones and all; if larger, the cooked meat easily flakes off the bones. The delicate skin is also eaten. Market average is 1 pound or less. Yield is 45 percent.

How to Choose:	Smelt are quite delicate and highly perishable. Select smelt with bright eyes, shiny taut skin, a minimum of bruising or dents, and a fresh cucumber smell.
Storage:	Store smelt up to 1 day refrigerated on ice.

 x 1

Preparation: **1.**	**Remove the heads and gut the fish. Rinse under cold water and then pat dry.**
2.	**Pan-fry, deep-fry, bake, broil, grill, or sauté.**
Suggested Recipe:	**Dutch Smelt** (serves 4): Cut 4 celery ribs into short sections, simmer in salted water until tender, drain, and keep warm. Boil 1¹/2 pounds gold potatoes until cooked through but still firm, about 15 minutes. Cool, then slice and pan-fry in 4 tablespoons butter until browned, about 10 minutes. Reserve. Season 2 pounds cleaned, headed smelt with salt and pepper, then dust with flour. Pan-fry in 4 tablespoons oil over high heat until brown and crisp, about 8 minutes. Serve with the celery and potatoes.
Flavor Affinities:	Almond, butter, celery, cucumber, daikon, dill, hot sauce, lemon, mustard, olive oil, paprika, potato, red onion, shallot, thyme, vinegar, white wine.

SNOOK

Other Names:	*Bicudo* (Portuguese); *brochet* (Haiti, Trinidad and Tobago); *brochet de mer* (Cuba, France); *camburiaçu, camorim*

(Brazil); *crossie-blanc* (French); *loubine* (French
Guiana); *quéquére* (Dominican Republic); ravallia;
róbalo (Latin America); *robalito* (Peru); saltwater pike,
sergeant fish; *snoek* (Dutch). **Centropomidae**.

General
Description:
*Snook (Centropomus undecimalis) are long, sleek,
and extremely strong fish revered for recreational fishing.*
Snook may live in shallow fresh, brackish, and salt
water but are temperature sensitive and must live in
warm waters. Snook have excellent flavor because they
eat crustaceans and other fish. They are fished commercially and raised in aquaculture, though they are
not available commercially in the United States. They
are a popular table fish in Latin America.

Locale and
Season:
Snook are native to the coastal waters of the western
Atlantic and the Caribbean, from Florida to Brazil.
They are illegal for commercial fishing in Florida
but are found in markets in Central America, the
Caribbean, and the north coast of South America.

Characteristics:
Snook may weigh up to 50 pounds, but average
weight is 5 to 8 pounds. The flesh is dense and firm,
delicate and flaky, and has moderate oil content and
full-bodied flavor.

How to Choose:
All snook in America are caught by recreational
fishers. Smaller fish will have milder flavor.

Storage:
Refrigerate whole, gutted snook covered in crushed
ice in a perforated pan inside a larger pan to catch
the drips up to 2 days.

Preparation: 1.   **Cut 3 slashes crosswise in each side of whole snook before grilling.**

 2.   **Grill whole or in fillet form, plank-roast, sauté, steam, pan-fry, hot-smoke, or broil.**

3.   **Remove the skin before eating, because it will impart a bitter, unpleasant flavor.**

Suggested Recipe: **Cajun Snook Stew** (serves 4): Fillet and skin a 2-pound snook and cut into bite-size chunks. In a large skillet, preferably cast iron, brown 1 chopped red onion, 1 diced green pepper, 2 sliced celery ribs, and 1 tablespoon chopped garlic in 4 tablespoons butter for 4 to 5 minutes. Add 2 diced tomatoes and 1 tablespoon Cajun seasoning, reduce heat, and simmer until sauce is thickened, 8 to 10 minutes. Add 1 sliced zucchini and/or yellow squash and simmer until crisp-tender, about 4 minutes. Add the snook, season with salt and pepper to taste, and simmer 6 to 8 minutes, or until the fish flakes. Serve over rice.

Flavor Affinities: Bay leaf, butter, fennel, lemon, lime, olive oil, onion, orange, oregano, red onion, tomato, vinegar, white wine.

44a–b.   ## STRIPED BASS AND OTHER AMERICAN BASS

Other Names: **Striped bass:** *Bar d'Amérique* (French); *felsenbarsch* (German); greenhead; linesider; *lubina americana*

(Spanish); *persico striata* (Italian); rockfish; roller; squidhound; striper; sunshine bass; *suzuki* (Japanese). **Moronidae** (striped and white bass); **Centrarchidae** (large- and smallmouth bass).

General Description:

Striped bass (Morone saxatilis) *is a large fish that gets its name from the dark horizontal stripes along its silvery sides.* They have been one of America's most prized fish since colonial times, because of their striking appearance and succulent, firm, white flesh. They are legendary among sport fishermen for their fighting ability. Seventy percent of the stock is born in the Chesapeake Bay, but overfishing has led to smaller catches and smaller fish. The smaller white bass (*M. americana*), also known as white perch, are freshwater fish related to the striped bass closely enough that they are cross-bred to create the hybrid striped bass.

There are several species of freshwater black bass, the most popular sport fish in America. The most important are the largemouth bass (*Micropterus salmoides*), weighing up to 15 pounds, and the small-mouth bass (*M. dolomieui*), weighing about 2 pounds. Both can make for good eating but have a distinctive flavor not pleasing to all.

Locale and Season:

Striped bass range from Canada to Florida and from Louisiana to the Atlantic. There was a complete moratorium on striped bass from 1985 to 1989 in Maryland and Delaware and from 1989 to 1990 in Virginia. Today, in the interest of conservation, striped bass may be fished only at specified times in limited quantities from each state. They are also farm-raised. White bass are native to the United States west of the Appalachians. Hybrid striped bass are all farm-raised, mainly in the western states. Large- and smallmouth bass live in lakes and ponds in the American East, Southeast, and Midwest.

Characteristics:

Striped bass weigh about 10 pounds. They have light-colored, delicate but satisfying flavor, and firm, succulent flesh with a large flake. White bass tend to be oily, and larger fish are muddy-tasting. Hybrid striped bass weigh 1 to 2 pounds with delicate, rather innocuous flavor and moderately firm flesh. Large- and smallmouth bass sometimes have a muddy taste that can be diminished by filleting and skinning.

How to Choose:

Wild striped bass (which will have a blue plastic tag attached) are long and narrow and have straight, uninterrupted stripes; hybrids are smaller and more rounded with broken stripes. There are many health advisories cautioning people with compromised immune systems against eating wild striped bass due to PCBs, mercury, and pesticides, problems that are more significant in larger fish.

Storage:

Refrigerate up to 2 days on ice.

Preparation: 1.

Scale hybrid or striped bass and thoroughly clean out the body cavity and gills through a slit along the belly. Rinse out with cold water and pat dry all over.

2.

Broil, grill, poach, sauté, or bake fillets or steaks; poach whole striped bass, stuffed or plain.

Suggested Recipe: 	**Stuffed Bass with Cranberries** (serves 4): Season a medium-sized striped or hybrid-striped bass (2 to 3 pounds) inside and out with salt, pepper, paprika, and ground celery seed. Combine 2 peeled and diced apples, 1/2 cup diced onion, 1 cup whole cranberries, 2 teaspoons chopped celery, and 1 cup mostly cooked rice. Stuff the fish, then sew or skewer closed. Place in an oiled baking dish and brush with 1/4 cup melted butter mixed with the juice and zest of 1 lemon. Bake 30 to 40 minutes at 350°F, or until the flesh flakes.
Flavor Affinities:	Apple, artichoke, avocado, basil, chervil, chives, corn, cured olives, dill, fennel, lemon, onion, orange, paprika, tarragon, thyme, tomato, white vermouth, white wine.

STURGEON

Other Names:	*Chôzame* (Japanese); *esturgeon* (French); *esturión* (Spanish); *esturjão solho* (Portuguese); *mersin baligi* (Turkish); *mouroúna stourióni* (Greek); *steur* (Dutch); *stør* (Danish, Norwegian); *stör* (German); *storione* (Italian). **Sevruga sturgeon:** *Pustruga* (Bulgarian); *sevryuga* (Russian); *storione stellato* (Italian). **Beluga sturgeon:** *Mersin morinasi* (Turkish); *morun* (Romanian); *moruna* (Bulgarian). **Green sturgeon:** Sakhalin or sterlyad sturgeon. **Acipenseriadae.**
General Description:	*Sturgeons are huge armored fish that are one of the oldest creatures on Earth, remaining unchanged for 300 million years.* These fish have a combination skeleton

with cartilage and rows of sharp, bony plates known as "buttons" along their bodies. They are renowned as the source of caviar (p. 286). European sturgeon (*Acipenser sturio*), rare today, was relatively common in the Mediterranean in ancient Greek and Roman times. Sterlets (*A. ruthenus*) are small, rare, freshwater fish that may venture into salt water, with good-tasting flesh and excellent caviar. The pointy-snouted sevruga sturgeon (*A. stellatus*) is most abundant in the Azov Sea. The rounded, plumper beluga sturgeon (*Huso huso*) is most abundant in the Caspian. Belugas are on the endangered list in the United States, so their prized caviar cannot be imported.

White sturgeons (*A. transmontanus*), the largest freshwater fish in North America, can reach up to 2,000 pounds. Called belusa when farmed, these firm, white-fleshed fish are raised indoors in recycled well waters. Only white sturgeon and the lesser green sturgeon (*A. medirostris*) are still harvested. The three main species of sturgeon used for aquafarming internationally are white sturgeon; Italian sturgeon (*A. naccaril*), found only rarely in the wild; and Siberian sturgeon (*A. baeri*).

Locale and Season:

Some European sturgeons live on France's Gironde River, others in the Black Sea, and a few in the Mediterranean, but they are quite rare. Sterlets are found in the Black and Azov Seas and in Siberia. White sturgeons inhabit large Pacific Northwest rivers. Farm-raised white sturgeons are available year-round from California. Wild sturgeon is in season in summer and fall.

Characteristics:	Most sturgeons sold in the United States are farm-raised white sturgeons. They have firm, dense meat similar in texture to veal. Raw sturgeon is pale pink and cooks up white with a tendency to dryness. The tough skin is not edible. Yield is 50 percent.
How to Choose:	Wild sturgeons can vary greatly in flavor depending on diet and whether they are caught in fresh or brackish water. Green sturgeons (not as highly valued for the table), with orange flesh, may be sold as white sturgeons, which are actually light gray. Farmed sturgeon is sold as skinless fillets that weigh 2 to 3 pounds each. Look for bright, shiny, moist fillets.
Storage:	Store sturgeon steaks refrigerated for up to 2 days.
Preparation: 1.	**Cut into thin slices like veal scaloppine for quick sautés; cut in chunks for skewers or stews; cut into fillet portions for pan-searing, grilling, or broiling.**
2.	**Broil, grill, sauté, pan-sear, or hot-smoke.**
Serving Suggestion:	Substitute sturgeon for any veal recipe, such as veal piccata or veal Marsala.
Flavor Affinities:	Capers, caviar, chives, dill, cream, lemon, Madeira, mushroom, onion, parsley, pine nut, shallot, sour cream, tarragon, thyme, tomato, veal stock, white wine.

45a–b. **SWORDFISH**

Other Names:
Broadbill; *emperador, espada emperado, pez espada* (Spanish); *espada* (Italian); *espadarte* (Portuguese); *espadon, poisson-épée* (French); *kilic baligi* (Turkish); *mechenos* (Russian); *mekajiki* (Japanese); *pesce spada* (Italian); *schwertfisch* (German); *sverdfisk* (Norwegian); *xifias* (Greek); *zwaardvis* (Dutch). **Xiphiidae.**

General Description:
The large and solitary swordfish (Xiphias gladius) roam temperate and tropical waters worldwide. Swordfish may reach 15 feet long with a huge sword as much as 5 feet long. Most swordfish are caught at night by longline during the final quarter of the moon and especially during bright, full-moon nights, when they feed heavily. The rest are caught by gill net and a very small number by harpoon. Fish stores buy sections of swordfish called wheels that may be cut into whole, half, or quarter-round steaks depending on size. Small swordfish may be sold headed and gutted as logs. Swordfish take well to marinades, especially those based on acids like vinegar and citrus juice. Steaks can be cooked from frozen. Take care not to overcook swordfish, because it quickly turns mealy and dry.

Locale and Season:

Swordfish are fished in 30 countries. In the United States, swordfish supplies are usually more plentiful and less expensive in summer and fall.

Characteristics:
Whole swordfish are mostly white with colored bands of blue or deep purple running lengthwise and can weigh more than 1,000 pounds, though 50 to 200 pounds is

most common. Its flesh ranges from pink-orange to
pink and ivory, and cooks up off-white. It has moderately high oil content and firm, meaty, moist, and
flavorful, though slightly mealy, flesh. Swordfish
steaks have a characteristic whorling pattern.

How to Choose: Choose swordfish steaks with firm flesh and no
raggedy edges, at least 1 inch thick for moist results.
Dull, discolored skin is a sign of poor handling, as
are steaks with signs of browning, called "burning,"
which happens when a caught fish struggles and gets
overheated. Frozen-at-sea (FAS), or "clipper," swordfish are of high quality and may be less expensive.

Storage: Swordfish bought in larger sections can be refrigerated,
covered with a damp cloth, for 3 to 4 days before
cooking. Swordfish purchased as individual steaks can
be refrigerated for 1 to 2 days before cooking.

Preparation: 1.   **Cut away any dark red areas, which should not show
any brownness, a sign of age.**

2.   **Cook swordfish as for tuna: grill, bake, sauté, broil,
or cube and thread on kebobs for grilling. Unlike
tuna, swordfish should be fully cooked.**

Suggested   **Swordfish with Sicilian Salmoriglio** (serves 4):
Recipe: Whisk 1/2 cup olive oil with 1/4 cup lemon juice, the
zest of 1 lemon, and 2 tablespoons hot water. Add
1/4 cup chopped Italian parsley, 2 teaspoons chopped
garlic, and 3 tablespoons chopped fresh oregano.
Sprinkle 4 thick swordfish steaks with salt and pepper

and brush with some of the sauce. Grill or broil until just cooked through, about 5 minutes per side. Serve with the remaining sauce.

Flavor
Affinities:
Anchovy, capers, chiles, chili powder, corn, lemon, lime, miso, olive oil, olives, oregano, red onion, red wine vinegar, tomato, white wine.

46.

TILAPIA

Other Names:
Chikadai, terapia (Japanese); *nil-buntbarch* (German); St. Peter's fish; sunfish; *tilapia del Nilo* (Italian, Spanish); *tilapia du Nil* (French). **Cichlidae**.

General
Description:
Tilapia are one of the most popular fish in restaurants and at retail fish counters. Native to Africa and Asia, tilapia have a long history of feeding pharaohs and kings. According to legend, they were the fish Jesus multiplied to feed the masses at the Sea of Galilee. Commonly known as St. Peter's fish, tilapia are the most common farm-raised fish in the world. In the United States they are raised in the South and West, with many producers using environmentally responsible closed recirculating systems. The most common species are *Tilapia nilotica*, emerald green and known for high yield and rapid growth; *T. aureus*, cold-resistant fish; and *T. mossambica*, with a reddish color that makes them popular for live fish tanks and displays.

Locale and Season:	Tilapia are farm-raised in 50 countries worldwide and available year-round at moderate prices.

Characteristics:

Tilapia is mild and sweet-tasting. The raw meat is pinkish-white to white and lean; cooked, the meat is white, tender, and slightly firm with flaky texture. Tilapia fillets have a thin layer of darker meat just below the skin that is often removed. These moderately priced fish are sold as whole fish or as fillets.

How to Choose:

Water quality and feed are critical. The best tilapia has clean flavor; poor quality tilapia can be muddy-tasting. Fresh tilapia in America mostly comes from Ecuador—it is imported frozen from Asia, usually China. Ecuadorian producers sell mostly deep-skinned fillets with the brown fat layer removed. Other Latin American producers leave the fat layer. Asian producers treat frozen fillets with carbon monoxide for reddish color and are known to pass it off as sashimi-quality snapper (*izumi dai snapper*). Filleted tilapia has probably been frozen in fillet form, so texture and taste can be compromised. Whole tilapia, found at Asain markets, are best.

Storage:

Refrigerate for up to 2 days after purchase. Defrost frozen fillets in the refrigerator overnight.

Preparation:

• **Bake, broil, sauté, pan-fry, or steam.**

NOTE:

Though attractive, the skin of the tilapia should be removed, because it can have a bitter taste. Either

remove the skin before cooking or pull it off after
cooking and before serving.

Suggested
Recipe:

Baked Tilapia with Tomatoes and Olives (serves 6):
Combine 1/4 cup extra-virgin olive oil, 3 diced tomatoes, 1/2 cup chopped red onion, 1/2 cup sliced green
olives, 2 teaspoons chopped thyme, 2 teaspoons
chopped garlic, 1/4 teaspoon hot red pepper flakes,
and the juice of 1 lime. Season 6 (6- to 8-ounce)
tilapia fillets with salt and pepper. Arrange in an oiled
baking pan and spoon the mixture over top. Bake at
400°F for 15 minutes, or until the fish flakes.

Flavor
Affinities:

Almond, dill, lemon, lime, mustard, olives, orange,
parsley, pecan, pistachio, red onion, shallot, tangerine,
tarragon, thyme, tomato, walnut, white wine.

47. **TILEFISH**

Other Names:

Amadai (Japanese); *blanquillo camello* (Spanish);
blauer ziegelfisch (German); golden bass or snapper;
khoklach (Russian); *peixe paleta camelo* (Portuguese);
rainbow tilefish; *tile chameau* (French); *tile gibboso*
(Italian). **Malacanthidae.**

General
Description:

Tilefish (Lophalatilus chamaeleonticeps) *are colorful
fish known as "the clown of the sea," with blue, green,
rose, and yellow skin that fades when removed from the
water.* These fish are found only in the United States,

in a warm band of water along a narrow stretch of ocean floor on the upper reaches of the continental slope from Florida to Nova Scotia.

Locale and
Season:

Tilefish are most abundant from Nantucket to Delaware Bay on the American Atlantic coast. It is available year-round.

Characteristics:

Though tilefish can weigh up to 80 pounds, market weight is 5 to 10 pounds. Tilefish fillets are thick and dense with a row of pin bones that must be removed. The raw meat is pinkish-white; the cooked meat is firm with flaky texture that retains moisture.

How to Choose:

Tilefish are sold fresh, graded, and priced by size. The bigger the fish, the higher the per-pound price. Smaller fish are also more perishable. Choose bigger tilefish for best flavor and longest shelf life; choose smaller tilefish for lower price and quicker cooking.

Storage:

x 3

Refrigerate large whole fish up to 3 days; store small whole fish 2 days. Use fillets within 1 day.

Preparation: •

Using fish or needlenose pliers, pull out the pin bones.

 •

Bake, broil, fry, poach, sauté, or use for sushi.

Suggested
Recipe:

Florida Fruit Tilefish (serves 4): Combine 3 cups diced tropical fruits (kiwi, pineapple, mango, papaya, star fruit, and/or banana) with 4 tablespoons melted butter, 3/4 cup orange or tangerine juice, and 1 cup grated coconut. Season 4 tilefish fillets with salt and

pepper and sprinkle with lime juice. Arrange in an
oiled baking dish, top with the fruit, and sprinkle
with 1/4 cup sliced almonds. Broil 10 minutes, or
until the fish flakes.

Flavor
Affinities:
Avocado, banana, bell pepper, butter, chiles, cilantro,
coconut, kiwi, lemon, lime, olive oil, orange, papaya,
passion fruit, pineapple, tomato, white wine.

48a–b.

TROUT

Other Names: **Rainbow trout:** *Lachsforelle, regenbogenforelle*
(German); *mijimasu, nijimusu* (Japanese); *péstropha*
(Greek); *regnbueørred* (Danish); *trota irdea* (Italian);
trucha arco iris (Spanish); *truite arc-en-ciel* (French);
truta-arco-íris (Portuguese). **European sea trout:** *Aure*
(Norwegian); *deniz alasi* (Turkish); *forel* (Russsian);
meerforelle (German); *péstrogha thalássis* (Greek);
salmon trout; steelhead; *trota di mare* (Italian); *trucha
marina* (Spanish); *truite de mer* (French); *truta marinha*
(Portuguese); *zeeforel* (Dutch). **Salmonidae.**

General
Description:
*The many species of trout, smaller members of the
salmon family, mostly live in freshwater lakes and
streams.* Trout flesh is quite delicate and ranges from
ivory to salmon-red with diet and habitat more
important to its character than species. Wild-caught
trout can be exquisite, and while farmed trout can
have good flavor and firm texture, poorly produced
trout can be mushy and muddy. Idaho produces

70 percent of American farmed trout.

Brook trout (*Salvelinus fontinalis*) are native to eastern North America but have been widely transplanted and farmed. Wild brook trout are considered by many to be the best-tasting trout. The brown trout (*Salmo trutta*) was the original European trout transplanted to America in the nineteenth century. They live in lakes and streams or migrate to the sea, where they are called sea trout or salmon trout, and are considered a delicacy in Europe. They are not the same as the American sea trout, or weakfish (p. 187). Dolly Varden trout (*Salvelinus malma*) are large, troutlike char (p. 9) closely related to brook and lake trout and usually found in cold mountain streams. Their flesh is delicious and often pink in color.

Lake trout (*Salvelinus namaycush*) are netted in cold-water lakes of northern North America. Their oil content varies greatly, so they range from delicious to too oily. These large fish are well-suited to hot-smoking. Rainbow trout (*Oncorhynchus mykiss*, called *Salmo gairdneri* until 1989), originated in the American West and are often used to stock rivers and streams there. When ocean-going, they are called steelheads and are even more highly prized. Rainbow trout are farm-raised in the oldest American aquaculture industry, dating back to the 1880s. All rainbow trout sold in America are farm-raised.

Locale and
Season:

Rainbow trout are farmed in the United States, Argentina, Chile, western Europe, and Japan. Late spring and early summer are their best seasons; they grow more slowly in winter. Steelhead are farm-raised

and harvested year-round in eastern Canada. Dolly
Vardens range from Korea to the Bergen Sea and
across to Oregon.

Characteristics: Whole trout have more flavor than boned trout.
Brown trout can weigh up to 40 pounds, but freshwater fish average 1 to 2 pounds, ocean-going fish 4 to
5 pounds. Farm-raised rainbow trout weigh 12 to
16 ounces and have soft, flaky meat with delicate,
nutty, herbal flavor. Steelhead may grow to 12 pounds;
2 to 4 pounds is average. Cooked, the meat is ivory
with fine flake, delicate flavor, and moderate fat.

How to Choose: Trout is covered by a layer of transparent slime. The
more slippery the fish, the fresher it is. They are available fresh, frozen, smoked, whole, or filleted (boned
or boneless). "Boned" does not mean boneless,
but rather that the backbone has been removed.
"Boneless" means the pin bones have been removed.

Storage: Trout is one of the longest-lasting freshwater fish and
can be stored refrigerated for 2 to 3 days.

□ x 2

Preparation: **1.** **Trout have such tiny scales that there's no need for**
scaling; the fish should be rinsed and dried. The tiny
pin bones can be picked out at the table.

2. **Bake, broil, grill, poach, sauté, or hot-smoke.**

Suggested **Pan-Fried Trout with Green Grapes** (serves 4):
Recipe: Season 4 butterflied bone-in or boned trout with salt
 and pepper. Dust with flour and sauté in 2 tablespoons

each walnut oil and butter. Cook 3 minutes per side, or until almost opaque, covering the pan to cook through. Remove the fish from the pan and keep warm. Add 1 cup halved seedless green grapes and sauté until caramelized, about 3 minutes, add a squeeze of lemon, swirl to combine with pan juices, and serve over trout.

Flavor
Affinities:

Almond, bacon, butter, capers, carrot, celery, chervil, chive, lemon, mint, orange, pine nut, scallion, shallot, tarragon, thyme, tomato, walnut, white wine.

49a–b.

TUNA

Other Names:

Albacore: *Atum voador* (Portuguese); *atún blanco, bonito del Norte* (Spanish); *binnaga* (Japanese); *germon, thon blanc* (French); *tombo* (Hawaiian); *tonáki* (Greek); *tonno bianco* (Italian); *weisser thun* (German); *yazili orkinos* (Turkish). **Bigeye:** *Atum barbatana negra* (Portuguese); *atún de aleta negra* (Spanish); *schwartzflossenthum* (German); *taiseiyo maguro* (Japanese); *thon à nageoires noires* (French); *tonno pinna nera* (Italian); *tónos marvrópteros* (Greek). **Bluefin:** *Atum rabilho* (Portuguese); *atún rojo, cimarrón* (Spanish); *kuromaguro* (Japanese); *orkinoz* (Turkish); *roter thun, thunfisch* (German); *tonno* (Italian); *tónos* (Greek). **Skipjack:** *Aku* (Hawaiian); Arctic bonito; *atún listado, bonito de altura, listado* (Spanish); *cizgiliorkinoz baligi* (Turkish); *echter bonito* (German); *gaiado* (Portuguese); *katsuo* (Japanese);

lakérada, palamida (Greek); ocean bonito; *tonnetto striato* (Italian). **Yellowfin:** *Ahi* (Hawaiian); *atum albacora* (Portuguese); *atún claro, rabil* (Spanish); *gelbflossen-thunfisch* (German); *kiwadamaguro* (Japanese); *tónos kitrinópteros* (Greek). **Scombridae.**

General Description:

Tuna are large migratory fish that travel in dense shoals. As early as the second century BCE, the Greeks knew of tuna's migratory habits, which are still not fully understood. Today tuna fishing is industrialized and scientific, with helicopters and satellites used to locate migrating shoals.

Albacore (*Thunnus alalunga*) are recognized by their extra-long pectoral fins. They are best known in the United States as canned "white meat" tuna (p. 286). Albacore is well suited to grilling and is best served rare. Bigeye (or blackfin) tuna (*T. obesus*) have fat bodies and large heads and eyes. Bigeye tuna is usually sold as fresh or frozen steaks, has rich and hearty flavor, and is popular for sushi and sashimi. Bluefins (*T. thynnus*) are the largest tuna. In Sicily, a long net intercepts the migrating fish, diverting them into a series of ponds and finally into a net where the fish are speared with gaffs. Bluefins are especially prized for use raw in sushi, ceviche, and tartars because of their high fat content. Skipjack tuna (*Katsuwonus pelamis*) are small fish that congregate in schools found in the warmer waters of the world. Nearly half the global tuna catch is skipjack. Larger, darker-fleshed skipjack are enjoyed in Japan for sushi and sashimi. Yellowfin tuna (*T. albacares*) have a long, bright yellow dorsal fin and a yellow stripe down their steel-blue backs. The Hawaiian name, *ahi*, means "fire." Yellowfins are fished in tropical waters and are widely canned as "light tuna."

Locale and
Season:

Fresh albacore are in season on the American Pacific coast from May through November. There are also fisheries in Korea, Japan, New Zealand, South Africa, Spain, and Taiwan. Frozen albacore are available year-round. In America, bluefins are in season in New England from July through October and in California from June through November. In America, high-quality yellowfin comes from Hawaii, Florida, Mexico, and California. They are available year-round, though supplies are greatest in summer. Yellowfins also come from France, Spain, Indonesia, Japan, Mexico, the Philippines, South Korea, and Taiwan.

Characteristics:

Albacore's creamy white, slightly rose-tinted meat resembles veal. Because they are soft, they are not suited to sushi. Bluefins are usually sold fresh and are the fattiest of all tunas, with cherry-red flesh when raw. When fully cooked, the meat is quite firm, dense, and ivory in color, though they are often seared and served rare to maintain moistness. The flavor is full-bodied with the firmness and look of beef. Skipjack average 5 to 8 pounds, with pale pinkish flesh; they can be used for sushi. Yellowfins are not as large as bluefins. The meat is mild, similar to sword-fish, with more flavor than albacore but less fat than bluefin. The skin of tuna is not eaten and is usually removed before cooking.

How to Choose:

High-grade clipper albacore loins have been cut from freshly landed tuna and frozen onboard. When grilling or broiling, cut steaks at least 1 1/2 inches thick and marinate before cooking. Look for bigeyes with glistening, bright color and firm, springy texture. Big bluefins are graded by taking sample "plugs" out of their flesh. Those with best color and richest in fat, Number 1, sashimi-grade, are destined for Japan's best sushi bars and return very high prices. Number 2 fish, grill-grade, are leaner; lower grades tend to be dry when cooked. Choose bluefin that is deep red with firm, springy texture. Cut steaks will quickly bleed their juices and look pale and dry. Skipjack are usually sold frozen because of their short shelf life. Look for tuna without any drying out, a sign of freezer burn. More than any other kind of tuna, fresh yellowfin is susceptible to scombroid poisoning if not kept chilled at all stages of handling. Choose yellowfin with glistening flesh and bright, clear, reddish-pink color and a fresh smell. Saku tuna is specially prepared by a "smoking" process (using carbon monoxide) that lends no flavor but helps to preserve sushi-ready rectangular sections of bluefin or yellowfin tuna that are sealed in plastic and frozen.

Storage:

All tuna quickly deteriorates, especially once cut into steak portions. Refrigerate (preferably uncut, rather than as steaks), covered with crushed ice, up to 1 day.

Preparation: **1.**

Cut out the blood line, the darker flesh near the backbone (although the Japanese prize this flesh).

2. **Albacore: broil, grill, or sauté. Bigeye: excellent raw; briefly pan-sear, grill, or roast. Bluefin: bake, broil, grill, sauté, smoke, or serve raw. Skipjack: broil, sauté, or pan-fry. Yellowfin: bake, broil, grill, sauté, poach in olive oil, smoke, or serve raw.**

Serving
Suggestion:
Substitute darker tuna for any beef steak recipes, lighter tuna for veal or chicken recipes.

Flavor
Affinities:
Anchovy, avocado, capers, celery, chiles, demi-glace, fennel, garlic, ginger, lemon, mango, mayonnaise, olive oil, onion, orange, rice wine, scallion, sesame, shallot, soy sauce, tomato, wasabi, white wine.

50. **TURBOT AND BRILL**

Other Names: **Turbot:** *Dornbutt, steinbutt* (German); *kalkan baligi* (Turkish); *kalkáni, siáki* (Greek); *meganemongara* (Japanese); *parracho, rémol, rodaballo* (Spanish); *pig-gvar* (Swedish, Norwegian); *pregado* (Portuguese); *psettod* (Russian); *rombo chiodato* (Italian); *sandhverfa* (Icelandic); *tarbot* (Dutch). **Scophthalmidae. Brill:** *Barbue* (French); *broit* (Ireland); *corujo, rapante, rémol* (Spanish); *glattbutt, kleist* (German); *griet* (Dutch); kite (British); *patrúcia, rodovalho* (Portuguese); *sleth-varre* (Danish). **Pleuronectidae.**

General
Description:
Turbot (Scopthalmus maximus) are large, diamond-shaped fish greatly prized for their firm and delicious flesh. Turbot are left-eyed flounder that are generally

brown for camouflage. Instead of scales, they have knobby, dark brown bony spots on top called tubercles; the fish are white and smooth underneath. Take care not to overcook, or they will be dry. Turbot make a superb, full-bodied fish stock. Brill (*S. rhombus*) are smaller, shallow-water versions of turbot that are oval in shape with scales instead of tubercles. The two fish sometimes form hybrids. Like turbot, brill does not appear in the western Atlantic. Less prized than turbot, brill are smaller and not as meaty, though still an excellent fish of good value.

Locale and
Season:

Turbot are found in shallow inshore waters throughout the Mediterranean and north to Iceland and Norway. Global supplies are quite limited, so turbot always commands a high price. The wild catch is now supplemented by farm-raised turbot from Spain, France, and Chile. Wild turbot are in peak season in spring and summer; farmed turbot is available year-round. Wild brill is found in the same areas and seasons as turbot.

Characteristics:

Wild turbot can reach 30 pounds, but 10 pounds is average. They have gleaming white flesh that is bright white even when cooked. The firm meat has a large flake, excellent flavor, and firm texture. Fillets from a 3- to 4-pound fish can be quite meaty; those from smaller fish will be thin. Farmed fish are generally smaller, 1 to 3 pounds, milder in flavor, and less firm. A rim of fatty tissue on the fin side of each fillet contains a row of "kernels" of snow-white meat, considered the best meat on the fish.

How to Choose: Note that other types of fish with softer flesh are sometimes sold as genuine European turbot, including Greenland turbot and West Coast arrowtooth flounder. Most of these fake turbot are sold as frozen fillets. The real thing is sold as whole, fresh fish.

Storage: Store whole turbot up to 2 days refrigerated; store fillets up to 1 day refrigerated.

x 2

Preparation: 1. **Remove the skin, especially from the dark top.**

2. **Bake or poach whole; grill, broil, poach, steam, or sauté fillets of both turbot and brill.**

Suggested Recipe: **Turbot with Sauce Vierge** (serves 4): Combine 2 cups diced fresh tomatoes with 2 teaspoons chopped garlic, the juice of 2 lemons, the zest of 1 lemon, 2 tablespoons chopped shallots, and 2 tablespoons each shredded basil, sliced chives, chopped dill, and chopped tarragon with 1/2 cup extra-virgin olive oil. Season 2 pounds turbot fillets with salt and pepper and dust with flour. Sauté in hot olive oil on both sides until opaque, about 8 minutes. Separately, wilt 1 pound baby spinach in olive oil and season with salt, pepper, and nutmeg. Serve the spinach with the turbot and spoon the sauce over top.

Flavor Affinities: Artichoke, bay leaf, basil, brandy, butter, chervil, chives, crayfish, cream, dill, lemon, lobster, mushroom, parsley, shallot, tarragon, thyme, tomato, white wine.

WAHOO

Other Names:
Acantocibio, maccerello striato (Italian); barracuda; *cavala da india* (Portuguese); jack mackerel; *kamasu-sawara* (Japanese); *kin fis* (Creole); kingfish; malata; *nguru-maskati* (Swahili); *ono* (Hawaiian); *paala* (Samoan); Pacific king-fish; *paere, thazard bâtard* (French); *peto* (German, Spanish); queen fish; *sierra* (Spanish); *serra-da-india* (Portuguese). **Scombridae.**

General Description:
Wahoo (Acanthocybium solandri) *is closely related to the king mackerel.* They have dark blue or electric blue upper bodies marked with waved stripes and a silver lower body, an overshot lower jaw, and razor-sharp teeth. There are no organized fisheries for wahoo, perhaps because the fish do not school. Wahoos are appreciated as game fish.

Locale and Season:
Wahoos are distributed worldwide in tropical and subtropical waters and are caught off South America and in the Caribbean, both commercially with longlines and recreationally. They are a bycatch of tuna and swordfishing in Florida. Most wahoos in America come from the Caribbean, Hawaii, Australia, and Fiji and are more abundant in summer months.

Characteristics:
Wahoos may weigh up to 100 pounds, but 8 to 30 pounds is average. Raw wahoo flesh is pale pink and slightly translucent, cooking up white with mild flavor, firm, lean texture, and large, round flake.

How to Choose:

In the areas where they are caught commercially, wahoos are marketed fresh, salted, spice-cured, or frozen. Day-boat wahoo from Hawaii is best. Wahoo has been linked to ciguatera poisoning, especially in larger fish. To avoid the poisoning, do not eat fish caught in affected areas. Clean the fish very well and do not eat the roe, liver, head, or innards, because they contain higher levels of the poison.

Storage:

Store whole wahoo hanging with its head down. Do not fillet this fish until ready to cook. Use immediately.

Preparation: 1.

Fillet (as directed on p. 3) or cut into thick steaks.

2.

Marinate, then grill, broil, sauté, or hot-smoke.

Suggested Recipe:

Caribbean Wahoo (serves 4): Season 1 1/2 pounds wahoo cut into chunks with salt, pepper, and lime juice and place in a baking dish. Combine 1 can unsweetened coconut milk with 1 finely minced Scotch bonnet or other hot chile, 1 each diced red and green bell pepper, 1 diced sweet onion, and 2 ripe plantains, sliced diagonally, and spoon over the fish. Cover and bake at 375°F for 20 minutes, or until the fish flakes.

Flavor Affinities:

Bell pepper, Cajun seasoning, chiles, cilantro, coconut, garlic, key lime, lemon, lime, mango, olive oil, orange, sweet onion, tangerine, tomato.

WALLEYE AND ZANDER

Other Names: **Pike-perch:** *Amerikanischer zander* (German); *doré jaune* (French); *lucioperca americana* (Spanish); *picão verde* (Portuguese); pickerel; *sandra americana* (Italian); yellow pike. **Zander:** European pickerel or walleye; *fogas* (Hungarian); *gjoers* (Norwegian); *kuka* (Finnish); *levrek*, *sudak* (Turkish); *lucioperca* (Spanish); *perche brochet*, *sandre doré* (French); sander; *sandra* (Italian); *snoekbaars* (Dutch); *sudak* (Russian); yellow pike. **Sauger:** Jack salmon; jackfish; *lucioperca canadiense* (Spanish); *picão canadiana* (Portuguese); river pike; *sandra canadese* (Italian); *sandre canadien* (French); spotfin pike. **Percidae.**

General Description: *Several fish in this genus are called pike-perch because of their resemblance to freshwater fish in the unrelated pike family (p. 118).* Walleye (*Sander vitreum*) are an American fish with long, tapering bodies that are brown and yellow on a silvery background. Like others in the lake perch family, they have spiny dorsal fins. The walleye gets its name from its smoky, silvery eye, said to resemble blinded or walleyed domestic animals. Almost all commercial pickerel sold in the Midwest is yellow walleye.

   The legendary zander (*S. lucioperca*) is a rare European freshwater fish that may be the most prized table fish in Europe, where it is also known as pike perch. It is almost identical to the walleye and can be prepared by any method. Sauger (*S. canadensis*), a close relative and lookalike of the walleye, inhabits large bodies of water like the Great Lakes.

Locale and Season:	Walleyes are commercially important in Canada, where the fishery is most active in winter months. Zander are found in northern Europe and Russia.
Characteristics:	Walleyes can grow up to 25 pounds, but 2 to 3 pounds is average. They have succulent, pure white, firm, clean-tasting flesh with few bones, very fine flake, and delicate flavor. The cheeks are also delicious. Zander from low-salinity seawaters, including the Aral, Baltic, and Black Seas, are less valued. Saugers weigh 3 to 5 pounds but because of their smaller size are not as prized as the nearly identical walleye. They all may be cooked with or without skin.
How to Choose:	Even when fresh, walleyes have opaque (rather than bright) eyes, adapted to the dim light in which they forage. Choose fillets from whole but small fish to get both the fattier, richer head meat and the leaner tail portion. Yield is 45 percent.
Storage: x 2	Store whole fish refrigerated up to 2 days; store fillets refrigerated up to 1 day.
Preparation:	• **Bake, broil, deep-fry, sauté, pan-fry, or poach.**
Suggested Recipe:	**Grilled Walleye with Tartar Sauce** (serves 4): Combine 1/2 cup mayonnaise with 2 chopped hard-cooked eggs, 2 tablespoons capers, 2 tablespoons chopped parsley, 2 tablespoons drained dill pickle relish, 1 teaspoon dry mustard, and the juice of 1 lemon to make the tartar sauce. Combine 4 tablespoons melted butter with the juice of 1 lemon and 1 table-

spoon chopped dill. Season 2 pounds walleye fillets with salt and pepper. Grill, covered, skin-up at first, brushing with the melted butter mixture, flipping once, until the fish flakes, 4 to 8 minutes total. Serve with tartar sauce.

Flavor
Affinities:

Almond, basil, butter, capers, celery, chervil, chives, dill, lemon, marjoram, mustard, paprika, potato, shallot, sweet onion, tarragon, tomato, walnut, white wine.

51. **WEAKFISH**

Other Names:

Accoupa pintade (French); corvina; *corvinata pintada* (Portuguese, Spanish); *gefleckter umberfisch* (German); *gevlekte ombervis* (Dutch); gray trout; *ombrina dentata* (Italian); spotted sea trout; squeteague. **Sciaenidae.**

General
Description:

Weakfish (Cynoscion regalis) are delicious and relatively inexpensive fish without pesky pin bones. Their name comes from their weak mouth, which easily tears and releases the hook. They are the most important member of the croaker-drum family (p. 39) in American waters.

Locale and
Season:

Weakfish is found along the Atlantic coast from Florida to Massachusetts in summer only.

Characteristics:

Weakfish may grow up to 40 pounds, but market weight is 2 pounds. They have complex coloring that varies, with dark olive above and varicolored sheen and small dark spots forming irregular, subtle stripes.

How to Choose: Choose weakfish that are fresh-caught and firm, with shiny skin and bright eyes. They deteriorate quickly.

Storage: Store whole weakfish up to 1 day refrigerated.
☐ x 1

Preparation: •   **Pan-fry weakfish whole or as fillets; it may also be grilled whole or used in chowders.**

Suggested   **Weakfish Almandine** (serves 4): Dredge a 2-pound
Recipe: whole cleaned weakfish in flour mixed with paprika.
                   Brown in butter mixed with bacon fat 6 to 8 minutes
                   and remove from the pan. Add 2 tablespoons chopped
                   or sliced almonds or hazelnuts and brown. Add the
                   juice of 1 lemon, combine, and pour over fish.

Flavor   Almond, bacon, butter, celery, chives, cream, hazelnut,
Affinities: lemon, lime, marjoram, oregano, paprika, pine nut,
                   scallion, shallot, thyme, white wine.

WHITEFISH

Other Names: *Corégone de lac* (French); *coregone dei grande laghe*
                   (Italian); *corégono* (Spanish); *felchen* (German); inland
                   whitefish; Labrador whitefish; *shiromasu* (Japanese).
                   Salmonidae.

General   *Whitefish (Coregonus clupeaformis) live in the cold*
Description: *deepwater lakes of the northern United States and
                   Canada.* The name whitefish is also used for various
                   mild-flavored, white-fleshed unrelated ocean fish.
                   Whitefish are one of the best-tasting freshwater fish

and are used traditionally for Jewish gefilte fish. The roe (p. 288), sold as golden caviar, is highly sought after. Because whitefish live in icy northern waters, they have a high fat content and are good smoked. Whitefish can be cooked in chowders and used fresh or smoked for salad because the meat is firm.

Locale and Season:

Most whitefish comes from Canada, where it is harvested commercially, but it is also caught by sport fishers in New England and the Great Lakes. Whitefish are most easily found at the market in winter and at Easter and Passover.

Characteristics:

Whitefish may weigh up to 20 pounds, but market weight is 3 to 5 pounds. When cooked, they have off-white, mildly flavored, medium-firm flesh with a large flake. Yield is 55 percent.

How to Choose:

Whitefish in winter are of better quality with firmer and fatter flesh. Whole fish harvested from cold, clear, clean northern waters will be of high quality. For whole fish, look for shiny skin, moist flesh, and bright eyes. Look for firm, shiny fillets with even color and pinkish tinge. Avoid dried-out or brown-tinted fillets.

Storage:

Store whole fish up to 2 days refrigerated; store fillets up to 1 day refrigerated.

Preparation: **1. Pull out the pin bones.**

2. Bake, broil, grill, hot-smoke, pan-fry, grind for fish mousses, or use for salad. Cook whole or cut into steaks or fillets.

Suggested Recipe:

Baked Whitefish (serves 4): Combine 1/2 cup white wine with 2 tablespoons Dijon mustard in an oiled baking dish. Season 2 pounds whitefish fillets with salt and pepper, sprinkle with chopped thyme, and add to the dish. Cover with 1 cup diced sweet or spring onion and 1/2 pound fiddleheads, snow peas, or cut lengths of asparagus. Cover and bake at 350°F for 20 minutes or until the fish flakes. Swirl 2 tablespoons butter into the pan juices before serving.

Flavor Affinities:

Asparagus, butter, celery, chives, cucumber, dill, green beans, horseradish, lemon, marjoram, mayonnaise, mushrooms, snow peas, sour cream, sweet onion, thyme.

WOLFFISH

Other Names:

Havkat (Danish); *katfisch* (German); lobo; *loup marin* (French); *merikissa* (Finnish); ocean catfish; pout; rock salmon; seacat; *steinbit* (Norwegian); *steinbítur* (Icelandic); *zebadz smugoway* (Polish); *zeewolf* (Dutch); *zubatka* (Russian). **Anarhichadidae**.

General Description:

Wolffish are ferocious looking creatures and are notable fighters. This bottom-dwelling, solitary, cold-water fish is primarily a bycatch of trawl fishing for cod and haddock. Striped wolffish (*Anarhichas lupus*) are one of three Atlantic species, all quite similar in the culinary sense. Highly appreciated in Europe, they are cooked like Dover sole. Wolffish are versatile and have firm flesh that holds together quite well. Spotted wolffish (*A. minor*) are now farm-raised in Norway and sold fresh throughout the year.

Locale and Season:

Wolffish range from Greenland to France in the east and Cape Cod to the west. Iceland has the largest targeted fishery for this species. Wolffish are most available in the spring and summer.

Characteristics:

Wolffish can reach 40 pounds, but market average is 10 pounds. They are dark blue-gray or greenish and may be spotted or striped. Wolffish are firm and can be cubed or cut into strips without falling apart. Wolffish are sold mainly as fillets but are also available as whole, cleaned fish or steaks. Farmed spotted wolffish yields almost 50 percent fish from 6 to 10 pounds. The lean, pearly white flesh is firm and has mild sweet flavor. Wolffish skin is edible.

How to Choose:

Properly processed wolffish are boneless. Fish containing pin bones are likely not the real thing. The fillets are long and narrow. Look for pinkish tinge without browning and shiny, moist flesh.

Storage:

Store wolffish up to 2 days refrigerated.

x 2

Preparation: •

Bake, broil, fry, grill, poach, sauté, or steam.

| Suggested Recipe: | **Wolffish Brabant Style** (serves 4): Slice $^1/2$ pound each Belgian endive and potatoes, season with salt and pepper, and fry separately in butter until the endive is wilted and soft, about 5 minutes, and the potatoes are browned and almost cooked through, about 10 minutes, and keep warm. Butter a metal baking dish and sprinkle with 2 finely chopped shallots. Lay $1^1/2$ pounds cleaned wolffish fillets on top, pour $^3/4$ cup white wine over, cover with foil, and bake at 375°F for 10 minutes. Transfer the fish, potatoes, and endive to a serving dish, cover, and keep warm. Place the baking dish over medium heat and boil the juices until syrupy. Swirl in 2 tablespoons butter and pour over the fish. |

| Flavor Affinities: | Belgian endive, butter, clam, lemon, lobster, mushroom, mustard, onion, oyster, potato, shallot, sherry. |

52. **WRASSE**

| Other Names: | **Ballan wrasse:** *Ballach* (Irish); *berggylte* (Norwegian); *durdo, maragota* (Spanish); *labre, vieille* (French); *lippfisch* (German); *lipvis* (Dutch); *margota* (Portuguese); sweetlips; *twrach* (Welsh). **Floral wrasse:** *Akatenmochino-uo* (Japanese); *bungat, maming* (Filipino); *cá mó* (Vietnamese); damelfish; parrotfish; *see fa* (Thai); *tsing yi* (Hong Kong). **Tautog:** *Austernfisch* (German); black porgy; blackfish; *bodião da ostra* (Portuguese); chub; *matiote, tautogue noir* (French); oyster-fish. **Labridae.** |

| General Description: | *There are about 450 species of wrasse mainly found in tropical waters.* Although they do not have high culinary reputations today, in Roman times, wrasse were prized, perhaps for their vivid coloring. Ballan wrasse (*Labrus bergylta*) are eaten in Scotland and Ireland, though they are considered by some to be insipid or coarse. Floral wrasse (*Cheilinus chlorourus*) are a Southeast Asian member of this family, usually sold live for high prices in Hong Kong and steamed whole. Hogfish (*Lachnolaimus maximus*) are colorful tropical fish with three distinctive long spines at the front of their bodies. The large, delicious California sheephead (*Semicossyphus pulcher*) is a Pacific wrasse occasionally caught or speared by sport fishers and sometimes seen in California retail markets. The plump, black calico tautog (*Tautoga onitis*) is a large member of the wrasse family. Tautogs are found near the mussel beds on which they feed. With its firm texture, tautog is often used for chowder on Cape Cod. |

| Locale and Season: | Ballan wrasse range from the Mediterranean to Norway. Floral wrasse range from eastern Africa to the western Pacific, as far south as northern Australia. Hogfish are found on the north coast of South America and the northern Gulf of Mexico to Bermuda and North Carolina. They are common year-round in shallow waters off Florida and the islands of the Caribbean. California sheepheads may be found from Monterey Bay to Baja California. Tautog range from Nova Scotia to South Carolina and are more abundant between Cape Cod and Delaware Bay. |

Characteristics:	They average 8 to 10 ounces in weight. Their sweet, delicate white meat is sold fresh and frozen. The fillets are small, 3 to 4 ounces each. Hogfish have been linked to ciguatera poisoning. Tautogs weigh up to 25 pounds, with 3 pounds average. They have lean, white, firm, and delicately flavored flesh with tight, white flake. Yield is 40 percent.
How to Choose:	Select brightly colored fish with shiny skin and clear eyes. California sheepheads are seldom found in retail markets but are a popular sport fish.
Storage: x 2	Store whole fish up to 2 days refrigerated. Store fillets up to 1 day refrigerated.
Preparation:	• **Remove the bitter-tasting skin from tautogs before cooking.**
	• **Steam, poach, bake, sauté, pan-fry, or use for fish soup, sandwiches, or tacos.**
Suggested Recipe:	**Island-Style Hogfish Sandwich** (serves 6): Soak 6 hogfish fillets (about 1 1/2 pounds) in 1 cup butter-milk seasoned with salt, pepper, and 1 teaspoon hot sauce for 1 hour. Drain and dredge in cornmeal. In a large heavy skillet, preferably cast-iron, heat 1 cup canola oil until shimmering. Shake off excess cornmeal and pan-fry the fish until well-browned, 2 to 3 minutes on each side. Drain on paper towels. Split open 6 (6-inch) sections of French baguette bread and spread each side with 1 to 2 tablespoons tartar sauce. Layer the fish, tomato slices, and lettuce leaves on the bread.

Flavor Affinities:	Apple, bay leaf, butter, capers, celery, chervil, chives, cider, dill, lemon, lime, key lime, marjoram, onion, parsley, shallot, tarragon, teriyaki sauce, thyme, tomato.

Mollusks

53. **ABALONE**

Other Names: *Aliótis* (Greek); *awaby, tokobushi* (Japanese); *deniz kulagi* (Turkish); green ormer (Great Britain); *orecchia marina* (Italian); *oreille de mer, ormeau* (French); *oreja de mar* (Spanish); *seeohr* (German). **Haliotidae.**

General Description: *Abalone is a delicious, expensive, rare single-shelled mollusk; its large, strong foot is the edible meat.* Its iridescent inner shell is used as mother of pearl. Unfortunately, wild abalone has been decimated worldwide. The red abalone (*Haliotis rufescens*) is most common in the United States from aquafarms in California and wild from Mexico. Black abalone (*H. cracheroddi*) is found off San Miguel Island in southern California. Abalones grown in onshore saltwater pens or suspended cages take 3 to 4 years to reach market size of 4 to 6 whole abalone per pound.

Locale and Season: More than 15 species of abalone are now farmed worldwide; China and Taiwan produce more than 90 percent. Farmed abalone is in season year-round.

Characteristics: Wild abalones average 12 inches, with meat averaging 1 pound. Farmed abalone is much smaller, at 2 to 4 inches, and is more tender. Cooked abalone is white to cream, moist, tender, and mild, with sweet flavor.

How to Choose: Live abalones should be lively and stick hard to the tank. If the foot muscle doesn't move or the flesh dents where touched, the animal is dead or nearly dead. Frozen abalone meat should be firm and ivory-colored. When thawed, it has almost no aroma. Abalone that is larger than 4 inches across is likely wild and may have been poached. It should be rejected to discourage environmentally destructive poaching. Circular, streaked cuttlefish mantles may be sold as abalone steaks. These are put through a meat tenderizer before sale, so look for cut marks as a clue.

Storage: Fresh abalone is highly perishable and should be cooked the same day it is purchased. Keep on ice and refrigerate until ready to cook. Defrost frozen abalone overnight in the refrigerator.

Preparation: 1. **Shuck live abalone by sticking a wide spatula between the meat and the shell and removing the meat. Trim off the organs and fringe.**

2. **Using a meat slicer, slice abalone muscle thinly crosswise. Or freeze until firm, slice thinly by hand, and pound each slice with a mallet or the side of a cleaver using persistent, firm strikes, flattening to 1/4 inch thick.**

⚠ NOTE: **Cook abalone less than 1 minute on a side in hot oil. Overcooked abalone will quickly toughen.**

Suggested Recipe: **Stir-Fried Abalone with Cucumber** (serves 4): Cut 1 pound abalone into thin steaks, pound until flattened, and then cut into 1-inch-wide strips. Mix

2 tablespoons rice wine with 1 tablespoon soy sauce, 2 teaspoons sugar, and salt to taste. Cut 1 large seeded cucumber into thin half moons. Heat 1 tablespoon oil in a wok and stir-fry the cucumber 2 minutes; add the abalone and stir-fry 1 minute. Pour the sauce into the wok and heat through. Serve over white rice.

Flavor
Affinities:

Basil, capers, cilantro, coconut, cucumber, dill, ginger, lemon, mint, olive oil, oyster sauce, rice wine, scallion, sesame, soy sauce, tomato, white wine, wild lime.

54a–c.

CLAM

Other Names:

Geoduck: *Geoduck-muschel* (German); king clam; *mirugai* (Japanese); *panope* (French). **Hiatellidae.** **Hardshell:** *Clame redonda* (Portuguese); *mercenaria*, *verigueto* (Spanish); *nimaigai* (Japanese); *palourde américaine*, *praire* (French); quahaug (Great Britain); quahog; *venusmuschel* (German); *vongola dura* (Italian). **Veneridae. Softshell:** *Almeja de rio*, *eito ama* (Spanish); belly clam, fryer clam; gaper; Ipswich; longneck; mainmose; *mia*, *mye* (French); *onogai* (Japanese); *sandklaffmuschel* (German); squirt, steamer clam; *vongole molle* (Italian). **Surf clam:** *Almeja blanca* (Spanish); bar, giant, hen, sea, or skimmer clam; *capa americana* (Italian); *mactre solide* (French); *nimaigai* (Japanese); *riesen-trogmuschel* (German); *spisula* (Italian). **Mactridae. Carpet-shell:** *Almeja fina* (Spanish); *amêijoa boa* (Portuguese); *chávaro* (Greek); *clovisse* (Provençal); *palourde* (French); *vongola verace*

(Italian). **Golden carpet-shell:** *Achiváda* (Greek); *clovisse jaune* (French); *margarita* (Spanish); *mouhar* (Tunisia); *vongola gialla* (Italian). **Razor shell clam:** *Cannolicchio* (Italian); *capa longa* (Venice); *couteau, rasoir* (French); grooved razor clam (Great Britain); *gross scheindenmuschel* (German); *navaja* (Spanish); *solina* (Greek). **Solenidae.**

General Description:

Clams are bivalve mollusks with two shells (valves). They are as valued today as they were when Native American tribes harvested them for food and used the violet inner shell as wampum (money and ornaments).

The hard-shell clam (*Mercenaria mercenaria*), also called quahog, has a thick grayish shell with a violet patch and can live for more than 150 years. They are harvested from sandy-bottomed bays and coves and along beaches by tongs, hand rakes, and hydraulic dredges. Eastern hard-shells, especially smaller little necks, are commonly served raw on the half-shell, but they are also used for clam chowder. Little necks, named after Little Neck Bay on Long Island, once a center of the clam trade, are the smallest hard clam. Somewhat larger cherrystones are often stuffed and baked. Smaller chowder clams may be cut into strips, breaded, and fried or used for chowder. The mahogany clam (*Arctica islandica*) is a small ocean quahog with mahogany-brown shells. Because they open up flat when steamed, they are not as desirable. American Mussel Harvesters has trademarked the name "golden necks" for their mahogany clams.

The surf clam (*Spisula solidissima*), served as fried clams at inexpensive restaurants, is dredged in large quantities off the East Coast. They are too big and tough to eat whole and are only sold processed. The Stimpson surf clam (*Mactromeris polynyma*), or hokkigai, which is native to the Canadian Maritimes, is prized in Japan as a delicacy for the red to purple-black tips of its foot. Look for frozen hokkigai in Asian markets.

Steamer clams (*Mya arenia*), also called Ipswich clams after Ipswich, Massachusetts, which is famed for them, have long necks, soft hanging bellies, and fragile shells that don't close completely. They are usually steamed or fried in batter or crumbs.

The Manila clam (*Tapes japonica*) was accidentally introduced to the United States in the 1920s in a shipment of Japanese seed oysters. They are the most common clam on the West Coast and can be served raw or steamed. The West Coast little neck (*Protothaca staminea*), not to be confused with the East Coast little neck, is harvested along with the Manila but costs less because it takes longer to steam open and has a shorter shelf life. The Venus clam (*Chione undatella*) is an excellent eating clam. The European carpet-shell clam (*Tapes decussatus*) is greatly esteemed by the French, Italian, and Spanish. They are essential to Neapolitan Spaghetti alle Vongole (steamed clams with spaghetti in garlic and white wine). The closely related golden carpet-shell (*Venerupis aurea*) is even smaller, not much bigger than a thumbnail, with beautiful zigzag patterns on the shell.

The Pacific razor clam (*Siliqua patula*) has a long, narrow, sharp-edged shell. They tend to be sandy and their tough meat must be cooked a long time or chopped up for tenderness. The European razor clam (*Solen vagina*) is similar in shape and may reach more than 5 inches in length. Much appreciated for their fine flavor, they are not easy to harvest, so they are not found in large quantities.

The geoduck clam (*Panopea abrupta*), pronounced "gooey-duck," gets its name from a Northwest Nisqually Indian term meaning "dig deep." The long, phallic siphon, the part eaten, protrudes from a pair of semi-open oval shells and has smooth, cream-colored flesh beneath the skin. Geoducks are harvested individually by divers who use water jets to loosen the sand around the clams. They are a delicacy in Asia. Dried geoduck is used in Chinese soups.

Locale and Season:

East Coast hard shells are found wild and farmed from the Canadian Maritimes to the Gulf of Mexico. Soft shells are found from Newfoundland to North Carolina with peak season May to September. Surf clams are at peak season in spring and summer. Canadian hokkigai are individually frozen for sushi, averaging 18 per pound, with peak season for fresh hokkigai June to September. Manila clams are harvested primarily from farmed beds in Washington and from natural beds in British Columbia. Razor clams are abundant on beaches from California to Alaska and may be found in Asian markets. Geoducks are found in Puget Sound and the inland waters of British Columbia and southern Alaska, both wild and farmed. Carpet-shell clams are found throughout the Mediterranean and into the eastern Atlantic.

Characteristics: One pound of hard-shell clams yields ¼ pound of meat. Littlenecks average 7 to 10 meats per pound, top necks 6 to 8, cherrystones 3 to 5, and quahogs 1 to 2. Darker, stronger-smelling ocean quahogs, usually labeled "ocean clams," are less expensive than surf clams, usually labeled "sea clams." A pound of soft-shell clams yields 6 to 8 ounces of meat and average 12 to 15 per pound with delicate, slightly salty meat and soft bellies. Mahoganies average 25 per pound; Manilas average 20 per pound. Geoducks weigh an average of 2 pounds. Clams have the firmest, best-tasting meat and longest shelf life in winter.

How to Choose: A live hardshell will have a tightly closed shell or will close if tapped. Avoid clams with broken or damaged shells; discard if the meat is dry when the clam is opened or the shell has dirt inside (called a "mudder"). The meat should be creamy tan and firm, the shell should be full of liquid, and it should smell briny. Take care that none are dead before cooking.

Choose soft-shell clams that are whole and clean, the siphon firm and plump, not flaccid or dry. If the clam moves when touched, it is alive. Though many people prefer geoducks with light beige siphons, the taste and texture is the same no matter what the color. Canned or fresh-shucked clams should be packed in plenty of sweet-smelling liquid.

Clams harvested in areas of pollution or naturally occurring red tide can cause serious infections or paralytic shellfish poisoning. Each bag of clams will carry a tag indicating its source and date of harvest, which should be checked. Clams from warm water in warm weather months may contain the vibrio bacteria that can sicken or even kill if eaten raw. Raw or partially cooked clams should not be eaten by people with compromised immune systems.

Storage: Cover clams with a damp towel to keep moist, and store in a cool, dark area of the refrigerator at 36°F–40°F. Don't store on ice, as it will be too cold and the freshwater will shorten shelf life. Under ideal conditions, clams will stay alive for up to two weeks, although shelf life is much shorter in summer.

Preparation: 1. **Scrub clams under cold running water using a stiff brush or an abrasive pad.**

2. **Soak clams in cold water to cover with 1 cup salt per 1 quart liquid for several hours, or overnight in the refrigerator. Scoop the clams from the water, leaving the sand behind.**

• **To prepare geoducks, cut the long trunklike siphon away from the body, peel off the tough outer skin, and split in half lengthwise. Cut into paper-thin slices.**

• **To prepare softshell clams, soak as in step 2, then pull off and discard the dark membrane that covers the siphon or "neck."**

3. **Serve raw, steamed, breaded and fried, stuffed and baked, or pan-roasted.**

• **To steam, set the clams over high heat in a small amount of liquid just until their shells open, removing each clam as its shell opens. Discard any clams that do not open after steaming for 5 to 10 minutes. Allow the broth to settle before serving, so any sand can fall to the bottom. Don't serve the last half cup of broth, which will contain most of any sand.**

Suggested Recipe:

Clams Casino (Serves 4): Combine 1 diced roasted red pepper with 2 tablespoons chopped parsley, 1/2 cup bread crumbs, 2 tablespoons olive oil, 2 teaspoons chopped garlic, the grated zest of 1 lemon, and hot red pepper flakes and black pepper to taste. Using a clam knife, pry open 2 dozen washed live littleneck clams, keeping all juices inside. Top each clam with a portion of the filling, mounding it up. Cover with several squares of diced bacon. Arrange on a metal baking pan and bake 15 minutes at 425°F or until browned and bubbling.

Flavor Affinities:

Bacon, cream, garlic, ginger, hot red pepper flakes, lemon, mushroom, olive oil, onion, pancetta, potato, rice wine, shallot, soy sauce, thyme, tomato, white wine.

55. **COCKLE**

Other Names:

Cockle: *Berberecho* (Spanish); *berbigão vulgar* (Portuguese); *coque commune* (French); *cuore edule* (Italian); *herzmuschel* (German); *kydóni* (Greek); *toni-gai* (Japanese). **Dog cockle:** *Amande de mer* (French);

almendra de mar, rabiosa (Spanish); comb shell; *castanhola do mar* (Portuguese); *gaidourokténi* (Greek); *gemeine samtmuschel* (German); *piè d'asino* (Italian). **Knotted cockle:** *Carneiro, marolo* (Spanish); *berbigão* (Portuguese); *bucarde tuberculée* (French); *cuore tubercolato* (Italian); *dickrippige herzmuschel* (German). **Cardiidae.**

General Description:

The common cockle (Cerastoderma edule) *has two hinged, heart-shaped shells and prominent rib markings.* Similar but not related to clams, they are smaller and have a briny flavor and an attractive look. The dog cockle (*Glycymeris glycymeris*) is smooth and almond- or chestnut-shaped with brown markings. The knotted cockle (*Acanthocardia tuberculata*) is highly ridged. The gray-white New Zealand cockle (*Austrovenus stutchburyi*) belongs to the family of ark shells said to resemble a species on Noah's Ark.

Locale and Season:

The dog cockle is found in northern Europe; the knotted cockle in the Mediterranean, West Africa, and Great Britain. While there are cockles on the American Atlantic coast, those in the market are usually imported from New Zealand.

Characteristics:

Cockles are small and tender with light, briny sea flavor. They may be eaten raw or cooked.

How to Choose:

New Zealand South Island cockles are larger, 15 per pound, than those from the North Island (20 to 25 per pound). Cockles with light-colored flesh are preferred to those with dark flesh.

Storage: Cover cockles with a damp towel and refrigerate 3 to 4 days. Don't use ice, as it will be too cold and fresh-water will shorten shelf life.

Preparation: 1. **Clean and soak cockles as for clams, page 203.**

2. **Serve raw, steamed, breaded and fried, stuffed and baked, or pan-roasted. Steam as for clams, page 204.**

Suggested Recipe: **Spaghetti with Cockles** (serves 4): Place 1/4 cup chopped shallots and 2 cups white vermouth in a large pot. Set over high heat; when the liquid comes to a boil, add 3 to 4 dozen washed cockles, cover, and cook until they open. Transfer to a bowl as they open, discarding any that remain closed after 5 minutes. In a pan, brown 1/4 pound diced Canadian bacon in 1/4 cup extra-virgin olive oil. Add 1 tablespoon chopped garlic, 1/2 teaspoon hot red pepper flakes, and the zest of 1 lemon and cook briefly. Toss with the cockles and any (strained) juices and bring back to a boil. Meanwhile, cook 1 pound spaghetti, drain, and toss with the cockles and 1/4 cup chopped Italian parsley.

Flavor Affinities: Bell pepper, cilantro, garlic, ginger, lemon, onion, oregano, pancetta, parsley, potato, rice wine, shallot, soy sauce, thyme, tomato, white wine.

56. 📷   **CONCH, MUREX, AND WHELK**

Other Names: **Conch:** Bahamas, Caribbean, pink, or queen conch; *cobo rosado* (Spanish); coo coo; *lambi*, *strombe rosé* (French); *sazae* (Japanese); *schneckenmuschel* (German); sea snail. **Strombidae**. **Whelk:** *Bai* (Japan); *bietunkóngur* (Icelandic); *bocina* (Spanish); *buccin*, *bulot* (French); *buccina*, *sconciglio* (Italian); *buoroú* (Greek); *búzio* (Portuguese); *é luó* (Chinese); ivory shell; *wellhorschnecke* (German). **Buccinidae** and **Melongenidae**. **Murex:** *Buzio* (Portuguese); *cañadilla* (Spanish); *herkuleskeule* (German); *murice commune* (Italian); *rocher épineux* (French). **Muricidae**.

General Description: *The queen conch* (Strombus gigas) *is a large saltwater gastropod that uses its large, edible, muscular foot to drag itself along the ocean floor.* Pronounced "conk," conch is popular for fritters, salad, and chowder. The whelk is a smaller gastropod with an edible muscular foot inside a spiral-coiled shell. The common whelk (*Baccinum undatum*) is the most popular type in Europe. In America, the channeled whelk (*Busucon canaliculata*) and the knobbed whelk (*B. carica*), known in Italian-American areas as scungilli, are most common. They are larger and more elongated than common whelks. The murex is a small gastropod with a fat, spiny shell ending in a thinner tail-like portion. The Mediterranean murex (*Murex brandais*) has been legendary since Phoenician times for the preparation of a rare purple dye used only for royal vestments. It is similar to whelk with good flavor, though tougher.

Locale and Season:	Once abundant, conch is now endangered, and commercial harvesting is banned in the United States. Jamaica, the Turks and Caicos Islands (which also farm conch), Honduras, and the Dominican Republic are major suppliers. Summer is peak season for wild conch; farmed conch is available year-round. Whelk is found in cold inshore North American waters, harvested May through November in northern inshore waters, and year-round on Newfoundland's south coast.
Characteristics:	Wild conch is usually sold frozen and is quite tough, so it is usually chopped or ground. The meat is often parboiled to eliminate compounds that may cause vomiting. Conch are also farmed; this type cooks more quickly than wild. Whelks average 2 to 4 ounces and have strong, clamlike flavor. They are sold fresh and frozen, whole and shucked, and pickled.
How to Choose:	Select farmed conch for tenderness, wild conch for flavor. Common whelks found inshore have a green-brown shell and are smaller; offshore they are larger and have a tan shell. In America, whelks are often sold cooked, cleaned, and trimmed so they are completely edible. Murex may be found in markets in the Mediterranean region. Look for unbroken shells with plump, sweet-smelling meat.
Storage:	Store whole conch, whelk, and murex up to 2 days refrigerated, covered with damp towels. Use frozen conch straight from the freezer.

Preparation: • **Tenderize conch by slicing thinly and pounding with a meat mallet as for abablone, page 197.**

• **Dice or grind conch for chowder or fritters. Marinate in lime juice for 2 hours for ceviche. Bake, broil, pan-fry, smoke, sauté, or steam.**

• **Cook whelk in gently boiling water 15 minutes, cool, then pick out the meat. Remove the tough disc that seals the shell's mouth before eating. Don't overcook, as the meat easily toughens. Cook murex similarly, in gently boiling water for 5 minutes.**

Suggested Recipe: **Caribbean Conch Chowder** (serves 6): In a large soup pot, brown 1/4 pound diced bacon, then reserve. Add 1/2 cup each chopped celery and green pepper; 1 minced Scotch bonnet or other fresh chile; and 1 tablespoon chopped garlic, and cook until softened. Add 4 cups chopped tomatoes, 1 1/2 quarts clam broth or seafood stock, and 1 1/2 pounds diced new potatoes. Make a spice packet of 6 whole allspice berries, 2 bay leaves, and 2 sprigs thyme wrapped in cheesecloth, and add to the pot. Bring to a boil and simmer for 20 minutes. Add 2 pounds ground conch and simmer 20 minutes, or until the conch is tender. Stir in the juice of 1 lime and 1/4 cup mixed chopped parsley and cilantro.

Flavor Affinities: Bacon, celery, chiles, cilantro, coconut, garlic, green pepper, hot sauce, lime, onion, parsley, potato, scallion, shallot, sherry, sweet onion, thyme, tomato.

57. **MUSSEL AND SEA DATE**

Other Names: **Mediterranean mussel:** *Cozza* (Italian); *mejillón mediterràneo* (Spanish); *mexilhão do Mediterrâneo* (Portuguese); *moule méditerranéenne, moule de Toulon* (French); *mydi* (Greek). **Common mussel:** *Mejillón* (Spanish); *mexilhao* (Portuguese); *miesmuschel* (German); *mitilo* (Italian); *moule commun* (French); *murasakiigai* (Japanese); *peocio* (Venice). **New Zealand green mussel:** Greenlipped mussel; green-shell mussel (Great Britain); *moule verte* (French). **Sea date:** *Dátil de mar* (Spanish); *datte de mer* (French); *dattero di mare* (Italian); *ishimate* (Japanese); *lithofágos, solína* (Greek); *meerdattel* (German); *tamr de bahr* (Tunisia). **Mytilidae.**

General Description: *The mussel* (Mytilus edulis) *was once held in low esteem in America, but it has become an aqaculture and culinary success story.* The Mediterranean blue mussel (*M. galloprovincialis*) is native to the Mediterranean and is preferred in Europe. It is smaller and a bit more rounded than the blue mussel. Wild mussels are found in intertidal zones on rocks and pilings and have "beards" (byssus threads) that they use to anchor themselves. Mussels are a Belgian national obsession. Mussels are farmed on ropes or in mesh bags suspended from rafts.

The New Zealand green mussel (*Perna canaliclus*) is native to New Zealand and only found there. Green mussels have a long, large shell that is a striking brown-green ranging to deep green at the lip. Growing standards, including water quality and production levels, are tightly regulated.

The sea date (*Lithophaga lithophaga*) is a prized but now rare and endangered mussel from the Mediterranean. It grows extremely slowly, taking ten years to reach maturity. It is difficult to harvest, and in most Mediterranean countries, harvesting has been banned. Sea dates are eaten raw, simmered in risotto, or added to fish and seafood stew.

Locale and Season:

Blue mussels are farmed in France, Great Britain, China, Spain, Korea, on both American coasts, and on Prince Edward Island, Canada. European mussels are farmed on the Pacific Northwest coast. Mussels are less plump for a few weeks after spawning in summer.

Characteristics:

Mussels are sweet, tender, delicate, plump, and juicy and vary from creamy colored in males to apricot for females. Color has no effect on flavor. Green mussels grow to more than 8 inches long, though market size is about 4 inches. Cultivated mussels are harvested at 2 to 3 inches and cost more than wild but are easier to use. Because they are grown on ropes suspended above the sea floor, they are quite clean with their beards removed before sale. Unlike blue mussels, the green mussel's shell gapes open naturally, which New Zealanders call "smiling."

How to Choose:

Mussels should taste and smell fresh and sweet and have tightly closed shells full of juice. Bags of mussels must display the license number of the shipper. Buy only from certified growers. New Zealand mussels are also frozen whole or on the half shell.

While there are many places where mussels can be gathered wild, these can be dangerous to eat because mussels are susceptible to pollution and disease.

Storage:

x 2

If possible, cook mussels the day you buy them. Mussels will stay alive longest if their beard is attached. Refrigerate covered with a damp towel up to 2 days. Store frozen mussels up to 3 months. Thaw in the refrigerator and eat within 2 days.

Preparation: 1.

Sort the mussels, discarding any that are broken or not tightly closed. If slightly open, try pressing the edges together. If the mussel closes up, it is alive. Often, the beard has already been removed. If not, pull off and discard just before cooking.

2.

Scrub with a brush under cold running water.

3.

Mussels can be steamed and grilled in the shells (remove each mussel once it opens); broiled, breaded and deep-fried, pan-fried, stuffed and baked, hot-smoked, or sautéed out of the shell.

Suggested Recipe:

Baked Mussels with Spinach and Saffron Cream (serves 4): Steam open 2 pounds cleaned mussels with 1/2 cup white vermouth in a large pot. Remove the mussels from their shells, reserving meats and shells. Strain the juices through a dampened paper towel set in a sieve and cook in a medium pot along with 1/4 cup each chopped shallots and fennel, a large pinch of saffron, and 1 cup heavy cream until thickened, about 5 minutes. Remove from heat, stir in

1/2 pound wilted and squeezed spinach and 2 tablespoons chopped tarragon. Season to taste with salt and pepper. Combine 1/2 cup bread crumbs with 2 tablespoons butter. Place the mussels back in half shells and spoon the spinach mixture over top. Sprinkle with the crumbs and bake at 425°F for 10 minutes, or until browned.

Flavor
Affinities:
Beer, celery, cream, curry, garlic, harissa, leek, mustard, Pernod, potato, saffron, shallot, spinach, tarragon, tomato, white vermouth, white wine.

58. **OCTOPUS**

Other Names:
Ahtapot (Turkish); devilfish; *gewöhnlicher krake* (German); *khtapodi, oktápous* (Greek); *kraak* (Dutch); *ma-dako tako* (Japanese); *moscardino, polpo di scoglio* (Italian); *pieuvre, poulpe* (French); *polvo* (Portuguese); *pulpo* (Spanish); *sprut* (Russian). **Octopodidae**.

General
Description:
Octopuses are cephalopods with eight tentacles. There are more than 140 species of octopus found in temperate and tropical waters around the world. The common octopus (*Octopus vulgaris*) is found in cooler waters worldwide. The large red octopus (*O. dofleini*) is found in cold waters of the northern Pacific. The white spotted octopus (*O. macropus*) is found in the Mediterranean and temperate waters worldwide. Floppy and grayish pink with suction-cupped tentacles, a large raw octopus resting on ice can look pretty scary. Many biologists consider octopus to be the

smartest of all invertebrates, with the same intelligence as a house cat. All parts are edible, except for the eyes, mouth area, and inner organs, although the tentacles are the most tender. Once poached for tenderizing, octopus can be grilled briefly, giving it a lightly charred flavor. Because of its natural gelatin, octopus can be made into a terrine simply by cooking and weighting it.

Locale and Season:

In the United States, octopus is harvested in California and Hawaii. The primary octopus suppliers are the Philippines, Thailand, and Korea. Octopus is in season year-round.

Characteristics:

Octopus bodies are covered by a thin, gelatinous layer of purplish-black spotted skin that may be removed. The raw meat is translucent and cream-colored with a pink tint. The cooked meat is smooth with a firm, satisfying bite and full-bodied flavor. Octopuses lose about half their weight in cooking, so allow 1 pound of raw octopus per portion.

How to Choose:

Fresh or frozen raw octopus is usually purplish in color and most commonly found at 3 pounds. Choose fresh octopus that is glistening and lively looking with a clean, pleasing smell. It's best to purchase octopus already cleaned. In America, much octopus is sold frozen, because it is so perishable.

Storage:

 x 1

Fresh and defrosted octopus is highly perishable and should be cooked within 1 to 2 days. Once cooked, the octopus will keep well for another 2 to 3 days.

Preparation: 1.   **Simmer a 3- to 4-pound octopus in broth for about 1 hour. Don't boil and don't overcook. Poke the thickest portion with a skewer; if tender, it is done.**

2.   **Rub off the pinkish gelatinous skin if desired.**

3.   **Grill, simmer in sauce, dress for salad, or cool and weight for a terrine.**

Suggested Recipe:

Grilled Octopus Salad (serves 6): Poach a 2- to 3-pound cleaned octopus in court bouillon (broth flavored with onion, celery, thyme, white wine, lemon zest, and black pepper) for 1 hour, or until tender. Drain, cool, peel, and cut into small pieces. Combine 1/2 cup extra-virgin olive oil, the juice and grated zest of 1 lemon, 2 tablespoons red wine vinegar, 1 teaspoon each dried oregano and hot red pepper flakes, 2 teaspoons chopped garlic, and salt and pepper to taste. Toss half the dressing with the octopus and marinate 1 hour, refrigerated. Drain, then grill the octopus until lightly charred. Toss with 1/4 cup kalamata olive halves, 1/2 cup diced red onion, 1 diced cucumber, and 1 cup diced fresh tomatoes, and the remaining dressing.

Flavor Affinities:

Bay leaf, capers, cured olives, dill, garlic, lemon, olive oil, onion, oregano, pomegranate, red onion, red wine, red wine vinegar, thyme, tomato, white wine.

59. **OYSTER**

Other Names: **European oyster:** *Auster* (German); *huître plat* (French); *istiridye* (Turkish); *kaki* (Japanese); *ostra* (Spanish); *ostra plana* (Portuguese); *strídia* (Greek). **Pacific oyster:** *Huître creuse* (French); Japanese oyster; *ostíon del Pacifico* (Spanish); *ostrica pacifica* (Italian); *Pazifische felsenauster* (German). **American oyster:** *Amerikanische auster* (German); blue point oyster; *crease de Virginia*, *hure* (French); *ostrica della Virginia* (Italian). **Ostreidae.**

General Description: *Oysters are saltwater bivalve mollusks.* Until early historic times, a great barrier reef made of European flat oysters ran from Scandinavia to Greece. Because oysters filter so much seawater, they are high in minerals. The risk in eating wild oysters is diminishing thanks to strict guidelines and monitoring of oyster beds.

   The thin, flat European oyster (*Ostrea edulis*), cultivated in western Europe, is prized as the Belon. Only oysters grown in Brittany's Belon River may by French law be termed Belons. American entrepreneurs now farm this tasty though expensive and highly perishable oyster in Maine. They are primarily served raw on the half shell. The native American or Eastern oyster (*Crassostrea virginica*) thrives from New Brunswick to the Gulf of Mexico and includes bluepoints from Long Island, Canadian Malpeques, and Wellfleets from Cape Cod. Beginning in 1842, express wagons carried oysters west to be served at feasts such as Abe Lincoln's famous oyster parties. The related Portuguese oyster (*C. angulata*), native to the Iberian peninsula, now thrives in France.

Japanese, or Pacific, oysters (*C. gigas*), found along the Pacific Coast, grow up to 1 foot long. They have deeply sculptured pearly shells with pure, clean flavor. Small Royal Miyagis have a deep cup, highly sculptured fluted shells, and smooth, slightly fruity flesh. Westcotts, from Washington, have meaty texture and creamy flavor. Yaquina Bays are premium oysters from Newport, Oregon, with deep cups holding sweet, briny meat in abundant liquor. Olympia oysters (*O. lurida*), native to the West Coast and found in Washington's Puget Sound, measure only about $1^1/2$ inches across. They are highly prized for their robust flavor, firm texture, and faintly metallic aftertaste. Kumamotos (*C. sikamea*) and the similar gigamotos are small oysters with a deep cup and excellent, briny, mineral-laden flavor.

Locale and Season: Oysters are at their best in the winter, with the main season lasting from late September to May. Oysters spawn in summer months; though edible, they tend to be flabby and insipid, the reason they are traditionally only eaten in months with names containing an R. Farm-raised oysters can be eaten year-round. The European oyster ranges from Norway to Morocco and is farmed and harvested. The Japanese oyster is found along the American Pacific coast and in Japan. Yields and quality are highest and prices lowest in winter.

Characteristics: American oysters have a moderately deep, elongated, spoon-shaped rough-textured shell that is grayish white to grayish brown. The tender meat is salty with meaty texture. European oysters have flat shells that vary from white to brown; the meats are rounded and creamy to light brown. Their meat has a distinct salty edge and a metallic flavor. Pacific oysters have deeply cupped elongated shells that are curly, thick, and silvery gray to gold. The meat is creamy white with hints of pink, green, or black and may have a dark fringe. They are mild and sweet.

How to Choose: Choose oysters without broken shells that are tightly closed. Tap on the shell. If it closes, the animal is alive. A dead oyster will have an unpleasant sulfur smell. Shucked oysters should be smooth and plump and covered in clear, grayish liquid with a briny scent.

Vibrio vulnificus is a bacterium that can cause severe illness or death in some people, especially those with compromised immune systems, who eat raw oysters or clams. It is found naturally in coastal waters and is not a result of pollution. It does not affect the appearance, taste, or odor of oysters (or clams, p. 198). It is most often found in oysters (and clams) harvested from warm waters in April though October, when bacteria counts are higher. Cold-water oysters are not affected, and cooking destroys the bacteria.

Storage: Store shucked oysters cup-side down to retain their liquor 2 to 3 days refrigerated, covered with seaweed or a damp towel. Freshly shucked oysters covered by their own liquor will keep for up to 1 week. European oysters don't last long because of their fragile shells.

Preparation: 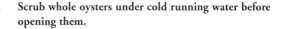 1. Scrub whole oysters under cold running water before opening them.

2. To shuck, use an oyster knife, table knife, or church-key can opener. (Do NOT use a sharp kitchen knife.) Holding the oyster in a thick kitchen towel or special oyster glove, turn it so the deep cup is down.

3. Find the point where the two shells hinge together. Just off to one side will be a small opening. Wiggle the implement at an angle into the opening to "pop" the shells apart.

4. Slide the implement flat across the underside of the top shell to release the meat without tearing it, and repeat on the bottom shell, cutting as close to the shell as possible.

5. Rinse briefly under cold water to get rid of any grit or shell pieces.

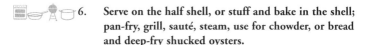 6. Serve on the half shell, or stuff and bake in the shell; pan-fry, grill, sauté, steam, use for chowder, or bread and deep-fry shucked oysters.

Suggested Recipe: **Dijon Deviled Oysters** (serves 4): Combine 2 tablespoons Dijon mustard with 1/4 cup sour cream, 2 eggs, and cayenne pepper to taste. Dip 24 fresh shucked oysters first in this mixture and then in soft, fresh bread crumbs. Pan-fry or deep-fry until browned and serve with lemon or a piquant sauce.

Flavor Affinities:	Bay leaf, black pepper, butter, cream, Dijon mustard, fennel, hot red pepper, lemon, Pernod, sesame, shallot, soy sauce, spinach, thyme, white wine.

60.

PERIWINKLE, LIMPET, AND TOP-SHELL

Other Names:

Periwinkle: *Alikruik* (Dutch); *bigaro, mincha* (Spanish); *bigorneaux, vigneau* (French); *burrelho* (Portuguese); *moustokarfi* (Greek); *strandschnecke* (German); *tamakibi* (Japanese); winkle. **Littorinidae. Limpet:** *Bernique, chapeau chinois, patelle* (French); *crogan* (Cornish); *lampa* (Spanish); *lapa* (Portuguese); *opihi* (Hawaiian); *patella* (Italian); *petallída* (Greek); *schusselmuschel* (German); *tepelhoidje* (Dutch); *venis* (Brittany); *yomegakasa* (Japanese). **Patellidae. Top-shell:** *Bigorneaux* (French); *caracol gris* (Spanish); *chiocciola marina* (Italian); *minare* (Turkish); *tróchos* (Greek). **Trochidae.**

General Description:

Periwinkles (Littorina littorea) *have been a popular food for a long time; large numbers of their small spiral shells were found in prehistoric mounds in northern Europe.* Today they are often served as a bite-size morsel called an amuse-guele ("tickle the throat") in European luxury restaurants.

The limpet (*Patella vulgata* and others) is a small gastropod with a shallow, cone-shaped single shell found all over the world clinging to rocks. There are several types of limpets in Hawaii, where they are a traditional food. Limpets have flavorful but tough meat that can be consumed raw or cooked. Their strongly flavored juices are used to make rich sauces. Top-shells (*Monodonta turbinata*) are small spiral-shelled sea snails with dark checkerboard-like marking so they resemble toy tops. They are popular in Europe and similar species may be found in Asian markets.

Locale and Season:

Limpets and periwinkles are found in the eastern and western Atlantic, but are most popular in Europe. Limpets are best from January to March.

Characteristics:

Most limpets are less than 3 inches long, usually gray, yellowish, or brown. European limpets are somewhat larger than American. Periwinkles are small with snail-shaped shells, usually dark gray or brown though sometimes white-green or rust red. Top-shells are a bit more than 1 inch long with small, flavorful meats.

How to Choose:

Choose periwinkles, limpets, and top-shells with their little doors securely shut (a sign that they're still alive). They should have a clean, briny sea aroma.

Storage:

Refrigerate 1 to 2 days, covered with a damp cloth.

x 1

Preparation:

1. **Wash periwinkles, limpets, and top-shells in a colander under cold water.**

2. **Boil 3 minutes in salted water with desired flavorings.**

3. **Pick periwinkles and top-shells out of their shells with a pin and pull off the operculum, the little door, before eating. Scrape or pull limpets away from their shells before eating.**

Suggested Recipe:

Poached Periwinkles or Limpets (Serves 4): Poach 6 dozen periwinkles or limpets 5 minutes in a wide pan in a little court bouillon (broth flavored with onion, celery, parsley, thyme, bay leaf, black pepper, lemon zest, and white wine) with the liquid coming only halfway up the shells. Spoon into hot bowls, swirl 2 to 4 tablespoons butter into the broth, and pour over the periwinkles. Serve with crusty bread.

Flavor Affinities:

Bacon, bay leaf, butter, capers, cayenne, celery, garlic, lemon, olive oil, onion, scallion, thyme, white wine.

61. **SCALLOP**

Other Names:

Queen scallop: *Akazaragai* (Japanese); *bunte kammuschel* (German); *canestrello, pettine* (Italian); *golondrina* (Spanish); *leque* (Portuguese); *tiganáki, kténi* (Greek); *volandeira* (French). **Great scallop:** *Cappasanta, ventaglio* (Italian); *concha de peregrino, pétoncle* (Spanish); *coquille St. Jacques* (French); *hotategai* (Japanese); *pilger-oder Jakobsmuschel* (German); pilgrim's scallop; *tarak* (Turkish); *viera* (Portuguese). **Bay scallop:** *Canestrello americano, ventaglio* (Italian); *itayagai* (Japanese); *karibik-Pilgermuschel* (German); *peine caletero* (Spanish); *piegne baie de l'Atlantique, pecten* (French); *vieira de baía* (Portuguese). **Pectinidae.**

General Description:

Scallops are bivalve mollusks with large, hard, white shells marked by radiating ribs and concentric growth rings. The entire scallop is edible, but it is the marshmallow-shaped adductor muscle that hinges the two shells, called the "nut," that is eaten. The decorative scallop shell is featured in Botticelli's famed painting *The Birth of Venus*.

The sea scallop (*Plactopecten magellanicus*) is the largest and the most important type of scallop. They are primarily harvested by dredging and are shucked on board, because scallops cannot hold their shells closed once they are out of the water and quickly lose moisture and die. However, dragging can damage the scallop population and all shellfish in the path. Harvesting sea scallops individually by divers is less destructive; these are known as diver scallops. In Europe, it is more common to find live scallops in their shells with their desirable bright orange roe for sale and on menus.

The small soft, fleshy, and delicately sweet bay scallop (*Argopecten irradians*) lives in bays and estuaries from New England to the Gulf of Mexico. The Nantucket bay scallop (*Pecten irradians*) has exquisitely delicate sweet flavor and firm, resistant texture. They are dredged using small day boats, with a daily 5 bushel limit, hand-opened, and rushed to markets, where they fetch a high price. Until the 1980s, Nantucket's bay scallop fishery thrived. Unfortunately, catches have been in decline in the past twenty years, and no one knows why. Calico scallops (*A. gibbus*) are quite small and can be a bit rubbery if cooked more than briefly. On the West Coast, the small and lovely pink scallop (*Chlamys rubida*) and spiny scallop (*C. hastata*) are similar, though the pink scallop has prominent ruffles on its ribs. Both are eaten whole, either steamed or raw.

Locale and
Season:

Sea scallops are harvested in Argentina, Canada, Chile, Iceland, Japan, New England, Newfoundland, and Russia. They are dredged year-round from Labrador to New Jersey with spring and summer peak season. Diver scallop season is from November 1 to April 15. Bay scallops are harvested from Maine to the Carolinas and are in season from October through January and April through May. Nantucket bay scallops are in season from November 1 through early January. Fresh calico scallops, from the southern Atlantic coast, are available from December through May. Pink and spiny scallops are harvested in Washington and British Columbia and are available year-round except for spawning season in summer.

Characteristics:

Sea scallops are commonly sized at 20 to 40 to the pound, though much larger scallops are sold (at a much higher price). Raw scallops will be creamy white to pink-beige and females may be tinted orange. Bay scallops average 60 to 90 meats per pound and are usually expensive, with sweet flavor and delicate texture. Nantucket bay scallops are commonly sized at 30 to 40 to the pound and are in high demand. Calico scallops are quite small, 70 or more meats per pound, and are heat-treated onshore for shucking, causing their tips to turn opaque white. Pink scallops may be chewy but have sweet flavor. Scallops are sometimes eaten raw or cured in ceviche, but anyone with a compromised immune system should avoid doing so.

How to Choose: The fresher the scallop, the more translucent it will be. Dragged scallops may be gray and are often soaked in a chemical solution to preserve them. These "wet" scallops will be flabby and opaque and will shed excess liquid as soon as they hit the pan. Dry-packed (untreated scallops) in a muslin bag are best. Scallops that grow in a fast-water current will have firm flesh with very little grit; those from areas with little water movement can be soft and grainy. Choose bay scallops with firm and moist texture, avoiding those that are slippery or spongy or have an unpleasant smell.

Storage: Store shucked scallops refrigerated up to 2 days. Cover

x 2   live scallops with a damp towel, refrigerate, and use at most one day later. A healthy live scallop should close tightly when tapped. Scallops freeze well.

Preparation: **1.** **If any shell bits or grit is visible, just before cooking rinse quickly under cold water and pat dry.**

2. **Pull off the thin rubbery band wrapped one third of the way around the scallop. Remove and discard the dark intestinal vein often attached to the band.**

 3. **Broil, skewer for kebobs, stir-fry, bake, bread or batter and deep-fry, sauté, steam, microwave, hot-smoke, use for chowder or stews, or use for sushi and ceviche.**

Suggested Recipe: **Bay Scallop Ceviche with Truffle Oil** (serves 6): Combine 3/4 cup lime juice, 1/4 cup orange juice, 2 minced serrano chiles, and 1 tablespoon kosher salt. Mix half the dressing with 1 pound trimmed fresh bay scallops or cut-up sea scallops. Cover and refrigerate 24 hours and then drain off and discard all liquid. Mix scallops with the remaining dressing, 1/4 cup diced red onion, 2 chopped tomatillos, 1/4 cup chopped cilantro, and 3 tablespoons truffle oil and serve.

Flavor
Affinities:

Avocado, brandy, cilantro, cream, garlic, lemon, lime, mango, olive oil, papaya, sweet corn, sweet potato, tarragon, thyme, tomato, vinegar, white wine.

62a–b.   **SQUID AND CUTTLEFISH**

Other Names:

Squid: *Akkar* (Norwegian); *calamar* (Spanish); *calamaro* (Italian); *gewöhnlicher kalmar* (German); *gewone pijlinktvis* (Dutch); *ika* (Japanese); *kalamári* (Greek); *lübje* (Turkish); *lula vulgar* (Portuguese). **Ommastrephidae** (summer squid); **Loliginidae** (winter squid). **Cuttlefish:** *Blekksprut* (Norwegian); *choco* (Portuguese); *inktvis* (Dutch); *jibia, sepia común* (Spanish); *ko-ika, ma-ika, mongoika* (Japanese); *sèche* (French); *seppia* (Italian); *sepya* (Turkish); *tintenfisch* (German). **Sepiidae.**

General
Description:

Squid have a fleshy, cigar-shaped, soft body with two fins on either side. A thin, transparent, flat, pen-shaped "bone" lies inside its body, and it has ten arms, two of which are long tentacles. There are more than 300 squid species worldwide, though only a dozen represent 90 percent of the harvest. Giant squid, over 100 feet long, are rumored to live in the depths of the

Atlantic Ocean. The long-finned or winter squid (*Loligo pealei*) is preferred for its finer, more tender meat to the less expensive, coarser, short-finned or summer squid (*Illex illecebrosus*). The Pacific squid (*L. opalescens*) is highly appreciated on the West Coast. Squid absorbs water quickly and should not be marinated more than overnight (refrigerated) or the meat will soften. Squid defend themselves by shooting dark ink at intruders. The ink is a salty, black liquid that makes an excellent flavoring. When heated, squid protein becomes firm rapidly and then turns chewy until long cooking breaks down the muscle, so squid should either be cooked briefly, no longer than three minutes, or simmered or braised no less than twenty minutes.

The closely related cuttlefish (*Sepia officinalis*) is also a ten-armed mollusk with a body larger and wider than the squid, so it is meatier, with narrow fins and obvious teeth. Its ink sac is larger than a squid's and the ink darker and more abundant. The ink was formerly used to make sepia pigment. Baby cuttlefish, called seppioline, are prized in Venice for risotto.

Locale and Season:

Squid and cuttlefish are all wild-caught. Squid are found in all the world's oceans. Long-finned squid are in season inshore from April to September and offshore (a much larger catch) from October to March. Short-finned squid are abundant from May to October. The roe may be present in females. Cuttlefish are harvested all over the Mediterranean, the west coast of Africa, northern Europe, and Asia, but they are not found in North America. Cuttlefish are best in spring and summer.

| Characteristics: | Young squid, as little as 1 inch long, are sought after for their tender texture and mild, delicate flavor and may be cleaned, then cooked whole. Large squid are often tough, will have a more pronounced flavor, and are best suited for stuffing and braising. Cuttlefish range in size from 2 inches to 2 feet. A thin, purplish-brown membrane covers the bodies of both squid and cuttlefish and is usually removed. Cleaned squid and cuttlefish will be bright white. The meat is tender and sweet as long as it is not overcooked. All parts of squid and cuttlefish can be eaten except for the eyes, mouth area, inner organs, and the clear, hard "bone." The cuttlefish's large ink sac ruptures easily and will usually be broken by the time of purchase, but the ink rinses off easily. |

How to Choose: Because fresh squid and cuttlefish spoil quickly, be especially attentive when purchasing them. Choose fresh squid with a clean, sweet smell and bright eyes. When properly frozen, both squid and cuttlefish will retain flavor and texture. Squid have usually been frozen and defrosted when sold at retail and may be purchased already cleaned. Choose cuttlefish that quickly change color when poked, darkening from brown to black, and that are glossy, sweet-smelling, and somewhat translucent. Frozen or bottled squid ink is sold by specialty suppliers.

Storage: Defrost frozen squid or cuttlefish in the refrigerator and use within 1 day. Refrigerate in a bowl and keep extra-cold by covering with a freezer gel-pack enclosed in a plastic ziplock bag for up to 1 day after purchase.

x 1

Preparation: 1. To clean whole squid, pull the head and everything that comes along with it from the body tube, including the clear, hard bone. Slice the head across just in back of the eyes and discard everything in back of the eyes. Reserve the head. Cut off and save the tentacles at the front of the head if desired, cutting them into smaller pieces or leaving them whole if the squid are small. To clean cuttlefish, place the knife over the hard cuttlebone that can be felt inside the body. Slice open to reveal the cuttlebone. Push back the skin and remove the cuttlebone. Slice across just behind the eyes and discard all the innards.

2. Push the head in, popping out the hard "beak." Discard the beak. Pull off the grayish membrane, leaving only shiny white meat. Rinse well on the inside and drain.

3. Cut off, skin, and reserve the side "fins."

4. Drain, rinse, and pat dry to cook immediately or marinate up to overnight refrigerated.

5. Slice the body into rings for salad or frying, or leave whole to stuff, or cut in half, turn inside-out, and cut shallow crisscrosses into the inner flesh for grilling. Cuttlefish tentacles are usually small and left whole. Serve squid raw in sashimi. Stew in wine, steam, stir-fry, sauté, or dip in batter or crumbs and deep-fry, or marinate and grill. Marinate cuttlefish strips and then grill briefly over high heat. Make black pasta or risotto using purchased squid ink.

Suggested
Recipe:

Crunchy Spiced Calamari (serves 4): Soak 2 pounds cleaned sliced calamari in 1 cup buttermilk mixed with 1 tablespoon chopped garlic up to overnight refrigerated. In a large bowl, mix together 2 tablespoons chili powder, 2 tablespoons paprika, 1 tablespoon ground cumin, 1 teaspoon black pepper, and 2 cups all-purpose flour. Heat 1 quart canola oil to 365°F, or until shimmering hot. Drain the calamari and toss with the seasoned flour. Shake in a sieve over a second bowl so excess flour is shaken off. Fry, without crowding, until crispy, about 6 minutes. Drain on paper towels, toss with fine sea salt, and serve.

Flavor
Affinities:

Chili powder, cilantro, cumin, garlic, ginger, lemon, lime, olive oil, onion, paprika, parsley, rosemary, scallion, sesame, shallot, thyme, vinegar, white wine.

Crustaceans

BLUE CRAB AND SWIMMER CRAB

Other Names:
Blue crab: *Blaukrabbe* (German); *cangrejo azul* (Spanish); *crabe bleu* (French); *galázios kávouras* (Greek); *gazami* (Japanese); *granchio nuotare* (Italian); *mavi yengec* (Turkish); *nalvalheira azul* (Portuguese). **Swimmer crab:** Flower crab; *radjoengan* (Dutch); sand crab (Great Britain); *schimmkrabbe* (German); *taiwangazami* (Japanese). **Portunidae.**

General Description:
The blue crab's scientific name, Callinectes sapidus, *tells us the essentials:* callinectes *is Greek for "beautiful swimmer," and* sapidus *means "tasty" or "savory."* Blue crabs have an olive-green top shell and white underbelly with blue-tipped claws on the male and red-tipped claws on the female. The blue crab fishery has a venerable history in the Chesapeake Bay. Most are harvested as hard-shells sold by the bushel. Another portion of the catch is steamed and the meat picked by hand, usually by women because of their smaller hands. Pregnant blue crabs carry their eggs in a sponglelike protrustion; to conserve the blue crab population and ensure their future, harvesting crabs with this protrusion visible is now illegal. Over its two- to three-year life span, a blue crab outgrows and sheds its shell about 20 times. Once the crab has molted, the new shell takes about four days to harden. Just after shedding, the blue crab's shell is soft enough to eat. Watermen harvest soft shell crabs as peelers

(about to shed), rank peelers (within hours of shedding) and busters (in the process of shedding). Because of their extreme perishability, soft shells must be alive until they're prepared for the pan. Soft shells are almost entirely edible with a salty, sweet taste. Hard shells must also be alive before cooking.

The swimmer crab (*Portunus pelagicus*) is sold in the United States primarily as less expensive pasteurized crab meant to mimic the blue crab. The males are bright blue with white spots and long pincers while the females are a duller green/brown and are more rounded. They stay buried under sand or mud, coming out to feed during high tide.

Locale and
Season:

Live blue crabs are in season from April through November. Live soft shells are in season from mid-May through September. More than 90 percent of American soft shells come from the Chesapeake Bay. Swimmer crabs are found in intertidal estuaries of the Indo-Pacific region on the Asian coasts, Australia, and into the Mediterranean where they have come through the Suez Canal.

Characteristics:

Blue crab meat has a rich, sweet, succulent, and buttery flavor. The body meat is white, tender, and delicately flavored, while the claw meat is brownish on the outside, nuttier, and rather stringy. Cooked shells of blue crabs turn orange-red. Pasteurized crabmeat is firmer and darker than fresh crabmeat. Whole swimmer crabs turn brownish red when cooked. Their meat is found in larger lumps ending in a characteristic brown tip. It is a bit stronger

in flavor and less succulent and tender than
blue crab.

How to Choose: For hard-shell crabs the larger, meatier males, called
"jimmies," are more desirable. The apron, the shape
on the belly, of a male is T-shaped and the prong
narrow. On a young female, or "she-crab," the apron
is triangular. A mature female crab, or "sook," has
a semicircular apron free of the bottom shell. Soft
shells are separated by size, not sex, with the largest
called whales, then smaller jumbos, then primes. The
smallest are hotels, usually the ones found for sale
in retail markets. Fresh-picked blue crab is sold in
America in 1-pound plastic containers kept on ice.
Jumbo lump is biggest and most expensive; lump is
a bit smaller, with backfin the smallest bits from the
body. Packages of claws are the darker, stringier, claw
meat, and they may include a partial shell to make
them easy to pick up. A bluish tint to pasteurized
crab is natural and has no bearing on quality.
Canned pasteurized crabmeat is common in retail
markets but less desirable because the meat tends
to be stringy. For live crabs, ensure they are alive:
They should wave their claws about.

Storage: Store live crabs and soft shells at 50°F, protected
by layers of dampened newspaper. If kept too cold
or too hot, the crabs will die. Don't freeze crabmeat because it will get stringy. Soft shells may
be found frozen. Precleaned soft shells are sometimes sold.

Preparation: ***For soft-shell crabs:***

1.   **Turn the crab over. Lift up the "tab" from the apron and bend it back. Twist and pull back to remove both the apron shell and the underlying intestinal vein.**

2.   **Lift up the sides of the top shell and scrape away and discard the inedible gills on both sides.**

3.   **Slice off a ¹/₂-inch strip at the front, including the eyes. Squeeze out the greenish bubble from behind the eyes and rinse in cold water.**

4.   **Pat the crabs dry. Cover and refrigerate until ready to cook, within 24 hours.**

    For hard-shell crabs:

1.   **Bring a large pot of salted water to a boil with crab boil spices added if desired. Add the (live) crabs and cook 6 to 10 minutes or until brightly colored.**

2.   **To eat cooked crabs, clean as above in steps 1 and 2. Break apart the body sections and crack the claws to get at the meat.**

Suggested Recipe: **Sautéed Soft-Shell Crabs with Orange-Tarragon Butter** (Serves 4): Combine 4 tablespoons softened butter with the zest of 1 orange and 2 tablespoons finely chopped tarragon. Sprinkle 8 cleaned soft-shell crabs with salt and pepper and dust with flour. Brown in a large skillet on both sides in a little hot oil starting with the top-side down. (Stand clear because soft shells tend to pop and splatter.) Remove from the pan and keep warm. Pour off any oil from the pan. Add 2 cups orange juice and boil until syrupy. Return the crabs to the pan along with the Orange-Tarragon Butter and swirl to combine.

Flavor Affinities: Almond, butter, capers, chervil, lemon, lime, orange, parsley, red chiles, saffron, scallion, shallot, tarragon, thyme, tomato, white vermouth, white wine.

64.   **CRAYFISH**

Other Names: **European crayfish:** *Cangrejo de rio* (Spanish); *ecrevisse* (French); *edelkrebs, flusskrebs* (German); *ferskvannskreps* (Norwegian); *flodkräfta* (Swedish); *gambero di fiume* (Italian); *karavída* (Greek); *kerevit* (Turkish); *lagostim do rio* (Portuguese); *zarigani* (Japanese). **American crayfish:** *Congrejo de rio rojo* (Spanish); crawdad; crawfish; *ecrevisse rouge de marais* (French); *gambero di palude* (Italian); mudbug; red swamp crawfish. **Astacidae.**

General Description: *Crayfish look like miniature lobsters with more than 400 species found in freshwaters worldwide, 250 in North America alone.* The most important farmed species is the red swamp crawfish (*Procambarus clarkii*) from southern Louisiana, with the next most important the white-river crawfish (*P. zonangulus*) from northern Louisiana. Both are favorites in Creole and Cajun cooking, most often boiled in a big pot of spiced water then served on large tables covered with newspapers to crack and eat their succulent, but small, tails and suck out the tasty juices from the head. The Pacific crayfish (*Pacifastacus leniusculus*) comes from California and Oregon, is larger, has a harder shell, and is meatier. The European crayfish (*Astacus astacus*) is found throughout Europe, but there is limited crayfish farming in Europe.

Locale and Season:

Crayfish live in rivers, lakes, swamps, canals, wetlands, and irrigation ditches. About 90 percent of American crayfish come from Louisiana, where they are trapped in the wild and farmed as a rotating crop with rice. Peak season for Louisiana crayfish is March to May. Farmed crayfish are also harvested in China, Japan, Norway, and Sweden.

Characteristics:

When alive, red swamp crawfish are red to nearly black; white-river crawfish are light to dark reddish-brown. Most crayfish shells turn brilliant scarlet when cooked. The raw meat is gray-white; the cooked meat is white covered by a reddish membrane and is sweet like lobster but more tender. The crayfish fat, also called head fat, contains much of the flavor and can be purchased separately. The tails have the most meat.

How to Choose:

Red swamp crawfish is preferred because it turns a striking lobster-red when cooked. Labels should distinguish between farm-raised and wild crayfish and should include the state and even river of origin. Rare soft-shell crayfish have just molted and are almost entirely edible. Live crayfish should be "alive and kicking" when purchased and should spread their claws when grabbed. Frozen crayfish tails may also be purchased in 1-pound pouches. There are 15 to 20 whole crawfish per pound.

Storage:
☐ x 1

Live crayfish are quite perishable and should be cooked within 1 day. Refrigerate covered by damp newspapers. Once cooked, the yellow head fat should be removed from the meat for better shelf life. Defrost frozen tails overnight in the refrigerator.

Preparation: 1. **Cook live crayfish by dropping into boiling water, usually heavily seasoned with Cajun spices and salt.**

2. **Cook only long enough for the crayfish to turn bright red and for the tail to begin to curl. Drain and serve immediately, or remove the tails, twist off the shells, and use the tail meat. If the tail doesn't curl up when cooked, discard.**

3. **To remove the intestinal vein, pull the fan-shaped shell at the base of the tail from side to side until it breaks off, usually with the dark vein attached. Or open the back of the tail and pull out the vein.**

4. **Serve crayfish in jambalaya, bisque, étouffée, and pasta sauces, or cold with flavored mayonnaise.**

5. **For soft shell crayfish, snip off the head in back of the eyes and squeeze out the hard "stones." The rest is edible. They are usually battered and deep-fried.**

Suggested Recipe:	**Crawfish Étouffée** (serves 6): Make a roux by cooking 4 tablespoons butter with 1/2 cup flour over low heat in a large heavy skillet, preferably cast iron, until the flour is deep brown, stirring constantly, about 20 minutes. Add 1/2 cup each chopped onion, green pepper, and celery, and 2 teaspoons chopped garlic and cook, stirring, until the vegetables are soft. Gradually pour in 2 cups fish or seafood stock, stirring until the liquid has come to a boil and is smooth. Add 2 pounds peeled, cooked crawfish tails, 4 tablespoons butter, 1 cup sliced scallions, and 1/4 cup sherry or brandy, and season with salt and pepper. Bring back to a boil, remove from the heat, and serve over rice.

Flavor Affinities:
Bay leaf, brandy, butter, celery, cream, dill, hot sauce, lemon, marjoram, mustard, onion, scallion, shallot, sugar, tarragon, thyme, tomato, white wine.

---

65. **DUNGENESS CRAB**

Other Names:
Cangrejo dungeness (Spanish); *danjinesukani* (Japanese); *dormeur du Pacifique* (French); *granchio* (Italian); market crab; *Pazifischer taschenkrebs* (German); San Francisco crab. **Cancridae**.

General Description:
Dungeness crab (Cancer magister) is one of the Pacific Northwest region's greatest delicacies. Dungeness, with its sweet, moist flesh and briny tang, has extraordinary flavor and buttery richness. Dungeness is usually eaten right out of the shell, though crab Louis, crab

cakes, and cioppino are also traditional. Dungeness crabs have been harvested off San Francisco Bay since 1848, and the crab industry is considered to be the best managed in terms of sustainability.

Locale and Season: Dungeness crab is found from Alaska to southern California. In Alaska and British Columbia, peak season is late spring and early summer; Washington and Oregon follow, and California is later.

Characteristics: Live Dungeness crabs are reddish-brown with short, thick legs. They weigh an average of 2 pounds. When cooked, the shell turns orange and the cooked meat will be opaque white with reddish-brown areas on the outside. The meat is sweet, flavorful, and semi-nutty; the leg meat is firmer than the rich body meat.

The internal organs of Dungeness crab may contain a natural toxin that can result in paralytic shellfish poisoning (PSP), so do not eat them.

How to Choose: Live crabs should be active in a holding tank and have bright shells. The back should not be cracked, and all legs should be attached. Local crabs harvested by small day boats, which return to shore every day, are best. Frozen crab is available but not desirable. Avoid lightweight crabs, which have been harvested before they can refill their shells after a seasonal molt. They are known as "air crabs" because they contain so little meat.

Storage: Store refrigerated in a perforated container over a second container to catch the drips and completely covered in crushed ice for up to 1 day before cooking.

Preparation: 1. Scrub the crabs with a brush and rinse thoroughly.

2. To cook live 2- to 2½-pound Dungeness crabs, boil in seasoned water for 18 minutes, or until brightly colored all over, drain, chill in an ice bath, and serve on newspapers, allowing one crab for every two people.

3. To clean whole cooked Dungeness crab, hold the crab with one hand and place the thumb of other hand under the shell at its midpoint to lift off the shell.

4. Scrape out and discard the orange-colored soft organs and the feather gills. Rinse the crab thoroughly under cool, running water.

5. Grasp the crab in both hands and break in half. Pull off the legs.

6. Crack the shell with a small meat mallet to expose the meat. Remove the meat using the tip of the leg shell, a small pick, or a fork.

7. Serve crabmeat in seafood stews, soups, sautés, and salads; in bisques, creamed dishes, and casseroles; or crack and serve with homemade mayonnaise.

Suggested Recipe: **Oven-Roasted Dungeness Crab** (serves 4): Preheat the oven to 500°F. In a large, heavy, ovenproof skillet, lightly brown ¼ cup chopped shallots, 2 tablespoons chopped garlic, 2 teaspoons hot red pepper flakes, and 1 tablespoon each chopped thyme and marjoram in ¼ cup each extra-virgin olive oil and butter. Add

2 large boiled, cleaned, and cracked Dungeness crabs, sprinkle with salt and pepper, turn and roast 12 minutes, or until sizzling, then transfer to a platter. Add $1/2$ cup orange juice and 2 tablespoons Pernod to the skillet; boil until syrupy, about 5 minutes, and spoon over crabs.

Flavor
Affinities:
Artichoke, bell pepper, butter, cilantro, cucumber, garlic, marjoram, olive oil, orange, oregano, Pernod, red onion, shallot, tarragon, thyme, white wine.

GOOSENECK BARNACLE

Other Names:
Balano, lepade cornucopia, pico (Italian); *balanus* (Turkish); *felsen-entenmuschle* (German); *fujitsubo* (Japanese); *lamperna* (Basque); *percebe* (Spanish); *perceve* (Portuguese); *pouce-pied* (French); *stidóna* (Greek). **Scalpellidae.**

General
Description:
The odd-looking gooseneck barnacle is a crustacean that attaches itself to rocks exposed to heavy surf. Two species, *Pollicipes cornucopia* and *Lepas anatifera*, grow in the same region and are prepared and eaten the same ways. Both have a tubelike appendage with dark, parchmentlike skin covered with tiny scales. The barnacles are topped by a pair of hooflike, bony white pads, from between which emerge the creature's edible feet. Barnacles are usually found in groups attached to rocks and are said to be most easily harvested at full moon when the tide is low. Demand for

them in Portugal and Spain is so great that they have become rare. A similar species (*P. polymerus*) is found on rocky cliffs on the Pacific Northwest coast, where they were a delicacy of native people.

Locale and
Season:

☀ ♻ ❄

Gooseneck barnacles are found in the Mediterranean and close-lying areas of the eastern Atlantic. Spaniards prize those from Galicia in northwest Spain. They are in season in summer but are most in demand for Christmas. They are farmed in Washington state and harvested in limited amounts from the wild in British Columbia and are considered to be best in summer.

Characteristics:

Gooseneck barnacles have a strong but pleasing taste of the sea. If the waters are relatively calm, the barnacles grow long and thin; when rough seas batter the rocks, they grow short and stubby and are considered to have the best texture and fullest flavor. These are also the most dangerous to gather. American gooseneck barnacles are fatter and less intense in flavor.

How to Choose:

Choose barnacles with a strong but sweet ocean smell. Spanish barnacles have a red fringe around the shell plates. They must be alive.

Storage:

🛋🗄 x 1

Store up to 1 day refrigerated topped with a damp towel to keep them moist.

Preparation: **1.**

🚰

Thoroughly rinse barnacles, rubbing gently to dislodge any sand.

 2.

Boil briefly in salted water, or steam until firm.

3. **Eat only the inner tube: Pinch the outer skin near the upper hoofs and pull it off. Inside is the edible part, a white, stalklike protuberance. Bite this off whole. When removing the skin, a bit of staining orange liquid sometimes spurts out, so take care.**

Serving Suggestion: Gooseneck barnacles are steamed in their shells above stock or seasoned wine for about 10 minutes, then peeled and served hot, allowing about 1 dozen per person, eaten as is or with drawn butter for dipping.

Flavor Affinities: Bay leaf, butter, coriander, lemon, mustard, oregano, paprika, parsley, thyme, white wine.

HAWAIIAN BLUE PRAWN

Other Names: *Bouquet* or *chevrette géante* (French); *camarão gigante do rio* (Portuguese); giant freshwater prawn; giant river prawn; *langostino de río* (Spanish); Malaysian prawn; *onitenagaebi* (Japanese); *rosenberg-garnele* (German). **Palaemonidae**.

General Description: *The Hawaiian blue prawn* (Macrobrachium rosenbergii) *is one of more than 200 species of freshwater prawns that are important commercially.* This fast-growing freshwater shrimp has a bright blue tail, long legs, and even longer antennae and can reach more than 1/4 pound, though farmed shrimp are harvested at about 6 per pound. Live whole prawns sometimes show up at high-end restaurants. Cooking with the

head makes for juicier results and more flavor,
although the tail is the only edible portion.

Locale and
Season:

Hawaiian blue prawns are found in the wild in the
Indo-Pacific and are farmed in Hawaii, California, the
Caribbean, and Southeast Asia. They are available
year-round with peak season in summer.

Characteristics: These freshwater shrimp have a delicate sweet flavor
and firm, white flesh.

How to Choose: There is limited availability of live whole fresh
prawns; most are sold as frozen tails. If chilled too
long with its head on, this shrimp can turn mushy.

Storage:

☐ x 1

Freshwater shrimp are quite perishable, and will only
keep for 1 day, refrigerated. Blanch before storing for
more than 1 day after purchase.

Preparation: •

**Cook whole by boiling in court bouillon (broth fla-
vored with onion, celery, thyme, white wine, lemon
zest, and black pepper) until opaque, about 4 minutes, or pan-sear, grill, or broil.**

Suggested
Recipe:

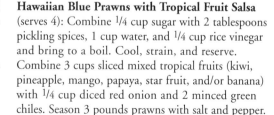

Hawaiian Blue Prawns with Tropical Fruit Salsa
(serves 4): Combine 1/4 cup sugar with 2 tablespoons
pickling spices, 1 cup water, and 1/4 cup rice vinegar
and bring to a boil. Cool, strain, and reserve.
Combine 3 cups sliced mixed tropical fruits (kiwi,
pineapple, mango, papaya, star fruit, and/or banana)
with 1/4 cup diced red onion and 2 minced green
chiles. Season 3 pounds prawns with salt and pepper.

Quickly sear the prawns in a preheated sauté pan in canola oil for 1 to 2 minutes on each side, or until done. Serve with salsa.

Flavor Affinities:

Avocado, banana, chipotle, coconut, green chiles, kiwi, macadamia, mango, papaya, passion fruit, pineapple, red onion, rice vinegar, saffron, tamarind, vanilla.

66.

JONAH CRAB, PEEKYTOE CRAB, AND SAWAGANI

Other Names:

Jonah crab: Atlantic Dungeness; *cangrejo* (Spanish); *granciporro atlantico rosso* (Italian); *jonahkrabbe* (German); *kani* (Japanese); *sapateira boreal* (Portuguese); *tourteau-jona* (French). **Peekytoe crab:** Bay crab; *felsenkrabbe* (German); *granciporro atlantico giallo* (Italian); *jaiba de roca amarilla* (Spanish); rock crab; *sapateira de rocha* (Portuguese); *tourteau poinclos* (French). **Sawagani:** Japanese river crab. **Cancridae**.

General Description:

The Jonah crab (Cancer borealis) *was once discarded by lobstermen.* In the 1990s, fishers found they could sell the crabs to processors, and it is now found on restaurant menus and at retail markets. Jonahs are close relatives of the peekytoe crab (*C. irroratus*) and are often treated as the same in markets. However, Jonahs are larger and have bigger claws and knuckles, which are the major source of their meat. The peekytoe crab was a throwaway byproduct of lobster fishing until a name change in 1997 from rock crab. The new name is credited to Rod Mitchell, owner of Browne Trading Company. Nowadays peekytoe crab is highly sought after. They are caught in waters 20 to 40 feet deep in traps baited with bits of fish. The meat is pink with a sweet, delicate flavor.

Sawagani crabs (*Geothelphusa dehaani*) are very tiny Japanese river crabs. They are eaten whole, shell and all. These freshwater crabs live in most parts of Japan in clear-water streams and average only 3/4 inch in diameter. Sawagani are usually eaten with sushi, but in Japan you can buy them in bags in roadside shops for munching on the go.

Locale and Season:

Jonah crabs range from Nova Scotia to northern Florida but are most abundant from Georges Bank to North Carolina. Supplies are less in summer, when fishermen focus on lobsters. The peekytoe crab comes from Maine. Both types range from light to dark brownish red; the further north they're caught, the darker their color. Sawagani are in season in summer and fall but are available frozen year-round.

Characteristics:

Jonah and peekytoe crabs are oval-shaped with big, hard claws. They have reddish-orange shells and a white underside. The raw meat is translucent white; the cooked meat is white with brown-red highlights. It is flaky and sweet. Japanese river crabs weigh 1 to 1 1/2 ounces each and are sold in an 8-ounce bushel. They may be sold frozen.

How to Choose:

Jonah crab claws and meat are sold already cooked and are often frozen. Break open a Jonah crab claw: If the meat sticks to shell, the claw wasn't cooked or frozen at peak freshness. Peekytoe crabmeat is sold already picked and is of high quality.

Storage:
x 1

Refrigerate Jonah and peekytoe crabs, covered by damp towels, for up to 1 day. Refrigerate crabmeat in its container and covered with ice for up to 2 days. Defrost frozen crab claws overnight in the refrigerator.

Preparation: • **Use peekytoe and Jonah crabmeat in salads, sauces, seafood cocktails, crab cakes, and other dishes. Eat sawagami whole.**

Suggested Recipe:

Capellini with Peekytoe Crab, Asparagus, and Saffron (serves 4): Soak a large pinch of saffron in 1 cup white wine mixed with 2 tablespoon Pernod until golden. Sauté 2 cups bias-sliced asparagus and 1 cup bias-sliced scallions in 2 tablespoons olive oil. Add the saffron-wine mixture, 1 cup tomato sauce, and 1/2 cup clam broth to the pan and bring to a boil. Remove the pan from the heat, add 1 1/2 pounds peekytoe crabmeat, and heat gently. Meanwhile, boil 1 pound capellini pasta 2 to 3 minutes until al dente. Drain well and toss with the sauce.

Flavor Affinities:

Asparagus, basil, brandy, butter, chervil, chives, cream, hot sauce, lemon, mayonnaise, olive oil, Pernod, scallion, shallot, tarragon, thyme, tomato, white wine.

67. ## KING CRAB, SNOW CRAB, AND EUROPEAN CRABS

Other Names:
King crab: *Crabe royal* (French); *kurzschwanz-krebs* (German); *tarabagani* (Japanese). **Lithodidae. Snow crab:** *Eismerkrabbe* (German); queen crab (Canada); spider crab; tanner crab; *zuwaigani* (Japanese). **Majidae. Common crab:** *Buey* (Spanish); *chancre* (Channel Islands); cromer crab (Great Britain); *dormeur, tourteau* (French); *granchio* (Italian); green crab; *pavurya* (Turkish); *siderokávouras* (Greek). **Crancridae. Shore crab:** *Cangrejo e mar* (Spanish); *crabe vert, crabe enragé* (French); *strandkrabbe* (German); *mouro* (Portuguese). **Portunidae.**

General Description:
The king crab (Paralithodes camtschaticus) *is the largest commercially harvested crab, with a spiny shell and long, spidery legs.* Most crabs have 10 legs, but king crabs have 6 walking legs, one larger crusher claw, and one smaller pincher claw. They often march in herds across vast expanses of underwater plains. Shell color varies according to the origin of the crab, with red the most common color, but there are also blue (*P. platupys*) and brown or golden (*Lithodes aequspina*). The southern king crab (*L. antarcticus*) is nearly identical to the king crab but found in the Southern Hemisphere.

Three species of snow crab are harvested in the cold waters of North America, all in the spider crab family. Bairdii (*Chionoecetes bairdi*) are the largest, averaging 5 pounds, found in the Pacific. Tanners (*C. tanneri*) are slightly larger with longer, skinnier legs, found in the Atlantic. Opilios (*C. opilio*) are smaller, about 1 pound, and are sometimes sold as queen crabs. Opilios are most important commercially and the only species caught in both the Atlantic and the Pacific. Snow crabs are taken in traps from sandy bottoms. They are smaller and more brown than king crabs. Although king crab and snow crab are only distantly related, they are often confused.

The large common crab (*Cancer pagurus*) is one of the most popular crabs in Europe, found in the Mediterranean, the North Atlantic, and the North Sea. It is a robust crab with a reddish-brown oval shell, a rippled edge, and black on the tips of its claws. The shore crab (*Carcinus maenas*) has a green shell with yellow spots and is most popular in the British Isles and Scandinavia.

Locale and
Season:

King crabs are found in shallow waters off the shores of Southeast Asia and in the Bering Sea. Live king crabs are available September through December. Frozen king crabs are available year-round, but the greatest supply and lowest prices are in November. Peak season for opilio snow crab is January to March. Bairdi snow crab is in season in November. Large common crabs are found in the eastern Atlantic and throughout the Mediterranean.

Characteristics:

King crabs grow up to 6 feet and weigh up to 10 pounds. Red king crab is in highest demand because of its large size. The spiky shell of the cooked crab leg is brilliant red, and the cooked meat is bright white with a scarlet membrane. The best meat is the merus, from the upper part of the walking legs and marketed as "fancy." The body meat is flakier than the leg meat. Snow crabs have longer, thinner legs than king crabs. When cooked, its shell is reddish-brown and browner at the shoulder. The meat ranges from snow white to reddish-brown and is sold cooked. It is sweet and delicate, though a bit fibrous. The shoulder has tender, long fibers; the claw meat is firmer. The common crab may weigh up to 6 pounds and has rather fibrous meat from its claws. Its flavor is moderately strong and redolent of the sea.

How to Choose: Almost all king crab in the United States has been cooked and frozen in brine. If processed correctly, the meat should not taste salty. King crab is sweet, moist, and rich. As snow crab ages, it shows black patches, barnacles, and mottling on the shell. This does not affect quality, but these crabs are likely to be meatier, because they haven't molted.

Storage: Store frozen crab legs in the freezer and do not pre-thaw, or they will become watery and lose their juices. Flavor is best just after thawing; use immediately.

Preparation: • **Add to soups and stews in the last 5 minutes of cooking or steam fresh or frozen until just heated through, about 5 minutes. Serve hot or cold, in chunks, flaked, or shredded, or brush with melted butter, season, and serve with cocktail or other cold sauce. Do not overcook.**

Suggested
Recipe:

Broiled Alaskan King Crab (serves 2): Cut 1 pound split king crab legs into 2- to 3-inch sections. Combine 1/4 cup melted butter with 1 tablespoon Old Bay or other seafood seasoning mix, the grated zest of 1 lemon, 2 tablespoons each grated onion and chopped parsley, and 1 tablespoon chopped tarragon, and brush over crab. Place the crab legs shell-side down on a broiler pan and broil about 5 minutes, brushing occasionally with sauce, or until sizzling hot.

Flavor
Affinities:

Bell pepper, butter, celery, cocktail sauce, dill, mayonnaise, mushroom, Old Bay seasoning, onion, parsley, scallion, shallot, tarragon, tomato, white wine.

68. 📷 **LOBSTER**

Other Names:

Astakós (Greek); *astice, lupicante* (Italian); *bogavante* (Spanish); *homard, homard Américain* (French); *hummer* (German, Norwegian); *iseebi* (Japanese); *istakoz* (Turkish); *omar* (Russian); *zeekreeft* (Dutch). **Nephropidae.**

General
Description:

The American lobster (Homarus americanus) *is a slow-growing, prized sea creature.* Native American tribes fished for lobsters that were so plentiful they were often found on the beach at low tide—they could be three to four feet long. High demand has led to higher prices, smaller lobsters, and smaller harvests. Steamed lobster with drawn butter and New England lobster roll sandwiches are East Coast favorites.

The European lobster (*H. gammarus*) closely resembles the American lobster but tends to be smaller with less robust tearing and crushing claws. Nicknamed "the cardinal of the sea" because of its bright red color when cooked, this lobster has been highly prized in France since the fifteenth century.

Locale and
Season:
☀ ❄ ❅

American lobsters are found in shallower water, especially in rocky areas where they can hide, from Labrador to North Carolina; those from colder waters are more highly regarded. Eighty percent of New England's lobsters are harvested from July to October, though some of those are kept in "pounds" for sale later in the season. Availability is lowest from March to July. The European lobster ranges from northern Europe as far south as the Mediterranean.

Characteristics:

A lobster's body is divided into two main parts: the head and thorax (midsection) and the abdomen (called the tail) with its small, scissorlike feelers. The color of live lobsters varies from olive green to dark green-brown with orange, reddish, dark green, or black speckles and bluish joints. The darker the live color, the brighter the cooked color. A genetic defect makes about one in two million lobsters bright blue when alive. Lobster meat is mild and sweet in flavor, with an incomparable meaty texture and satisfying flavor. The tail meat is firmer, the claw meat stringier. Lobsters cooked at high heat, either in oil or by steam, will be brightest.

How to Choose: A live lobster should look lively and wiggle its claws. Its tail should snap back when straightened, and the shell should be hard and thick. Although a newly molted lobster may be larger, it will have limited amounts of watery, flaccid meat. Female lobsters are plumper and mature females will usually carry the flavorful dark green roe that turns coral red when cooked. Look at the first set of feelers below the thorax: They are soft on a female, hard on a male, and females have shorter, wider tails. A cull has one or both claws missing or has a tiny replacement claw and may sometimes be found at a lower price. A chicken or chix lobster is between 1 and 1^{1}/4 pounds, the minimum size sold, and less desirable, because the proportion of meat is low. A 1^{1}/2-pound lobster is most common and works well for most recipes. Larger lobsters not only weigh more but also cost more per pound. The greenish tomalley, a set of glands, has the texture of scrambled eggs and is considered a delicacy. People are now advised not to eat the tomalley because it accumulates contaminants from the environment. Yield is about 25 percent meat from hard-shelled lobsters.

Storage: To store a live lobster, place in a box or shallow pan
x 1   in the refrigerator and cover with a dampened cloth, seaweed, or layers of damp newspaper for 1 day. Do not use fresh water or ice. Cooked lobster meat may be stored in the refrigerator for up to two days. Culls must be cooked the same day they're purchased. Hard-shelled lobsters live longer than those with soft shells.

Preparation: 1.   To cut up a live lobster, grip it on the back of its thorax. Plunge the point of a sharp chef's knife between the shell sections where the head meets the body, killing the lobster instantly.

 2.   Twist off the tail. Remove and reserve any dark green roe sacs. Split the tail lengthwise, then remove and discard the (usually clear) intestine that runs down the center and the small stomach sac from inside the head. Crack the claws and "knuckles," the upper portion of the claw. Sauté, pan-sear, roast, broil, or grill in the shell. Or, cook briefly by poaching or boiling in court bouillon, then cool and remove the meat from the shell and briefly sauté, broil, or grill until fully cooked.

3.   To boil whole lobster, bring a large pot of salted water to a rapid boil, then plunge the lobster head-first into the water. Boil 12 to 15 minutes for smaller lobsters, 17 minutes for larger lobsters. The lobster is cooked when it is bright red and the legs and antennae can be pulled off easily. The tail shell should be curled, but not too tightly, an indication of overcooking. Serve with melted butter or other sauce.

4.   To remove the meat from a cooked lobster, twist off the claws. Using a mallet, crack the claws and knuckles. Remove the claws from their shells, trying to leave them as intact as possible. Twist off the tail from the body and, using scissors, cut along the underside of the shell. Pull off the tail shell, leaving the meat intact. Twist off the small pincers from the

body and pull out the long thin meat on the inside (only worth doing on larger lobsters).

Suggested Recipe:

Maine Lobster Roll (Serves 2 to 3): Steam or boil 1 (1½-pound) lobster, cool, remove the meat, cut into small pieces, mix with mayonnaise to taste, and serve in hot dog buns with lettuce.

Flavor Affinities:

Artichoke, basil, brandy, coriander, cream, dill, fennel, garlic, lemon, lime, onion, orange, saffron, shallot, sherry, tarragon, thyme, tomato, truffle, white wine.

69. 📷 **LOBSTERETTE AND LANGOSTINO**

Other Names: **Lobsterette:** *Akazaebi* (Japanese); *cigala, maganto* (Spanish); *demoiselles de Cherbourg, langoustine* (French); Dublin Bay prawn; *dybvandshummer* (Danish); *kaisergranat* (German); *karavída* (Greek); *logostim* (Portuguese); *nefrops* (Turkish); Norway lobster (Great Britain); *scampo* (singular), *scampi* (plural) (Italian); *sjoekreps* (Norwegian); *tiefseehummer* (German). **Galatheidae. Langostino:** *Galthée rouge, munida* (French); *langostino* (Italian); *langostino amarillo* (Spanish); *langostino colorado* (Chile). **Nephropidae.**

General Description: *The lobsterette (Nephrops norvegicus) is famed as the original "scampi" cooked in garlic, butter, and white wine sauce.* The shell of this thin, elongated, lobster-like creature is pale pink to rose-orange with claws that have red and white bands. Until the 1950s, fishers in Great Britain usually discarded them. They are now hugely popular but can be hard to find in American markets. They are usually cooked with their heads on. The similar New Zealand lobsterette (*Metanephrops challengeri*) is now beginning to be exported.

The langostino (*Pleuroncodes monodon*) is a smaller crustacean often confused with lobsterette or the unrelated langoustine. The most important species is found in the deep, cold waters off the coast of Chile. After the fishery nearly collapsed in the early 1980s, strict regulations were enacted in Chile to ensure their sustainability. Langostino tail meat can be used in recipes calling for cooked crab, lobster, or shrimp.

Locale and
Season:

The lobsterette, found on muddy sea bottoms, is now the most valuable crustacean harvested off the Scottish coast. The langostino is harvested off Chile during its tightly regulated season, from May to September.

Characteristics:

Lobsterettes resemble shrimp but have long, slender pincer claws and a narrow body. They are usually sold whole, alive or cooked. They are brownish pink and don't change color much when cooked. The meat is full-bodied in flavor with sweet, tender meat. Langostinos range from 4 to 6 inches in length and resemble a short, wrinkled crayfish with extra-long pincers. It is seldom seen whole in the marketplace but is usually sold as frozen cooked tail meat.

How to Choose:

Lobsterettes should smell sweet; larger ones yield more meat. Precooked shelled langostino tails are easy to use.

Storage: Store live lobsterettes as for lobster; defrost frozen lobsterette meat in the refrigerator overnight. Defrost frozen langostinos in the refrigerator overnight.

Preparation: 1. **Cook lobsterettes and langostinos as for shrimp, either whole or just the tails, or use to make bisque.**

2. **For grilling or roasting, butterfly the tail meat by cutting up the back and opening up flat.**

Suggested Recipe: **Dublin Bay Prawns with Lemon and Pepper** (serves 4): Heat 2 tablespoons butter in a pan over medium heat, then add 1 tablespoon chopped garlic, and cook 2 to 3 minutes, until fragrant. Add 8 whole butterflied Dublin bay prawns with 1/2 cup white wine, the grated zest of 1 lemon, and salt and freshly ground pepper to taste. Cook 3 to 4 minutes or until the tail meat is opaque, then add the juice of 1 lemon and a pinch of hot red pepper flakes.

Flavor Affinities: Brandy, butter, chiles, chives, cilantro, cream, garlic, lemon, lime, marjoram, olive oil, oregano, parsley, shallot, soy sauce, tarragon, thyme, tomato, white wine.

MANTIS SHRIMP AND SLIPPER LOBSTER

Other Names: **Mantis shrimp:** *Cannocchia, pannocchia* (Italian); *galera* (Spanish); *heuschreckenkrebs* (German); *mante, squille* (French); mantis squillid (Great Britain); sea scorpion; *shako* (Japanese); squilla; *zagaia-castanheta*

(Portuguese). **Squillidae**. **Slipper lobster:** *Barenkrebs* (German); *cicala di mare, magnosella* (Italian); *cigale, petite cigale* (French); *cigarra de mar, santiaguiño* (Spanish); *cigarra do mar, lagosta da pedra* (Portuguese). **Scyllaridae**.

General
Description:

The mantis shrimp (Squilla mantis) *looks like a flattened, pale lobster tail with a whitish shell and two distinctive eye-shaped spots at the end of its tail and famously powerful claws.* It is quite popular and sought after on the Adriatic coast for its sweet and mild flavor and soft, tender texture. An American species, *S. empusa*, is light yellowish to gray-green. Mantis shrimp are rarely, if ever, seen in American markets outside of Hawaii.

The slipper lobster (*Scyllarus arctus*) looks like a flat lobster without claws. Though the meat of the tail tastes good, there is not much of it. The Balmain bug or butterfly slipper lobster (*Ibacus peronii*) is the most common member of this family in Australia and makes for excellent eating. The Moreton Bay bug (*Thenus orientalis*) from Australia is prized.

Locale and
Season:

The mantis shrimp is found in the Mediterranean and the eastern Atlantic. It is fished year-round but especially in the fall. Slipper lobster is found in the Mediterranean and the waters surrounding the Iberian Peninsula. The butterfly slipper lobster comes from southeastern Australia. The Moreton Bay bug is in the Indo-Pacific from East Africa to the northern half of Australia's coast, including Moreton Bay, from which it derives its common name.

Characteristics: Both mantis shrimp and slipper lobster have soft, tender, mildly flavored meat. The Moreton Bay bug has sweet, succulent meat that is quite adaptable.

How to Choose: Choose lively-looking creatures that move their claws.

Storage: Store refrigerated up to 1 day, covered by damp towels.

Preparation: 1. **If alive, place mantis shrimp, slipper lobsters, or Moreton Bay bugs into the freezer for 30 minutes and then boil briefly in salted water until the tails begin to curl. Refresh in iced water and peel the tails.**

2. **Grill or pan-sear raw tails, use in soup, steam with herbs, or boil and serve like shrimp with a sauce.**

Suggested Recipe: **Cannocchie Adriatica** (Serves 4): Split 1 pound mantis shrimp tails lengthwise down the center and open up to expose the flesh. Combine 1 tablespoon chopped garlic, 2 tablespoons olive oil, 1/2 cup breadcrumbs, and salt and pepper. Place the tails in a single layer in a baking dish and pat with the crumb mixture. Pour 1 cup white wine around the shrimp and bake at 400°F for 15 minutes or until opaque.

Flavor Affinities: Basil, butter, coconut, coriander, cumin, curry, garlic, ginger, lemon, lime, macadamia, mint, olive oil, parsley, red chiles, scallion, tarragon, tomato, white wine.

70. 📷   **ROCK SHRIMP**

Other Names: *Boucot ovetgernade* (French); brown rock shrimp; *camarón de piedra* (Spanish); *furchen-geisselgarnele* (German). **Sicyoniidae.**

General Description: *Rock shrimp* (Sicyonia brevirostris) *get their name from their rock-hard shell.* A deepwater cousin to the shrimp (p. 262), their meat is quite firm, more lobsterlike, and lower priced than other shrimp. Shrimpers started pulling these up as a bycatch in the 1960s but kept them for themselves, figuring people wouldn't be able to crack the shell. When a gadget was invented to split the shell and devein the shrimp, they started to gain popularity. Rock shrimp are harvested by trawling with reinforced nets to protect against the coral and rocky bottoms where they live. They are commonly served as "popcorn" shrimp in chain restaurants.

Locale and Season: ☀ ⌘   Rock shrimp are found from Virginia to the Yucatan. Rock shrimp are mostly fished in the late summer and fall.

Characteristics: Because they are so difficult to peel, almost all rock shrimp are sold peeled. Rock shrimp meat is transparent white with fine pink or purple-tinged lines. It has delicate, sweet flavor.

How to Choose: Look for rock shrimp with mild, briny smell. Rock shrimp are generally small; the largest size is usually 21 to 25 per pound. Avoid rock shrimp with black spots or orange striping, an indication that they have been mishandled.

Storage: Refrigerate up to 2 days in a container surrounded by crushed ice.

Preparation: 1. **Rock shrimp are sold already peeled and cleaned, making them easy to cook.**

2. **Sauté, boil, broil, or deep-fry. The small size of rock shrimp makes them cook very quickly.**

Suggested Recipe: **Popcorn Rock Shrimp** (serves 4): Combine 1/2 cup heavy cream, 2 teaspoons Creole seasoning, and salt, pepper, and hot sauce to taste. Add 1 pound peeled rock shrimp and toss well. Cover and chill 30 minutes in the refrigerator. Drain. Combine 1 cup cornmeal with 1 tablespoon Creole seasoning. Dredge the shrimp in the cornmeal mixture, coating them evenly and tapping off any excess. Heat 1 quart canola oil to 365°F in a large, heavy pot. Fry the shrimp a few at a time until crispy, about 3 minutes each. Drain on a wire rack and serve with lemon wedges.

Flavor Affinities: Basil, brandy, butter, capers, chervil, chiles, coriander, cream, cumin, dill, fennel, garlic, oregano, saffron, shallot, tarragon, thyme, tomato, white wine.

71a–b.   **SHRIMP**

Other Names: **Black tiger shrimp:** *Ebi* (Japanese); *garnele* (German).
Endeavour prawn: *camarón devo* (Spanish); *crevette devo* (French). **European common prawn:** *Bouquet, crevette rose* (French); *camarão branco* (Portuguese); *camarón, gamba* (Spanish); *corgimwch* (Welsh).
European gray shrimp: *Camarão negro* (Portuguese); *crevette grise* (French); *gamberetto grigio* (Italian); *garída* (Greek); *garnaal* (Dutch); *hestereke* (Norwegian); *kahverengi karides* (Turkish); *quisquilla gris* (Spanish); *sandgarnele* (German); *tekke* (Turkish). **Gulf white shrimp:** *Camarón blanco norteño* (Spanish); *crevette ligubam du Nord* (French); *kurumaeibi-zoku* (Japanese); *mazzancola bianca atlantica* (Italian); *nördliche weiss geisselgarnele* (German). **Gulf pink shrimp:** *Camarón rosado norteño* (Spanish); *crevettte rose du Nord* (French); *kurumaeibi-zoku* (Japanese). **Gulf brown shrimp:** *Azteken-geisselgarnele* (German); *camarón café norteño* (Spanish); *crevette royale grise* (French); *mazzancolla caffè* (Italian). **Pacific white shrimp:** *Camarão pata branca* (Portuguese); *camarón patiblanco* (Spanish); *crevette pattes blanches* (French); *gamberone centramericano* (Italian); *geisselgarnele* (German); whiteleg shrimp. **Spanish red shrimp:** *Crevette rose du large* (French); *camarão da costa* (Portuguese); *gambero rosso* (Italian), *langostino moruno* (Spanish); *tsunogachihiroebi* (Japanese). **Crangoniae, Aristaeidae, Peneidae, Palaemonidae.**

General
Description: *There are a vast number of different kinds of shrimp throughout the world, all divided into three basic cate-*

gories: cold-water (northern), warm-water (southern or tropical), and freshwater. You may find all three categories in your local market. In the United States, *prawn* commonly refers to freshwater shrimp or large saltwater shrimp. In the British Isles, *prawn* is equivalent to U.S. *shrimp.* The misnomer *scampi* is often used in restaurants to describe shrimp cooked in butter and garlic. True scampi are actually another creature entirely called the lobsterette (p. 257). Warm-water shrimp from the Gulf states represent the overwhelming majority of shrimp harvested in the United States.

Black tiger shrimp (*Penaeus monodon*) are the largest of more than three hundred commercially sold shrimp species, and can be up to 1 foot long. They are mostly farmed as one of Asia's most important aquaculture species, though they are also harvested by trawlers. Farmed black tigers have a mild, rather bland flavor, and their texture is soft. Some producers treat these shrimp with sulfites and other chemicals to prevent deterioration. Shrimp with too many additives will have an unpleasantly soapy flavor. Cook shrimp only long enough for them to turn opaque, as they quickly overcook and toughen.

The European common prawn (*Palemon serratus*) is found in inshore waters, walking forward in search of food. Almost translucent when alive, they turn bright orange-red when cooked. The endeavour prawn (*Metapenaeus endeavour*) from Australia is prized for its excellent eating qualities. A white prawn, it has a hard shell and firm flesh with sweet flavor.

Tiny gray shrimp (*Crangon crangon*) belong to the sand shrimp family and are highly prized in Europe. They are gray or brown and translucent. This burrowing species is usually found in shallow, muddy, inshore waters. They are cooked and eaten whole, shell and all, or the meat may be picked out of their tiny tails. They have an intense "shrimpy" flavor.

Gulf whites (*Penaeus setiferus*) are sought after for their sweet, firm meat and have been fished commercially as far back as 1709. Gulf pinks (*P. duorarum*) are the largest Gulf species, up to 11 inches long and usually sold whole because two-thirds of their body length is in the head. They are tender and sweet with firm texture. Gulf browns (*P. aztecus*) have reddish brown shells and stronger flavor because of higher iodine content, so they are generally less expensive.

Northern pink shrimp are probably the most important commercial shrimp in the world, found in most northern waters. *P. borealis* is caught in the northern Atlantic, *P. jordani* in the northern Pacific. They are quite small, about 50 per pound, and are known as salad shrimp.

The large, mild, and sweet Pacific or Panamanian white shrimp (*P. vannamei*) is the leading farm-raised species in the Americas, especially in Ecuador, Venezuela, and Panama, and in the United States in Texas and South Carolina. Native to the Pacific coast from Mexico to Peru, these white-fleshed shrimp are flown to America during their short summer season for top-tier restaurants. They are also trawler-caught, though farmed are much more prevalent. Chinese white shrimp (*P. chinensis*) have soft, fragile, mild-tasting meat and grow to more than 7 inches. Because they sell for much less, they are sometimes passed off as more expensive Gulf or Pacific whites.

The Santa Barbara spot shrimp (*Pandalus platyceros*), or California spot prawn, is named for the four bright white spots on its body. It has a pink to red shell and sweet, firm flesh. Called *tarabaebi* in Japanese, they are a highly prized sushi bar item. Look for the delicious roe under their belly shells. The giant red shrimp (*Aristaeomorpha foliacea*) is a vibrant, deep red color and is harvested in many parts of the world, though not in large quantities.

Locale and Season:

Black tiger shrimp are found in Indo-Pacific waters with supplies at their peak June through November. The common prawn and the gray shrimp range from the Mediterranean to Norway. The endeavour prawn is harvested on the northeast coast of Australia. Gulf brown shrimp are found off the Texas-Louisiana coast; pinks on Mexico's Gulf coast; whites south of the Carolinas and in Florida, with the main harvest from the Gulf of Mexico. Prices for Gulf shrimp are highest in early summer, falling toward the winter holidays. Northern pink shrimp are in peak season from April through October. Pacific white shrimp are in season in summer. Santa Barbara spot shrimp are found from Alaska to San Diego year-round, though supply is greater in summer. Chinese white shrimp are farmed and wild-caught by trawlers in China and Korea. Peak season is from late September to October just after harvest.

Characteristics: Shrimp in retail markets are almost invariably frozen and defrosted, except near areas where they are caught. Tiger shrimp have dark stripes on grayish shells and stripes on the meat. When cooked, their shells turn bright red and the white flesh is tinted orange. Gulf brown shrimp have a special groove in the last tail segment that differentiates them from the more expensive whites. Small pink cold-water shrimp do not have to be deveined before eating.

How to Choose: In the food trade, shrimp are sold by count, or number per pound, and frozen in standard 5-pound (and 2 kilo) boxes in counts ranging from the largest U 10s (under 10 per pound) to the smallest 51–60s (51 to 60 per pound). The smaller the count, the larger and more expensive the shrimp. In retail markets, shrimp are sold as small, medium, large, or jumbo. Avoid black tiger shrimp with pitted shells or black spots on the shell. Choose shrimp that are resilient and moist; improperly frozen shrimp will be tough, dry, and fibrous. Look for shrimp from aquafarms that follow U.S. HAACP food safety protocols. Avoid Chinese white shrimp with chlorine, sulfur, or ammonia odors. An undesirable grassy odor is associated with pond-raised shrimp. Number One Pacific Whites are Mexico's top-grade of these desirable shrimp. Peeled shrimp are dipped in phosphates to minimize shrinkage. Avoid those that feel soapy; they have been soaked too long.

Storage: Refrigerate up to 2 days. Frozen shrimp may be stored
☐ x 2 up to three months in the freezer as long as they never melt or defrost; use within 2 days of thawing.

Preparation: • **To devein, cut along the back of the shrimp tail. Remove the long black vein and discard. Rinse under cold water, and drain well.**

• **Grill, poach, broil, sauté, bake, hot-smoke, bread or batter and deep-fry, or pan-fry. Take care to cook only until the tail meats are opaque and lightly curled. Save the shells for seafood stock.**

Suggested Recipe: **Shrimp Provençal** (serves 4): Sauté 1 1/2 pounds peeled, deveined shrimp in a large skillet just until pink, about 2 minutes. Transfer to a plate. Add 1/2 cup diced colorful bell peppers, 1/2 cup chopped red onion, 1 tablespoon each chopped garlic and thyme, and 1 teaspoon fennel seeds and cook until softened. Add 2 cups diced tomatoes, 1/2 cup halved Provençal olives, and 1/2 cup white wine and cook 10 minutes or until thickened. Add the shrimp and simmer 3 minutes, or until opaque. Mix in 1/2 cup shredded basil, season to taste with salt and pepper, and serve with rice.

Flavor Affinities: Basil, brandy, butter, chervil, coriander, cream, fennel, garlic, lemon, marjoram, oregano, paprika, red onion, saffron, shallot, sugar, tarragon, thyme, white wine.

STONE CRAB

Other Names: *Kani* (Japanese); *steinkrabbe* (German).

General
Description:

Stone crabs come from the southern United States, especially Florida, and get their name from their rocklike oval shell. Three species are harvested: the Florida crab (*Menippe mercenaria*); the Gulf crab (*M. adina*); and a hybrid of the two. The crabs are captured with traps and only one of the large, orange-tinted, black-tipped claws can be kept. If removed correctly, the crab can regenerate its claw in about three molts, 1 year to 18 months. It is illegal to land whole stone crabs. Stone crabs were made famous by Joe's Stone Crabs in Miami, Florida, which sells an enormous number every year, served cold with mustard sauce.

Locale and
Season:

Stone crabs are found only in the United States along the Atlantic and Gulf coasts from Texas to the Carolinas, but almost all the commercial harvest is from Florida. Stone crab season runs from October 15 to May 15, though they are also frozen.

Characteristics:

Claws are classified from medium (about 7 per pound) to the far rarer colossal (1 to 2 per pound) and are purchased already cooked and chilled. The shells turn orange when cooked. The raw meat is grayish-white; the cooked meat is white, mild, firm, succulent, and a bit stringy.

How to Choose:

Stone crab claws must be cooked immediately after harvest to prevent the meat from sticking to the inside of the shell and often have a slight sea odor. Check that the claw meat is free of the shell.

Storage: x 1	Store 1 day at most in the refrigerator, covered with damp newspapers. Freeze for up to 3 months. Do not leave at room temperature. Thaw frozen claws in the refrigerator overnight.
Preparation:	• **Claws are sold already cooked. Crack them with a mallet, hammer, or nutcracker. Serve with drawn butter and lemon, or mayonnaise and lime, or dill and lime vinaigrette.**
Suggested Recipe:	**Joe's Stone Crab–Style Mustard Sauce** (makes 1 1/4 cups): Combine 1 tablespoon dry mustard with 1 cup mayonnaise, 2 teaspoons Worcestershire sauce, 1 teaspoon A.1. steak sauce, 1/4 cup heavy cream, and salt and pepper to taste, mixing until creamy and smooth. Serve with chilled stone crab claws.
Flavor Affinities:	A.1. sauce, butter, cream, curry, dill, garlic, key lime, lemon, lime, mustard, olive oil, Pickapeppa sauce, white wine vinegar, Worcestershire sauce.

72a–b.

SPINY LOBSTER

Other Names:	**Caribbean spiny lobster:** *Iseebi-zoku* (Japanese); *lagosta das Caraíbas* (Portuguese); *langosta del Caribe* (Spanish); *langouste blanche* (French). **Baja blue lobster:** *Langosta azul* or *pinto* (Spanish); spiny lobster. **European spiny lobster:** *Aragosta* (Italian); *astakos* (Greek); *böcek* (Turkish); *iseebi* (Japanese); *lagosta* (Portuguese); *langosta* (Spanish); *langouste*

(French); *languste* (German); lobster tails; rock lobster.
Palinuridae.

General
Description:

Rock or spiny lobsters have wide, spiny tails without the large claws of the Atlantic lobster. Thirty species are found worldwide in tropical and subtropical waters, and they are prized for their firm tail meat, which accounts for one-third of their body weight. They are caught with traps and by divers. They are usually sold frozen, or live in season.

The Caribbean spiny lobster (*Panulirus argus*) accounts for 65 percent of the American market. Almost all the domestic American catch is from the Florida Keys, where stocks are well-managed. In the Caribbean, many populations are heavily fished and there are significant concerns about illegal catch. The California spiny lobster (*P. interruptus*) is caught in smaller numbers in California with more from the large Mexican fishery, which is certified sustainable by the Marine Stewardship Council. The Baja blue lobster (*P. inflatus*) is found along the California and Mexican Pacific coasts. Brilliant red-shelled when cooked, the Baja blue lobster's tail meat is firm, sweet, rich, and supple. The west Australian rock lobster (*P. cygnus*) is the second most important species in the United States. It is highly sought after and has been certified sustainable by the Marine Stewardship Council. The South African lobster (*Jasus ialandii*) is an important commercial species.

Locale and
Season:

Brazil and the Caribbean are the main sources of warm-water tails in the United States, while Australia, New Zealand, and South Africa supply most of the cold-water tails. The Caribbean spiny lobster is found from Bermuda to Brazil. Cold-water lobster is in peak season September through mid-March; warm-water lobster January through October. Fresh Florida spiny lobster is in season August through March.

Characteristics: Rock lobster tails range from 5 to 22 ounces with 8 ounces the most common size. Coldwater lobster tails tend to be more tender and succulent than those from warm waters. The cooked tail meat should be white with red tinges, firm, mild, and sweet. Pacific spiny lobsters will have green to orange shells; those from the Atlantic will be brown.

How to Choose: Coldwater tails are more expensive than warmwater tails, so substitutions are sometimes made. Warmwater tails are smooth with a greenish shell; coldwater tails are rough with a deep red-purple shell. If the cooked tail meat is gray rather than white, it was probably dead when processed and should be avoided. The sand vein in the center top of the tail should be completely clean. Any black spots may give the tail a strong ammonia taste. Cold-water tails are usually packed dry-wrapped in plastic. Avoid warmwater lobster tails that have been overglazed with too much ice. Frozen lobster tails tend to be tougher and may be a bit more rubbery than fresh. Caribbean spiny lobsters are often caught by divers who pull off the tails and hold them on ice, resulting in mushy texture if kept on ice too long.

Storage:
□ x 2

Freeze well-wrapped for up to 2 months. Defrost frozen lobster tails overnight in the refrigerator and use within 2 days. They may be cooked from frozen, but they tend to be more tender if thawed.

Preparation: •

To keep the tails from curling, run a skewer through the length of each tail. Brush thawed tails with butter or olive oil and bake, grill, broil, or steam until the meat is completely opaque, about 10 minutes. Serve with lemon, butter, hollandaise, or other sauce. Or remove cooked meat and sauté or use for crepe filling, salad, pasta sauce, or seafood casseroles.

Suggested
Recipe:

Broiled Rock Lobster with Citrus Butter (Serves 4): Butterfly 4 thawed rock lobster tails and arrange on a broiler pan shell-side down. Combine 1/4 cup melted butter, 1 tablespoon lemon juice, 1 tablespoon frozen orange juice concentrate, 1 tablespoon each grated orange zest and ginger, 1 teaspoon paprika, and salt and pepper to taste. Brush over lobster tail meat. Broil about 10 minutes, or until the meat is opaque.

Flavor
Affinities:

Basil, butter, chiles, cilantro, coconut, coriander, curry, fennel, fenugreek, ginger, lemon, lemongrass, scallion, shallot, soy sauce, tomato, turmeric, wild lime.

YABBY

Other Names: *Australischer flusskrebs* (German). **Parastacidae.**

General
Description:

Yabby (Cherax destructor) *is a large Australian freshwater crustacean with a delicate, sweet flavor.* The Queensland red claw has a bright red patch on the outside of the large claw; the marron is dark brown or black and sometimes bright blue. Farmed yabbies are raised in clean water, fed grains, and carefully processed. They are excellent steamed in spicy broth and served on a cold seafood platter. They are available in the United States, especially in restaurants.

Locale and
Season:

Yabbies come only from Australia and are found year-round, with peak season mid-October to mid-June.

Characteristics:

Yabbies are brown, green, and pale blue with mottled claws. They are meaty and don't have the muddy taste common to other freshwater shellfish. They are delivered chilled and live to the United States.

How to Choose:

Yabbies are graded by size and are classified buffet (1 to 2 ounces), medium (2 to 2 1/2 ounces), large (2 1/2 to 3 ounces), and extra-large (over 3 ounces).

Storage:

⊟ x 7

Yabbies will survive, live, for up to 7 days under refrigeration.

Preparation: 1.

Cook yabbies live in boiling water, court bouillon, or other flavored liquid, 5 to 6 minutes, or until the meat is opaque and the tail starts to curl.

 2.

Cool, remove the tail shell only, and serve. Or remove cooked tail meat from shell and sauté or use for crepe filling, pasta sauce, or seafood casseroles. They can be

split and grilled, or cooked, shelled, and used in
pasta dishes, salads, and stir-fries.

Suggested
Recipe:

Yabbies with Lime and Coriander (serves 4):
Combine 2 finely chopped green chiles, 2 teaspoons
chopped garlic, 1 diced tomato, 1 tablespoon sugar,
1 tablespoon olive oil, and salt to taste. Cook over
medium heat 2 to 3 minutes, or until soft. Cool, then
whisk in the juice of 1 lime, 1/4 cup chopped cilantro,
and 3 tablespoons more olive oil and reserve. Bring
1 quart water, 1 cup dark beer, 1/2 cup brown sugar,
and 2 tablespoons salt to a boil and boil for 5 minutes. Add 2 pounds live yabbies, and boil for 5 to 6
minutes or until opaque. Remove the yabbies from
the pot, cool, then remove the tail shell only and
serve with the sauce.

Flavor
Affinities:

Bean curd, butter, cilantro, garlic, green chiles, lemon
myrtle, lime, mustard, olive oil, scallion, sesame, snow
peas, tomato, white wine, wild lime.

Other Water Creatures

73a-b.

FROG LEGS

Other Names:
Ancas de rana (Spanish); *cosce de rana* (Italian); *cuisses de grenouille* (French); *froschschenkel* (German); *hanyu pinyin* (Chinese). **Ranidae**.

General
Description:
The edible frog (Rana esculenta) is an amphibian that has long been enjoyed for its tender, delicate rear legs. Chinese, Germans, and Italians eat them in quantity, and in America they're a specialty of Cajun Louisiana. Sautéed frog legs is a dish of French haute cuisine, while garlicky frog legs Provençal is a rustic dish.

Locale and
Season:
Frog legs are both wild and farmed. Peak season for wild frogs is in the rainy months from May to October. Fresh frog legs from Florida are in season in early spring. Frozen frog legs are available year-round.

Characteristics:
Frog legs are mild in flavor. Their tender meat is most similar to chicken wings. They are sold by the number of leg pairs per pound, ranging from the largest at 2/4 count to the smallest at 16/20 count; the most popular are 4/6 and 6/8 count.

How to Choose:
Frog legs are removed either at or below the pelvis and called either saddle-on or saddle-off. Saddle-off are preferred because they're fully trimmed. All frog legs are sold skinless. Aquacultured frog legs are lighter in color and milder in taste than wild; they

are also cleaner. This is significant, as wild frog legs are susceptible to salmonella contamination.

Storage: Store fresh frog legs up to 2 days refrigerated. Store
x 2   frozen frog legs up to 3 months frozen.

Preparation: 1. **Rinse thawed or fresh legs in several changes of cold**
              water and pat dry.

    2. **For larger frog legs, scald 3 minutes in 2 quarts boil-**
              ing water mixed with ¹/₂ cup lemon juice and salt.
              Remove, dry with clean towel, season to taste with
              salt and pepper, and then proceed with recipe.
              Smaller frog legs may be seasoned, then cooked.

    3. **Sauté, batter and deep-fry, bake, pan-fry, or broil.**

Suggested   **Cajun Fried Frog Legs** (serves 4): Beat 4 eggs, then
Recipe: mix in 2 cups of flour. Add ¹/₂ cup milk and mix,
            then add ¹/₂ cup wine. Season to taste with salt and
            reserve. Combine ¹/₂ cup each cornmeal and flour
            with 1 teaspoon each cayenne, garlic powder, and
            onion powder. Dip 12 frog legs into the egg mixture,
            then the cornmeal mixture. Heat 1 quart canola oil
            to 365°F or until shimmering hot, then deep-fry the
            frog legs until brown and crispy, 6 to 8 minutes.

Flavor   Butter, cayenne, celery, cornmeal, garlic, lemon, hot
Affinities: sauce, mushrooms, onion, paprika, parsley, shallot,
            thyme, tomato, white wine, Worcestershire sauce.

SEA CUCUMBER

Other Names:
Beche-de-mer, holthurie (French); *hai shén* (Chinese); *hoy sum* (Hong Kong); *loli okuhi kuhi* (Hawaiian); *namako* (Japanese); *olothuria* (Italian); sea rat; sea slug; *seegurke* (German); *tripang* (Indonesia). **Holothuroidae**.

General Description:
Sea cucumbers are an abundant and diverse group of cucumber-shaped, soft-bodied echinoderms related to sea urchins and starfish. Prized for its gelatinous texture and supposed aphrodisiac qualities, the sea cucumber is a delicacy in Chinese cuisine. Rather bland on their own, sea cucumbers absorb and accentuate the flavors of the ingredients in which they are cooked. Sea cucumbers are usually purchased already cleaned, in a complex process that takes several days, and then rehydrated before use.

Locale and Season:
In Canada, sea cucumbers are a byproduct of the scallop fishery in May through November. In China, *Stichopus japonicus* are farm-raised and harvested in spring and fall.

Characteristics:
Sea cucumbers can be held live in seawater until they are processed. Their average weight is $1/2$ to 1 pound. They are gelatinous and mildly clamlike in flavor.

How to Choose:
The main species found in Canadian waters, *Cucumaria frondosa*, is reddish purple with five bands of tube feet and ten tentacles. In China, the best kind of fresh sea cucumber is black with a smooth surface

and fine gloss.

Storage:
🗄️ x 1

Store dried sea cucumber at room temperature. Store soaked dried cucumber for 1 to 2 days, refrigerated. Store fresh cleaned sea cucumber 1 day, refrigerated.

Preparation: 1.
🚰

Rinse and boil fresh cleaned sea cucumber before further cooking.

🥘 🍲 2.

Stir-fry, simmer in rich stock, braise, or stew.

Suggested Recipe:
🥣 🔪 ⏳ 🥣

Chinese Hacked Chicken with Sea Cucumber (serves 4): Marinate 1 pound hacked chicken drumstick pieces with 1/4 cup soy sauce for 20 minutes. Place 1 pound soaked, rinsed, and sliced sea cucumber with a 1-inch section of smashed ginger in a nonstick skillet and stir-fry without oil until almost dry. Add 2 tablespoons rice wine and cook 2 minutes. Remove the sea cucumber and reserve. Separately, briefly fry 1 tablespoon each chopped shallots and garlic and 2 tablespoons chopped ginger in a thin layer of canola oil. Add 8 to 10 soaked and dried shiitake mushrooms, the chicken pieces, and the sea cucumber. Add 2 cups chicken stock, 2 tablespoons soy sauce, 1 tablespoon oyster sauce, a pinch of sugar, and salt and pepper to taste. Cover and simmer 45 minutes or until sea cucumber is tender. Thicken with cornstarch mixed with water.

Flavor Affinities:

Abalone, dried shiitake mushrooms, garlic, ginger, ham, oyster sauce, rice wine, shrimp, soy sauce.

74.   **SEA URCHIN**

Other Names: *Achinós* (Greek); *deniz kestanesi* (Turkish); *erizo de mar* (Spanish); *morskoy yezh* (Russian); *orsino, riccio di mare* (Italian); *ouriço do mar* (Portuguese); *oursin* (French); *seeigel* (German); *sjoeppinsvin* (Norwegian); *uni* (Japanese). **Echnidae**, **Stronglyocentrotidae**.

General Description: *Sea urchins are spine-encrusted globes that resemble seagoing porcupines.* There are about 500 species of sea urchins, but the most valuable commercially are the red (*Echinus esculentus*), the green (*Strongylocentrotus drobachiensis*), and the purple (*Paracentrotus lividus*). They are considered a great delicacy in many parts of the world. These baseball-sized, spiny creatures have a hard shell containing a star-shaped, orange-colored mass that is the edible portion and is either the gonads of the male or the eggs of the female. In America, West Coast urchins are harvested by divers; East Coast urchins are harvested by divers and by trawlers. The roe may be found in Asian markets.

Locale and Season: The red sea urchin is found throughout northern Europe and the Mediterranean. Red, green, and purple sea urchins are harvested on the American Pacific coast. Green sea urchins are commercially harvested on the American Atlantic coast. The largest American producers are California for red urchins and Maine for green urchins. Peak season for red urchins is October to May; peak season for green urchins is November to March.

Characteristics:	The red is the largest, about 7 inches in diameter. The green is the smallest, at 1^1/$_2$ inches in diameter. The roe ranges in color from bright yellow to deep orange. Sea urchin roe should taste sweet and have a smooth, rich, buttery texture. The male "roe," actually the gonads, is fine and silky, the female's more grainy.
How to Choose:	Choose sweet-smelling live sea urchins. Choose sea urchin roe with the membrane enclosing the roe completely intact. Preserved roe, or uni, at the market has been soaked in an alum and salt solution to firm.
Storage:	Prepare live sea urchins the day they're purchased or harvested. Store the roe refrigerated 2 to 3 days.

Preparation:

1. **To clean live sea urchin, insert heavy shears into the hole on the domed top. Cut around the top of the shell, cutting toward the outer edge, exposing the flesh. Pour away the liquid and the dark viscera.**

2. **Inside are 5 pairs of roe that go from top to bottom on the inside of the shell. Carefully run a rubber spatula under the roe, along the inside of the shell. The roe is incredibly fragile; try to keep it whole. Use your fingers or tweezers to remove any viscera.**

3. **Rinse the roe in cold water and drain well.**

4. **Sauté, steam, add to sauces, or eat raw with a squeeze of lemon.**

Suggested
Recipe:

Creamed Sea Urchin on Toast (serves 6): Sauté 3 tablespoons chopped shallots in 2 tablespoons butter until softened. Add 1 cup white wine and cook until syrupy, about 6 minutes. Add 2 cups heavy cream and cook down again until thickened, about 8 minutes. Press 3/4 pound sea urchin roe through a sieve into the mixture. Combine gently, season with salt and white pepper, and stir in 2 tablespoons sliced chives. Serve on toast spread with garlic butter.

Flavor
Affinities:

Butter, cayenne, chives, cream, dashi, garlic, lemon, lime, mirin, mushroom, nori, olive oil, scallion, shallot, shiso, soy sauce, water chestnuts, white wine.

TURTLE

Other Names:

Caguama (Mexico); *schildkröte* (German); *tartaruga* (Italian); *tortue* (French); *tortuga* (Spanish). **Cheloniidae** (sea turtle), **Eemydidae** (freshwater turtle), **Testudinidae** (tortoise).

General
Description:

The turtle is an ancient four-limbed reptile topped with a hard shell that lives on land and in the sea and fresh water. Freshwater turtles live and are eaten in most regions of the world. Terrapins are freshwater and salt-marsh turtles; tortoises are land turtles. The diamondback terrapin (*Malaclemys terrapin*), from the Chesapeake Bay region, is reputed to be the best for eating and for its eggs, though it is illegal to eat in many places in the United States. The leatherback turtle (*Dermochelys coriacea*) has eggs that are regarded as an aphrodisiac. The loggerhead turtle (*Caretta caretta*) is used to make a famous Maltese stew called *stuffat tal-fekruna*. There are seven surviving species of large slow-growing sea turtles, all of which are endangered. Early explorers on long voyages captured live turtles and kept them on board for food as needed, especially the Caribbean green turtle (*Chelonia mydas*), still a favored island meat. Sea turtle soup became a standard in English cookery. Today in America, snapping turtle (*Chelydra serpentina*) is used for soup.

Locale and
Season:

Snapping turtles live in freshwater in the Western Hemisphere only. Diamondback terrapins live along the American Atlantic and Gulf coasts. Soft-shelled turtles live in freshwater in Africa, America, and Asia. Tortoises are found in Africa, Asia, Europe, and the Americas.

Characteristics:

American snapping turtles can be dangerous to handle. They account for about half the turtles eaten in the eastern United States. They average 15 to 25 pounds and can live in a wide range of freshwater habitats. The calipee and calipash found inside the green sea turtle impart the characteristic gelatinous quality to British turtle soup. The calipee is a light yellow, fatty gelatinous substance in the upper part of the shell; the calipash is a dull green similar substance found in the lower part of the shell. Connoisseurs judge whether turtle soup is authentic by the lumps of calipash and calipee it contains. Because sea turtles lay their eggs in deep holes on shore, they are vulnerable and the eggs are illegal to eat in most places.

How to Choose: Snapping turtle has the texture of frog legs or lobster. The four legs and the tail are dark meat; the neck and back straps are white meat. The meat is sold semi-boneless and boneless and is frozen. Asian soft-shelled turtle is found for sale, also frozen, but may be from illegal species.

Storage: A live snapping turtle should be kept in a tub of clean water for 1 to 2 weeks, changing the water every few days until it remains relatively clear.

Preparation: • **Because of the complicated purging, cleaning, and preparation involved, many feel that turtle soup should be purchased rather than making it at home.**

• **The best results are obtained by parboiling the meat until it can be easily removed from the bone.**

Suggested Recipe: **Turtle Soup with Sherry** (serves 6): Melt $1/2$ pound butter in a heavy pot, add 1 cup flour, and cook, stirring frequently, over medium heat until the roux is light brown. Set aside. In a large soup pot, melt 2 tablespoons butter and add 1 pound diced turtle meat. Brown over high heat, about 8 minutes. Add 1 cup each diced onions and celery, 2 teaspoons chopped garlic, 3 bay leaves, 2 teaspoons dried oregano, and 1 teaspoon dried thyme and cook until the vegetables are soft. Add $11/2$ cups tomato puree and simmer 10 minutes. Add 1 quart rich beef or veal

stock and simmer 30 minutes. Add the roux by the
spoonful until the soup is thickened. Season with salt
and pepper, add $1/4$ cup lemon juice and $1/2$ cup
chopped parsley, and serve. Garnish with sliced
hard-cooked eggs and sherry.

Flavor
Affinities: Bay leaf, brandy, butter, celery, cream, egg, garlic,
lemon, onion, oregano, thyme, tomato, white wine.

Preserved Fish and Seafood

75. 📷 Anchovies

Acchiuge, *alici* (Italian); *anchois* (French); *boquerones* (Spanish). Anchovies are a small, highly perishable warm-water fish (p. 7) that are often salted to preserve them. Once rinsed, the anchovies are quite mild and firm in texture. Before using, rinse under tepid water, discarding the bones and innards. Eat right away, or layer with olive oil and refrigerate up to three weeks. Salted anchovies have been popular since ancient times and are ingredients in pizza, Provençal pissaladière, and salade niçoise.

Tinned anchovies are salted, washed, filleted, and packed in olive or other vegetable oil. White anchovies (or boquerones), which are filleted and lightly cured in vinegar and oil, are more perishable than canned or salt-packed anchovies but delicate and mild enough to enjoy right out of the package. They will usually be found in clear plastic modified-atmosphere packaging in specialty markets. Store all types of cured anchovies in the refrigerator for up to 6 months, because they will deteriorate if not kept cold. Opened jars of anchovies will keep, closed tightly and refrigerated, for up to 1 month.

76. 📷 Asian Fish Sauce

Fish sauce is a pungent-smelling, salty, thin, clear brown liquid made from fermented fish and is important to the cuisines of Southeast Asia. Used like salt in western cooking and soy sauce in Chinese cooking, it is directly related to the garum fish sauce made in classical times by the Romans. Many brands of fish sauce can be found in Asian markets.

Bombay Duck

Bamaloh (Bengali); *bumla* (Gujurati); *bombii* (Marathi); *bummalo* (Bengali). Called Bombay duck in English for unclear reasons, this is a dried, salted lizardfish (*Harpadon nehereus*) found in the Arabian Sea and the Bay of Bengal. After drying, Bombay duck has an extremely strong aroma and must be packed in airtight containers. It is commonly used as a condiment for curries. The bones of the fish are soft and edible. The importing of dried Bombay duck had been banned by the European Union because of health concerns about drying methods, though that ban has been rescinded.

77. 📷 Bottarga

Botargo (north Africa); *boutargue* (French). Sometimes called "poor man's caviar," bottarga (the name comes from the Arabic *butarikh*, "salted fish eggs") is the dried roe of tuna or gray mullet, or occasionally swordfish. In Italy, it is a condiment typical of Sardinia but also found in Sicily, Liguria, and Calabria. The roe is sold in small blocks that are shaved, chopped, grated, sliced, or ground to use as a seasoning for pasta sauces, rice, salads, or spreads. Sardinia prefers the gray mullet roe, whereas Sicily prefers tuna roe. In Japan, the similar karasumi is made from mullet roe that is salted then soaked in fresh water before drying. See also tarama, p. 293.

78. Canned Tuna

In the Mediterranean, which has a 2,000-year-old tuna fishing industry, there is a long tradition of preserving tuna by canning it in olive oil. The best canned tuna can be likened to a confit of tuna, oil-poached tuna that melts in your mouth. Tunisian, Spanish, French, and Italian canned tuna can be superb. Ventresca, or belly, the fattest portion, is considered the best. Water-packed solid white-meat tuna has been the gold standard in America, but it can be mealy and dry. Yellowfin (also called light tuna), packed in olive oil, is the type used in the Mediterranean. Solid-pack tuna consists of large pieces tightly packed together; chunk tuna has small fragments. Use canned tuna in mixed salads, stuffed vegetables, hors d'oeuvres, or sandwiches.

Caviar

Ikra (Russian); *khag-avar* (Persian). Caviar is the processed, salted roe of sturgeon mostly fished from the Caspian and Black Seas; beluga, ossetra, and sevruga caviars are the most expensive. Beluga, with its large smooth eggs, varies from pale to dark gray and is known for the "pop" of the egg bursting in the mouth. This delicately flavored, buttery, and creamy caviar is among the rarest of caviars and commands a high price. Ossetra is smaller than beluga, most commonly dark brown in color, with a more assertive, nutty, and rich flavor. Sevruga is smaller and is light to dark gray with an intense, rich flavor. The rare golden sterlet caviar was once the favorite of royalty, but the species is now nearly extinct. Pressed caviar is a blend of ossetra and sevruga that consists of broken fish eggs pressed to remove excess salt and oil and contains four times more roe than fresh caviar of the same weight. It is dry, spreadable, and considered a delicacy, especially in Russia, where it is preferred for its highly concentrated flavor.

In the United States, only the roe of sturgeon and paddlefish may be termed caviar. Malossol caviar means "little salt" in Russian and indicates that the caviar has been processed with a minimum of salt. Caviar usually contains 4 to 8 percent salt, with the better types containing less salt. Slow-growing prehistoric sturgeons have been over-fished, and illegal trading of Caspian caviar has led to their near extinction, so farmed caviar has become more common.

White sturgeon (p. 164) is farm-raised in California for its caviar and is most similar to ossetra. Lake sturgeon (*Acipenser fulvescens*) produces caviar comparable to Russian beluga but is only available from Canada. Hackleback sturgeon (*Scaphiryhnchus platory-hnchus*) is native to the Mississippi and Missouri Rivers and faster growing and smaller than most sturgeon. Its roe is dark and medium-sized with sweet, buttery, nutty flavor. Paddlefish (*Polyodon spathula*), or spoonbill, are cartilaginous cousins to the sturgeon and also native to North America. Their roe ranges from pale through dark steel-gray to golden and is smooth and silky with a rich, complex flavor. Paddlefish are considered endangered, so only one American company, Osage Catfisheries, is permitted to sell both the fish and the roe. Farmed caviar is available year-round, with some variability of supply and winter the best season. Caviar has a shelf life of up to 1 year, if kept tightly sealed and extra-cold in the refrigerator. It is served with gold, horn, wood, mother-of-pearl, or plastic utensils because other metals may alter its taste and color. In the United States, the import of beluga caviar from the Caspian and Black Seas has been banned since September 2005.

79. Colatura di Alici

Colatura di alici is a strong, salty, clear liquid sauce made from the juices of salt-packed anchovies. This artisanal product from southern Italy is the modern equivalent to the ancient Roman garum and is similar to Asian fish sauce (p. 285). Add a few drops to pasta sauces or fish and seafood dishes for seasoning.

Dashi

Dashi is a delicately flavored Japanese stock essential to Japanese cuisine, often sprinkled on food as a seasoning. Fresh dashi is rare today, even in Japan; instead, people use granulated or liquid instant substitutes. To make it, bonito (p. 26) are boiled whole and cut into halves. The bones and skin are removed, and the good parts are smoked and dried in the sun repeatedly for about six months, finally yielding hard blocks. A small part of the washed block is shaved thinly, using a special plane. The slices, called *katsuo-bushi*, are boiled with kombu (kelp) to make dashi. Prepared dashi can be found bottled in Asian markets.

Dried Scallops

Gan bei (Chinese). Dried scallops are one of the four treasures of Chinese cooking (p. 291) and are a prized ingredient sold for high prices as a flavoring for soups, sauces, and other dishes. The scallops, once soaked to rehydrate, are shredded and used in small quantities. Store them in a covered jar at room temperature.

80. 📷 **Dried Shrimp**

Camarão seco (Brazil)*; ebi* (Japanese); *eibei* (Indonesian); *goong haeng* (Thai); *hay bee* (Chinese); *tom kho* (Vietnamese); *udang kering* (Malaysian). Dried shrimp are commonly added to stir-fries and soups in Asian, African, and Brazilian cuisine for their pungent flavor. These small dried shrimp are sold in plastic packets either whole or shredded (labeled powder or floss), with the whole shrimp preferred. Dried shrimp should be deep salmon pink and yield only slightly to the touch; avoid woody shrimp or any that smell strongly of ammonia. Kept refrigerated, they should last for up to 6 months. If they become powdery or start to disintegrate, discard.

81. 📷 **Dried Squid**

Considered a delicacy to the Chinese, dried squid is produced from cleaned squid that are sun-dried. It has a strong smell and chewy texture and is used to add a distinctive flavor to soups and other dishes. Dried squid is soaked in water overnight to soften before using. Some cooks add a pinch of baking soda so the squid will expand and soften further. Some dried squid are cut in a special machine that slits them so they're ready to eat as a snack popular in Korea, especially with drinks.

Finnan Haddie

Also called finnan or findan haddock, finnan haddie is cleaned and headed split haddock from Scotland that is lightly salted and cold-smoked. Finnan haddie can be simply grilled with butter for a British-style breakfast, simmered with milk and onions for a delicately flavored fish stew, or used for chowder.

82. 📷 **Fish Roe**

The roe of many types of fish are enjoyed around the world, though in the United States, only the roe of sturgeon may be termed caviar (p. 286). Brook and rainbow trout roe is orange in color; it looks similar to but is smaller than salmon roe. It can be sticky in texture. Cod roe is packed in tubes, especially in Scandinavia, as a cheaper version of caviar used as a sandwich topping. Masago is the orange roe of capelin, a small fish related to smelt. It is popular for sushi, especially for the outside or as a topping for maki rolls. Salmon roe, sold in Japan as *kura* (eggs) or *sujiko* (whole skeins), is now widely available in the United States. Eggs from chum salmon are most desirable because of their thin outer membrane, tender texture, and appealing orange color. Salmon roe is harvested from wild salmon during their season, May to November. Whitefish roe is apricot-colored and has a mild flavor. See tarama (p. 293) and tobiko (p. 293).

Gravlax

Graavilohi (Finnish); *graflax* (Icelandic); *gravad laks* (Danish); *gravlaks* (Norwegian). Gravlax is salmon cured in a mixture of sugar, salt, and dill until it is firm enough to slice thinly, usually 2 to 3 days. Popular in all countries of Scandinavia, gravlax is traditionally served with a sweet and sour dill and mustard sauce and crispbread.

Gulbi

Gulbi is dried salted yellow croaker; in Korea, where it is popular, it is thought to stimulate the body. Fishers have to be very careful when catching the fish, as just a scratch will diminish its freshness. The taste of the yellow gulbi can vary in accordance with the weather. Only natural salt stored for over a year is used to prepare this fish, which is sun- and wind-dried for preservation. This rather oily fish has a full-bodied, rich flavor when dried. Its salted roe is also eaten.

83. Herring

Herring (p. 77) are cured in many styles and are most popular in northern Europe, Scandinavia, and eastern Europe. Bismarck herring is a vinegar-cured skin-on herring fillet, usually packed with sugar and sliced onions. Bloaters are whole salted and smoked herring, prized in Great Britain. Herring in sour cream is common in New York's Jewish community. Kippers are split whole herring with both sides attached at the back that is cold-smoked. The best kippers have a silvery-red color from long smoking, though they may also be artificially dyed. Rollmops are pickled herring fillets (Bismarcks) rolled up and fastened with a toothpick. Cured or pickled herring will keep up to one year, refrigerated. Smoked whole kippers and fillets have a limited shelf life but can be kept frozen for up to 1 year.

Lutefisk

Lutefisk is a highly pungent traditional food of Scandinavia made from air-dried stockfish (p. 292) and caustic lye. In Scandinavia and American Scandinavian communities, lutefisk is typically served for the Christmas season. Lutefisk prepared from cod is notorious for its intense odor; if made from pollock or haddock, it has little odor. To cook it, lutefisk is steamed at low heat for about 20 minutes until soft. It is mild and mellow in flavor and is often served in a spiced white sauce. Many Scandinavians claim their strength and longevity are derived from eating lutefisk at least once a year, and it is a point of pride to do so.

Mojama

Mochama (Portuguese); *musciame* (Italian). This Spanish salt-cured, air-dried tuna loin is comparable to prosciutto (air-dried pork leg). Mojama is most commonly found in southern Spain. Mojama is most often served in thin, translucent slices, drenched in fine extra-virgin olive oil. In Italy a similar salt-cured air-dried tuna loin, called *musciame*, is a Sardinian specialty. Originally it was made with dolphin loin, now illegal.

84. 📷 **Salt Cod**

Bacala (Spanish); *baccalà* (Italian), *bacalao* (Portuguese), *morue* (French). By the year 1000, Basque fishers were fishing cod in a major way off the coast of Newfoundland and preserving it with the salt they had in abundance. When purchasing salt cod, look for ivory-colored flesh with a faint tint of green or yellow. Bright white color can mean that the fish has been artificially treated or is overly salty. Soaked salt cod can be cooked directly in a sauce, as long as the liquid is kept to a bare simmer (boiling toughens salt cod and turns it stringy), though it is often pan-fried first. Whole salt cod has more flavor and more natural gelatin to give extra body to a sauce, but boneless, skinless fillets are easier to handle. Salt cod will keep perfectly for months if well wrapped and refrigerated.

To prepare salt cod, rinse the fish under cold running water until there are no more hard salt crystals on the surface. Place the fish in a large bowl, cover with cold water, and soak overnight, refrigerated, changing the water once or twice. Once the fish has soaked sufficiently, it will be plump and pliable and the soaking water will not taste unpleasantly salty. Drain the salt cod and place in a large pot with cold water to cover. Bring to a boil, then reduce heat and simmer for 10 minutes, or until the fish flakes easily. Drain the fish, flake into large chunks, making sure to remove and discard any bones, and reserve. Caribbean, Asian, Portuguese, and Italian markets are the places to find whole salt cod, especially for Christmas.

85. 📷 **Sardines**

Sardines (p. 141) were first canned at the beginning of the nineteenth century, when Napoleon recognized the need to preserve food. Sardines are so popular that their population has been depleted considerably. Sardines are commonly packed in olive or other vegetable oil, tomato sauce, or mustard sauce with seasonings such as cayenne pepper and salt. Good sardines have silvery skin with firm, pinkish flesh and meaty flavor. They should be uniform in length and width and tightly and evenly packed in the tin. Their aroma should be mild and pleasant and the oil heavy and clear.

Shark Fin

Dried shark fins are used to make a soup, *yú chì*, served for prestige at Chinese special occasion feasts, such as weddings. It is made from the skinned, trimmed, and dried cartilaginous pectoral and dorsal fins from several shark species, especially the hammerhead, mako, and blue shark. Though it has little flavor, the individual shark fin "needles" have a flexible consistency, light brittle crunch, and impart their slippery and glutinous texture to the soup. Genuine shark fins are in high demand in Hong Kong. Shark fin is one of the four treasures of the sea in Chinese cuisine, including abalone, sea cucumber, and dried scallops. Fake shark fin is made from mung bean pasta shaped like shark fins. According to conservationists, much of the shark fins are cut from living sharks in a process called finning, leading to a rapid decline in global shark populations. Shark fins have also been reported to have high levels of toxic mercury.

Shrimp Paste

Belacan, *balachang* (Malay); *bagoong alamang* (Filipino); *kapi* (Thai); *terasi* or *trassi* (Indonesian). Dried shrimp paste is a common ingredient used in Southeast Asian and southern Chinese cuisine; it is made from fermented ground shrimp. It has a notoriously pungent aroma and powerful flavor that provides an essential undertone to these cuisines. Shrimp pastes range from pale, thin liquids to solid, chocolate-colored blocks. While all shrimp paste has a strong smell, higher grades can have a more pleasant aroma. Shrimp paste is commonly used in Malaysian sambal belacan, an intensely flavored sauce made by mixing belacan with chile peppers, minced garlic, shallot paste, and sugar. Terasi, from Indonesia, is usually sold in dark blocks but is also sometimes sold ground. Bagoong alamang is Filipino shrimp paste, made from tiny shrimp; it ranges from pink and salty to brown and sweet. Dried shrimp paste does not require refrigeration, but it should be wrapped in aluminum foil to contain its potent odor. ˙

Smoked Eel

Smoked eel is a specialty of Quebec, Canada, where there has been an active fishery since colonial times. It is also quite popular in northern Europe, much of it imported from Ireland. Large silver eels are preferred because their size and higher fat content yield a better smoked product. Most is sold whole and should be skinned, then thinly sliced. The jelly and oil from inside the skin is served with the sliced eel as an appetizer.

86a-b. 📷 Smoked Fish

Smoked sable or black cod (p. 37), known as "the poor man's sturgeon," is highly prized for its mild and juicy flavor. It is usually lightly coated with paprika. Smoked sturgeon is the queen of all smoked fish, rich and buttery and considered a delicacy. Smoked whitefish is a specialty of Jewish delis. Whitefish (p. 188) from the Great Lakes are smoked whole to a golden color. The fish are then filleted and mixed with mayonnaise and other ingredients to make the popular whitefish salad. Smoked chubs are a smaller version of a whitefish with tender and mild meat. Smoked trout are hot-smoked for a delicately flavored, tender meat that may be served as is or crumbled on top of salads or other appetizers. Cold-smoked yellowfin tuna is firm with mild flavor. It is served in thin slices like smoked salmon with lemon and pepper or with crème fraîche. Peppered mackerel is infused with honey, black pepper, and spices to make a small hot-smoked fillet with soft, flavorful meat. It is usually served whole as an individual portion. Smoked whiting is soft and moist and is sold head-off. See unagi (opposite).

87. 📷 Smoked Salmon, Lox, Kippered Salmon, and Salmon Jerky

Smoked salmon is usually a fillet that has been cured with salt and often sugar and then hot or cold smoked. Cold-smoked salmon, in which the smoke does not cook the fish, has a characteristic smooth, firm texture, close to that of the raw fish. It usually sells for a high price, especially if prepared from wild fish. Cold-smoked salmon is served thinly sliced and garnished with chopped onion and hard-cooked egg, capers, and lemon. The best wild Scottish smoked salmon is lean, gamey, and creamy-smooth, with a light oak smoke flavor. Russian style is a steak-cut fillet of salmon that is lightly smoked. Hot-smoked salmon has been cooked by the smoking process and has the texture of cooked salmon; it is known as kippered salmon. Hard-smoked salmon or salmon jerky is a traditional way of preparing salmon for Amerindians of the Pacific Northwest coast, often smoked over alder wood. Smoked salmon may be used as a cooking ingredient, in quiche, pasta sauce, scrambled eggs (lox and eggs), or even pizza. Lox refers to the stronger-tasting salted and cured salmon that has not been smoked.

Stockfish

Stoccafisso (Italian). Stockfish is unsalted fish dried naturally by sun and wind on wooden racks, or in special drying houses, in the world's oldest known preservation method.

Stockfish keeps for several years. Cod is the most common stockfish production, but other lean white-meat fish, such as pollock, haddock, ling, and cusk, are used. Stockfish is a specialty of Norway, from whence it is exported to market, especially to Italy and Croatia. Drying evaporates 70 percent of the water in the fish so that it is board hard. Cooked stockfish is a specialty of Venice, Italy, where is it known as *baccalà*, elsewhere a name for salt cod.

88. Surimi

Surimi, meaning "ground meat" in Japanese, is made from lean white-fleshed fish, often pollock or hake, ground to a fine paste so that it is rubbery and firm when cooked. Surimi is available in many shapes, forms, and textures. The most common surimi product in the West is imitation king crab legs, often called sea legs. In Asia, surimi is eaten as a food of its own and is seldom used to imitate other foods. In Japan, fish cakes, called *kamaboko*, and fish sausages, as well as other extruded fish products, are commonly sold as cured surimi.

Tarama

Tarama is a Greek specialty of salted carp, cod, or gray mullet roe traditionally preserved in a layer of dried beeswax. There are two types of tarama: white, considered superior, and dyed pink, which is most common. Taramasalata is a spread made with the salted roe mashed with bread, olive oil, and lemon juice.

89. Tobiko

Tobiko is the roe of Japanese flying fish (*Exocoetus volitans*), used to create certain types of sushi. The very small, loose, salted eggs are usually orange or pale yellow with light briny flavor and a crunchy, popping texture. It is now available in a range of colors, from green to gold to red to black, and flavors, including wasabi and jalapeño.

90. Unagi

Unagi is broiled eel glazed with a sweet basting sauce and is a delicacy in Japan traditionally eaten during one of the hottest days of summer to provide strength and vitality for the rest of the year. Unagi combines rich flavor with a crisp, caramelized outside and tender light inside. It may be purchased at Asian markets.

Table of Equivalencies

Weight

U.S.	Metric
1 oz	28 g
16 oz (1 lb)	454 g
2.2 lb	1 kg

Length

U.S.	Metric
1 in	2.5 cm
1 ft	30.5 cm
1 yd	91.4 cm

Volume

U.S.	Metric
1 tsp	5 ml
1 tbsp (3 tsp)	15 ml
$^1/_2$ cup	120 ml
1 cup	240 ml

Oven Temperature

Degrees Fahrenheit	Degrees Centigrade	British Gas Marks
325	165	3
350	175	4
375	190	5
400	200	6
450	230	8
500	260	10

Index

Numbers in **bold** (for example, **1**) can be used to locate fish and seafood in the photograph section. All other numbers are page numbers.

Sources: Books

Bittman, Mark. *Fish: The Complete Guide to Buying and Cooking*. New York: Macmillan Publishing Company, 1994.

Brown Jr., Paul B., ed. *The Commercial Guide to Fish and Shellfish*. Tom's River, New Jersey: Urner Barry Publications, 2006.

Davidson, Alan. *North Atlantic Seafood: A Complete Guide to the Fish and Shellfish of the North Atlantic with Over 270 Recipes from 20 Countries*. New York: The Viking Press, 1979.

Davidson, Alan. *Mediterranean Seafood: A Comprehensive Guide with Recipes*. Berkeley, California: Ten Speed Press, 2002.

———. *Seafood of Southeast Asia: A Comprehensive Guide with Recipes*. Berkeley, California: Ten Speed Press, 2003.

Gibbons, Euell. *Stalking the Blue-Eyed Scallop*. New York: David McKay Company, 1964.

Goodson, Gail. *Fishes of the Pacific Coast*. Stanford, California: Stanford University Press, 1988.

Johnson, Howard, and Peter Redmayne. *Sourcing Seafood: A Professional's Guide to Procuring Ocean-Friendly Fish and Shellfish*. Washington, DC: Seafood Choices Alliance, 2004.

Kurlansky, Mark. *Cod: A Biography of the Fish That Changed the World*. New York: Penguin Books, 1997.

McClane, A. J. *McClane's New Standard Fishing Encyclopedia and International Angling Guide*. New York: Holt, Rinehart, and Winston, 1965.

———. *The Encyclopedia of Fish Cookery*. New York: Holt, Rinehart, and Winston, 1977.

———. *McClane's Fish Buyer's Guide*. New York: Henry Holt and Company, 1990.

Olney, Richard, ed. *The Good Cook: Fish by the Editors of Time-Life Books*. Alexandria, Virginia: Time-Life Books, 1979.

Pernot, Guillermo, with Aliza Green. *Ceviche!: Seafood, Salads, and Cocktails with a Latino Twist*. Philadelphia: Running Press, 2001.

Peterson, James. *Fish & Shellfish: The Cook's Indispensable Companion*. New York: William Morrow and Company, 1996.

Scandinavian Fishing Year Book. An Illustrated Dictionary of Fish and Shellfish. Hedehusene, Denmark: 2003. CD-ROM.

Schmidt, Arno. *The Chef's Book of Formulas, Yields, and Sizes*, 2nd ed. New York: John Wiley and Sons, 1996.

Skinner, Linda, ed. *Seafood Business Professional Edition Seafood Handbook: The Comprehensive Guide to Sourcing, Buying, and Preparation*. Portland, Maine: Diversified Business Communications, 2005.

Whiteman, Kate. *The World Encyclopedia of Fish and Shellfish*. New York: Lorenz Books, 2000.

Sources: Web sites

www.americanmussel.com

www.asudoit.com/pdfs/sea_food_foraging_recipes.pdf

www.australis.us

www.bcsardines.ca/sardinefest.htm

www.bcseafoodonline.com/files/seafood-factsheet.html

www.canadiansablefish.com/sablefishinfo.htm

www.costante.com/pescinewestero.asp

www.explorecrete.com/nature/fish-2.html

www.fao.org/fi/default.asp

www.flmnh.ufl.edu/fish/Education/bioprofile.htm

www.geocities.com/TheTropics/Shores/6794/f-fish.html

www.globalchefs.com/article/archive/art033oys.htm

www.inspection.gc.ca/english/anima/fispoi/fispoie.shtml

www.kashrut.com/articles/fish/

www.mareinitaly.it/pesci.php

www.mbayaq.org/cr/seafoodwatch.asp

www.mdc.mo.gov/conmag/1996/06/50.html

http://myfwc.com/marine/fishinglines/fish_id2.pdf

www.net.org/marine/csb/

www.npr.org/programs/talkingplants/features/2003/fugu/list.html

www.oceansalive.org/home.cfm

www.parl.ns.ca/lobster/index.htm

http://rgmjapan.tripod.com/SUSHI.html

www.samuelsandsonseafood.com

www.sciencenews.org/pages/sn_arch/8_10_96/food.htm

www.seafoodfromnorway.com/page?id=24

www.seagrant.wisc.edu/greatlakesfish/becker.html

www.taylorshellfishfarms.com

www.tomzap.com/fish.html

www.trawl.org/wcfish.htm

www.urnerbarry.com/fyearbook/index.asp

www.webseafood.com/index.htm

www.westcoastaquatic.ca/article_goosebarn_fishery0204.htm

Acknowledgments

This, my fourth Field Guide, is without a doubt the most complex book I've worked on yet. I could never have done it without the support of Quirk Books and its capable, hard-working, and dedicated managing editor, Erin Slonaker. Erin always knows when to ask the right questions to make sure I'm on track. The careful reading by assistant project editor Kevin Kosbab helped clarify and organize the myriad details in this book. Karen Onorato, talented art director at Quirk, kept everything in order, lent the book her superb design sensibility, and leavened our long days at the wholesale seafood market with her wry humor. Steve Legato (www.stevelegato.com), the food photographer with whom I've now worked on six food books, has once again shown his sensitive eye, technical skill, and willingness to do what it takes to get the shot.

I couldn't have written this book without the help of some extraordinarily knowledgeable and helpful people in the fish and seafood industry. My special thanks go to Samuel D'Angelo, owner of Philadelphia's Samuels and Son Seafood (www.samuelsandsonseafood.com), a company his grandfather started out of a pushcart. As chef, I had the pleasure of buying from his company for many years. Joe Lasporgata, a certified marine biologist and the skillful buyer at Samuels, cheerfully answered my endless questions and came up with all the species we photographed. Today Samuels and Son supplies top restaurants from Pennsylvania to Virginia.

Several years ago, I attended the Boston Seafood Show as a guest of German and Luis Dao, owners of Standard Seafood of Venezuela and Miami (www.standardseafood.com). It was a fascinating chance to understand more of the world of seafood. This year, the brothers invited me to visit their state-of-the-art shrimp farm and processing plant and blue crab processing plant in Maracaibo, Venezuela. I learned much about raising quality seafood and the economy of the seafood export business. I also had the pleasure of touring Taylor Shellfish Farms (www.taylorshellfish farms.com) in Puget Sound with Bill Taylor, a fourth-generation shellfish farmer, and Jon Rowley, a noted oyster expert, to learn about West Coast oysters, mussels, scallops, and clams (including the extraordinary geoduck).

More Quirk Field Guides

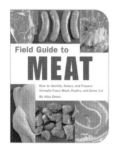

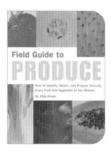

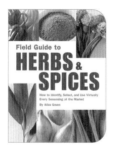

Available at www.quirkbooks.com
and Wherever Books Are Sold